MIRACLE HILL

Miracle Hill

The Story of a Navajo Boy

Blackhorse Mitchell

WITH A NEW FOREWORD BY
PAUL G. ZOLBROD

THE UNIVERSITY OF ARIZONA PRESS
TUCSON

ABOUT THE AUTHOR

Blackhorse Mitchell was born on Palmer Mesa, known as Popping Rock Ranch Mesa today, in the northeast corner of New Mexico near Colorado and the Ute tribal boundary. He left in 1951 to attend boarding school and learn English in Ignacio, Colorado. After completing his junior year in the spring of 1963, he left for the Institute of American Indian Arts in Santa Fe, New Mexico. It was there in the fall of 1963 that Mitchell began his studies in literary writing and where his book *Miracle Hill* was born. It was published in 1967 by the University of Oklahoma Press. Mitchell went on to attend the University of New Mexico, where he earned his BS in elementary education; in 1993 he earned his MA in secondary education with a minor in modern classical language (Navajo language). He currently teaches at Shiprock High School in Shiprock, New Mexico, and is an adjunct teacher at Diné College of Shiprock, where he gives workshops in Native Navajo pottery, basketry, moccasin making, and Navajo music. His other creative endeavors include two CDs, *Where Were You When I Was Single: Old Time Sheepherder Songs* and *Don't Let Go!* (both produced by Cool Runnings, Window Rock, Arizona), and a documentary DVD, *MUD: The Creation of Traditional Navajo Pottery* (sponsored by www.nativechild.com in Flagstaff, Arizona). More information can be found at his Web site: www.blackhorsemitchell.com.

Publisher's note: The text of this edition is a facsimile reproduction of the original 1967 printing published by the University of Oklahoma Press, and therefore the spellings of terms such as *Navajo* have not been updated.

Library of Congress Control Number 2004105480
Manufactured in the United States of America on acid-free, archival-quality paper containing a minimum of 30% post-consumer waste and processed chlorine free.

13 12 11 10 09 08   7 6 5 4 3 2

Originally published as *Miracle Hill: The Story of a Navaho Boy*, by Emerson Blackhorse Mitchell and T. D. Allen (Norman: University of Oklahoma Press, 1967)

In memory of
my loving mother, Emma B. Mitchell,
and my aunt, Amy B. Mitchell

The Drifting Lonely Seed

From the casein dark-blue sky,
  Through the emptiness of space,
A sailing wisp of cotton.
  Never have I been so thrilled!
The drifting lonely seed,
  Came past my barred window,
Whirling orbit, it landed before me,
  As though it were a woolly lamb—
Untouched, untamed, and alone—
  Walked atop my desk, stepping daintily.
Reaching forth my hands, I found you,
  Gentle, weightless, tantalizing.
I blew you out through barricaded window;
  You pranced, circled round me,
Sharing with me your airy freedom.

  —Blackhorse Mitchell, 1963

Contents

	Foreword by Paul G. Zolbrod	xi
	Acknowledgments	xxv
I	"I Do Have a Name"	3
II	Hello, World	12
III	Grandfather's Surprise Comes True	21
IV	There Is a Way!	33
V	"I Am Lost"	44
VI	A Miracle Thing	52
VII	A Gift for Grandmother	63
VIII	"These Things I Can't Forget"	73
IX	Birthday Gift for Broneco	84
X	The Shared Love	95
XI	Home for Christmas	109
XII	And New Year's Eve	121
XIII	Original Tea and the Dream	137
XIV	Once in a Lifetime	148
XV	So This Is the Institute of American Indian Arts!	156
XVI	Tears Raining in My Heart	171
XVII	Graduation	181
XVIII	After Graduation	188
XIX	Stranger on the Hill	196
XX	Miracle Hill	211
	Index	225

Foreword

PAUL G. ZOLBROD

It is good to see this unique volume reappear. Even though it has been out of print for many years, it stands alone for a variety of reasons, not only in the annals of Native American studies in particular, but among personal memoirs in general. Its author's persistence in acquiring exclusive publication rights is fortunate, and I myself am grateful for the opportunity to replace the original foreword with one of my own. Unfolding in a voice that marks the strains and triumphs of a Navajo youth learning to speak and write English, the story exhibits a remarkable capacity for observation in one so young, expressed with disarming grace in an idiom governed by its own rules of grammar. With refreshing unself-consciousness, it recites not only the details of a pure, mid-twentieth-century Navajo existence, but also those of a subsequent transition to mainstream culture by way of formal schooling. Thus it records fluid cultural change offset by a secure native identity through first-hand experience, offering sharp contrast between what was and what is in the Navajo community—mediated by what comes to pass in a world far different from that one. On the surface it gives an account of a successfully undertaken rite of passage through the institution of the Indian boarding school. More deeply, however, it remains as significant for what it does not say about that experience as for what it does, leaving the story vexingly incomplete, its great charm notwithstanding; yet it ultimately records one Navajo's triumph in behalf of an entire culture that somehow endures.

With the publication of this new edition, more than thirty-five years have passed since *Miracle Hill* first appeared in print—just over sixty since its author was born. As readers will recognize, conditions have altered considerably during that time, and Navajo life has not been immune to the impact of that change. Paved roads, the Internet, cell phones, and state-of-the-art communications make getting back and forth across the vast Navajo Reservation and keeping in touch with the outside world much easier. All along the high plateau where Broneco[1] and his sister Annie were raised without electricity, push-button and keyboard technology now bring football scores and rap music into Navajo homes. In households still without computers, the information highway extends at least as far as the local chapter house. Newly erected dwellings—now equipped with indoor plumbing and electricity—dot the countryside around the Shiprock area, which means more lights and more people than young Broneco ever dreamed of seeing. Today very few, if any, Navajo children would grow up in the isolation that the opening chapters here describe. Fewer as well can now speak the language, although they suffer less resistance from their school teachers for doing so than before.

Older now and hence a different person, Blackhorse Mitchell himself has changed. Part of that is the result of coming of age, of course, and moving confidently through adulthood. In having undergone the transition from boy to man, he has done what any society expects of its children. In traditional and modern societies alike, it is a given that youngsters become adult participants in the wider community that reared them. For Navajo kids being educated in the "White Man's" system thirty-five or so years ago, how-

---

1. "Broneco" is a variant spelling of "Bronco," which is the name the author originally meant.

ever, that expectation had a peculiar spin. Those who went to school were trained to contribute to the dominant society in some expected way—whether as laborers, clerks, entrepreneurs, professionals, or artists. They were still taught then to read and write primarily to fit into an economy alien to the old Navajo way of life. Prevailing wisdom held that Native Americans would blend into the melting pot anyhow. The sooner they were assimilated into mainstream culture, the better.

Thus, as the boy who called himself Broneco grew into Blackhorse Mitchell the man, he underwent the prescribed passage in a dominant culture that expected Navajos to change. And change he did, but only to a degree. He left the Reservation to attend school; he learned to speak, read, and write English; he rode the Greyhound bus back and forth to off-Reservation places; he wore sunglasses, watched movies, and drank Seven-Up. All of that is anticipated in the way this narrative begins by describing how young Broneco allows his hair to be cut as a white boy's would be, and in how the story he tells concludes with his high school graduation. Yet he returns home more consciously aware of his place of origin than he was when he first left for school.

In regard to his capacity to change, English teacher and first-edition editorial guide T. D. Allen's recognition of his potential has been fully justified, even if she may not have recognized the depth of his Navajo identity. "He is learning," she asserted in her foreword to the original text, pleased with the enthusiasm he displayed for books, and with his eagerness to write. And indeed, Mr. Mitchell went on to earn a master's degree in education and for a time considered beginning work toward a doctorate. Society's investment in his schooling secured a place for him in the professional world. He is a certified history teacher; he has been a school administrator and an educational consultant to Anglo employers of Navajos. He has traveled broadly, performs and lectures widely, and moves comfortably in mainstream society.

Yet something distinctly Navajo about the Dinébikayah of Blackhorse Mitchell's childhood prevails here; something acquired during his early childhood in Navajo Country remains deeply rooted in what he now does as an adult. An indelible Diné influence survives the education chronicled in these pages; that persistence supplies a thematic constant in this book about going to school in a system that at the time expected young members to subordinate their Native identity to the dominant culture. This is not only a story of a Navajo who comes of age by taking the Greyhound to and from boarding school year after year or being driven by a rela-tive, living in dorms and attending compulsory church services, celebrating Christian holidays, following rock groups to teen dances, learning to read and write English and to love books. It is also a tale of an abiding Navajo identity that withstands cultural accretions without thwarting them.

That identity persists down to young Broneco's very syntax, which simply will not relent entirely to the conventions of standard written English. After he sees his friend Johnnie disappear into a car that takes him away from the Ignacio boarding school, for example, Broneco reacts in a characteristically Navajo way. He tells of watching "almost everything he sees" and knowing how different the world now seems for him with the possible loss of a friend. "For the weather is cool and the wind kept on blowing and lots of dirts went up in the air each time the wind would blow, messing up the sharp-combed hairs of every students that are strolling along the walk. Some talking together and smaller kids running and racing together to see who's the fastest" (91). Other passages and episodes similarly reveal an underlying Navajo distinctiveness of expression throughout this book, and a deep pleasure awaits the reader who comes to recognize and accept it.

The hill southward of his early boyhood home retains its Navajo magic for him throughout his youth and adolescence. On the threshold of his adulthood, Blackhorse finds that it yields a visionary awareness that only a Navajo can describe so believably. While ready for the next set of hurdles white culture sets before him as his learning continues, he is fortified by his grandparents' abiding legacy. His affinity for those who raised him and were raised with him lingers as he gradually becomes attuned to the culture of the Ignacio Indian agency and its boarding school, the shops in downtown Farmington, the lights of Santa Fe, and the University of New Mexico's graduation requirements.

As T. D. Allen explained in her foreword to the first edition, *Miracle Hill* started out as a schoolroom assignment at the Institute of American Indian Arts in Santa Fe in 1962. She taught creative writing there at the time, and there Mitchell had matriculated to complete the twelfth grade after attending a BIA boarding school in Ignacio, Colorado, for his first eleven. It was her practice to begin the school year by having students write their life story. Tell her everything, she instructed them; write about their homes, their families, how they played as small children, and their early schooling (x). As he relates in chapter XV, Blackhorse had signed up for that course after sampling other arts classes at the institute and finding that he favored the one she offered. His response to the assignment, she went on to say, was to write and write, page after beautifully handwritten page, where other students presented her with no more than a single, hastily dashed-off sheet.

For two years he continued to submit manuscript, she explained (x), evidently continuing to do so even after receiving his diploma. Taken—as readers of the current volume themselves will be—by the keenly observed details in his descriptions and the unfettered charm of his unique idiom, she continued reading, aware that she was in possession of a significant document. Initially she made an effort to correct his prose, mindful of her responsibility "to teach grammar [and] syntax"; but as he continued handing in pages of this "delightfully unfolding story told in his aborted English," she found that she could not "correct [it] without draining life from it." In spite of the "confused tenses and genders and sound-alike words," she "urged him to keep going" (xi). But as Broneco's "story began to unfold as that of a Navaho [*sic*] boy determined to get an English education," she wrote, she "began to feel guilty" because she "wasn't doing to it what a teacher is supposed to do" while at the same time feeling "obligated to do something" (xii).

That "something," she decided, was to send a portion of the manuscript to Savoie Lottinville at the University of Oklahoma Press with a cover letter containing the "wild idea" of turning what he was submitting into a published volume. "How about a book," she offered, "that both tells and shows how a small Navaho boy with an active mind grows up on the reservation, first becomes acquainted with white people, longs to learn English, finally gets to go to school (against his grandmother's wishes), has both satisfying and disrupting experiences with white people, etc.?" (xii–xiii). There followed a sequence of two responses, both positive. In the first, Mr. Lottinville promised to review what had been sent as quickly as possible, and he added that "A first glance indicates the kind of charm you detect, and I must say that you have an excellent eye for this sort of thing." Soon thereafter he wrote, "Why don't you go ahead and have him complete his story. . . . If the book-length work holds up as well as it has begun there's a possibility . . . that we could publish it." However, he added, "we could stand a little more proficient use of English, without losing the charm of his own expression, which is partly that of a youngster, partly that of an Indian" (xiii).

Thus T. D. Allen took on something of an editorial balancing act, struggling to preserve Mitchell's beautifully idiosyncratic idiom while maintaining the called-for proficiency. In her foreword she revealed little about that process, other than to acknowledge that she had "taken the liberty of changing personal pronouns which prove such a problem for those who move from the Navaho language into English" (xvi). And elsewhere she spoke knowingly about the way a Navajo can be expected to write or "sound" in English. But to exactly what extent she imposed an editorial hand, she never disclosed. In any event, her participation led to the publication of a book that was met with enthusiasm and went through four printings before it disappeared from the University of Oklahoma Press's list.

It is to T. D. Allen's great credit, of course, that *Miracle Hill* found its way into print as an upbeat account of a Navajo boy's coming of age within the framework of a boarding school education. However, this new edition needs to be put into a broader context than she was able to place it in when she agreed to apply her editorial hand to the manuscript Broneco handed her. Given what has been learned about the Native American educational experience since its initial publication, this work can now be read against a template shaped by recent studies of Native American autobiography, by what can now be said about boarding school education, more specifically by Blackhorse Mitchell's own life since his graduation from the Institute of American Indian Arts, and more specifically still by how his relationship with Ms. Allen evolved since he was her pupil.

To be all too brief here, scholars like H. David Brumble who have examined the issue of American Indian autobiography have demonstrated the degree to which those who have told their life stories have by necessity filtered what they say through a medium not native to them—that of print—as well as through a language not their own. Furthermore, in many cases what came to be written down was relayed indirectly by way of an amanuensis—or scribe, as it were—whose greater degree of literacy imposed control not necessarily available to the teller, often leading to editorial distortion—sometimes naively, sometimes with disingenuousness, sometimes by way of oversight, sometimes with interpretive bias, and sometimes by sheer censorship. Something would happen to reshape what was originally offered by the native "author," who either recited the story or whose lesser writing ability required the work of an editor. As Brumble says, in many cases the process would require "hours of transcription . . . editing . . . ordering, cutting, and sometimes . . . rephrasing, and . . . additions" (10).

It is well to keep all of that in mind as this volume is read. As T. D. Allen indicated, whether unwittingly or not, she raised an issue of editorial interference here, which scholars like Brumble serve us well by observing. We do not know specifically what she omitted from what Mitchell handed her, or whether she rearranged anything. I do know, however, that he submitted what originally amounted to 625 typed pages of manuscript—later destroyed in a fire so that no measured comparison can today be made—not all of it included in what she sent to the publisher. And while the first edition was favorably received and makes for delightful and even enlightened reading, that something is missing should be acknowledged, as should the institution in which Blackhorse was placed when he began his schooling as a nine-year-old.

Initially sponsored by the government and reinforced by missionaries, the Indian boarding school movement was established "to teach Indian children English, Christianity, and the moral superiority of a clean life of honest labor" (Lomawaima 2, see also Adams 5–27). Whether misguided or not, those ideals were compromised by insensitivity and abuse, so that the record of educating young Indians remains uneven. True, many children learned to read and write and went on to live productive lives both on and off the reservation. Older Navajo veterans of the boarding-school experience whom I have directly spoken with acknowledge the advantages of having attended. But even at best, results were mixed. The regimentation was good, I have been told by some, while others now resent having endured it. Former students I have consulted speak nostalgically of taking showers for the first time in their lives, enjoying electricity, sleeping in sheeted beds, and most significantly, acquiring mastery over the printed page. For many, the formal classroom was invigorating, with teachers like T. D. Allen having encouraged them the way she professed to have supported Blackhorse. But those same individuals also tell of unbearable homesickness, emotional disorientation, unprincipled capital punishment, and even sexual abuse. Teachers and preceptors would call them "heathens" and "savages" and insist that they reject what their parents and grandparents had taught them. If they spoke their own language, they would be beaten or locked up or made to eat soap. Those anecdotal accounts I have heard are now being cor-roborated in written testimony, particularly by Native Americans themselves in both the United States and Canada, where elders have gone on record thirty, forty, and fifty years later to tell of mistreatment ranging from outward denunciation of their lifeways to malnourishment and severe beatings (Kelly). Less widely reported at first but now being acknowledged, too, is the issue of sexual abuse, "whispered today but seldom mentioned publicly" (Archuleta et al. 42–43, see also Krauss 11, Levchuck).

What Blackhorse witnessed and experienced at Ignacio Consolidated Agency Indian School takes no exception to what is now being revealed, although none of that is mentioned in this text. During one long conversation he and I once had, he offered specific instances of what he and his classmates endured. The story is his alone to tell if he so chooses, but he made it clear that harsh treatment mitigated the joy of his having learned to read and write there. He has tailored his activities as a medicine man, in fact, to treat elders who once attended boarding schools as he did and are still suffering from the lingering effects of what is now recognized as post-traumatic stress. So there was another side to the chipper account that comes through in the narrative offered here. Some of what he and others withstood he wanted to include in the book but could not. "At the time," he later corresponded when I wrote him to ask about the extent of her editing, "T. D. Allen said that all those things she [deleted] were not necessary and that I should not speak of the terrible things in the Bureau school system. . . . " With the understanding of the school's stated mission that he now has, however, especially after reading other things she had published, he can recognize the perspective she brought to her teaching and applied in editing his manuscript. With something of a missionary's outlook, he added, "T. D. Allen's idea of educating 'little brown Indians'" was to "get them away from the world of heathen thinking." In his correspondence with me, he goes on to tell of disagreeing with her while the manuscript was in preparation. "I remember times when I came clashing and arguing about the choice of words that I used," or whether to include "lines of writing I had done at the time." And when I asked him if he was satisfied with what he had written when he read the published version, he replied, "I was too eager to have what was left of the cut to get published. Nothing mattered, just so it was off the press. . . . The initial core of the subject was English. . . . That English was everything. It was the key to the other side of the culture. It was a key to many drawers with many growing roots, and to read and understand each word was a never-ending dream."

As his teacher, T. D. Allen thought she knew what was best, and as her student, he sometimes acquiesced to the editorial decisions she made and sometimes simply surrendered to her authority. With the passing years, however, Blackhorse has come to reevaluate his attitude toward her. Ten years prior to this writing, he proposed to her that *Miracle Hill* come out in a new edition with his byline alone. While it had gone out of print, it was still being read and discussed, and he wanted to see it reissued under his exclusive ownership. But when he made that suggestion, she resisted. There followed an exchange of letters over a period of several years; a visit to her home in California, where she had retired; and some negotiation with the original publisher, punctuated with her continued objection until she finally relented with the provision that along with her name, her foreword would have to be omitted from any subsequent edition.

Although I have seen some of the correspondence between them, her reasons for resisting remained unclear to me beyond my sensing some disappointment in what she expressed to Blackhorse after all she felt she had done for him. What came across in the letters I read was that for her the relationship between them had not changed; he was still the young Navajo boy learning to master written English, she still the teacher who continued to know what was best for him. For his part, Blackhorse explains it this way: Originally it was she who initiated a new edition and had begun negotiating for one in 1990, while he was occupied with graduate work at the University of New Mexico. Meanwhile, she took it upon herself to write a new foreword, which she then sent to him, but only at his request, and which he disputed. Objecting that she no longer knew him, he requested an altogether different foreword by someone who did know him, whereupon negotiations with the original publisher collapsed. By then he had read her other books, understood that they were the work of a missionary intent on "saving souls" and acculturating Indian children, and realized that he had acquired a purpose of his own in advancing his education. "I think she still saw me as . . . that little red man in the [BIA] school," he later wrote me, whereas "I have grown up and have a life of my own."

Yet even with T. D. Allen's failure to realize as much, and for whatever may be missing from the story as young Blackhorse might have wanted it told, something substantial survives here. And I repeat my assertion that she deserves credit for the way she encouraged her students to express themselves in written English, recognized young Broneco's singular talent, encouraged him to keep writing, and facilitated the production of the original volume. Omissions not withstanding, it fills a gap in the broader awareness of the Native American experience that would not otherwise exist. Thanks to writers like Peter Iverson, the full panorama of Navajo history is unfolding with renewed accuracy; and ethnographers like Charlotte Frisbie have improved the technique of compiling an autobiography so that a more individually human side of Navajo history becomes accessible. So it is to first-person accounts that we would wish to turn to particularize the American Indian past in ways once overlooked.

"No Native autobiography is a 'true' representation of the self in any absolute sense," warns Brumble (11). Yet here we can get as close to such an absolute sense as we can, for the point of view is Blackhorse Mitchell's own, allowing readers to experience sensations and see details from an authentically Navajo perspective, with its unique awareness of motion and sensation as seen by a boy whose youthful experiences are brand new. Look, for example, at how the merger of vision and smell filters through his consciousness when he speaks of "the scent of spiral shaping clouds of the steaming puffs float[ing] about his nose" in describing the freshness of his grandmother's adobe oven–baked bread during a summer at home (96). This text is full of such details, described with the sensory alertness of a highly perceptive youth experimenting with a second language. So, too, is this voice his, clear down to the pure rhythm of the language, with its powerful resonance of oral expression in what gets written down. In its purest sense, voice becomes a leitmotif throughout this text, as it remains in his life now as a singer. In his introduction, Adams acknowledges that "the problem involved in giving voice to Indians, a group for whom the documentary record is both sparse and unreliable, are legion" (x). Yet this work makes young Broneco's language virtually audible. I have heard him lecture and sing as an adult, both in public appearances and in the ceremonial hogan, and what I cull here from the silent medium of print resonates for me with the sound of his recitations, whether spoken or chanted, together with a story of triumph—no matter what has been excised by a well-meaning but culturally insensitive editor. I perceive a uniquely Navajo inquiring eye and an energetic voice, offering small details vividly re-created so that we both see and hear a process of transition set against a background of cultural persistence. In that respect *Miracle Hill* is as pure, true, and direct an account as we are likely to find in the written record of outward movement from tribal to modern, set against an inward resistance so that the old ways might yet prevail.

Clearly, the person Blackhorse Mitchell has become is a grown-up version of the Navajo he originally was, and while T. D. Allen failed to anticipate such an outcome, that is the person I have come to know. If, as an educated Navajo, Blackhorse Mitchell now differs from what his grandfather was or what his grandmother had foreseen his becoming when she chastised him for playing in a white boy's home, he still retains much of what they endowed him with. So if, as T. D. Allen prophetically remarked, he is still learn-ing, his learning remains characteristically Navajo. His cer-emo-nial hogan occupies the family site, a stone's throw from the sheep corral with its large herd. There he constructs intricate sand paint-ings and recites timeless chants, retained over generations by way of the traditional manner of serving years of apprenticeship. The songs he sings and the mythic events he celebrates help to pre-serve an ancient legacy—one that is not to be relinquished. His life as a student, in fact, has come full circle with something of an ironic twist. For if Anglo teachers at the Ignacio boarding school and the Institute of American Indian Arts trained him to become an Anglo, he now advises businesses learning to understand the traditional ways of its Navajo employees and to deal fairly with Native clients. Or he shares his Navajo elder's knowledge and wis-dom with scholars like myself, and he himself becomes teacher and guide.

If I may end on a personal note, I have one example to offer that has enriched my life with a lasting memory. One summer after-noon some dozen or so years ago, Blackhorse led me and an an-thropolo-gist friend around the far side of the north rim of a mesa overlooking Horseshoe Canyon, not many miles from the home-stead he describes in *Miracle Hill*, and very near the spot where his family had main-tained a summer home during his boyhood. Guiding us across that high mesa, he repeated the Navajo names of each species of flora with a botanist's precision, detailing its medicinal use or describing its harmful effect. He led us to a small Ancestral Pueblo ruin and explained its purpose. He then calmly took us to the south face—a sheer cliff that towered five hundred feet above the canyon floor. Fif-teen years his senior and long since having given up rock climbing, I first regarded that descent with terror. But as he patiently directed my every step, taking my hand or offering me his as a foothold, I quickly understood that I had little to fear. His was the superior knowledge in this native envi-ronment, where Navajo remains the dominant culture, and ours, the subordinate. As someone who neither compromises his own way of life nor bitterly rejects the mainstream, he exhibits an ad-mirable precept. Comfortably straddling both worlds, he projects the ideal that learning goes both ways to mediate between them. The example Blackhorse sets remains all too rare, and once the story of its publication and re-publication is known, this book offers an unparalleled explanation of how that can be.

References

Adams, David Wallace. 1995. *Education for Extinction: American Indians and the Boarding School Experience, 1875–1928.* Lawrence: University of Kansas Press.

Allen, T. D. 1967. "Please Read Loose," foreword to the first edition of *Miracle Hill*. Norman: University of Oklahoma Press.

Archuleta, Margaret L., Brenda J. Child, and K. Tsianina Lomawaima, eds. 2000. *Away From Home: American Indian Boarding School Experiences, 1879–2000.* Phoenix: The Heard Museum.

Brumble, H. David. 1988. *American Indian Autobiography.* Berkeley: University of California Press.

Frisbie, Charlotte, ed. 2001. *Tall Woman: The Life Story of Rose Mitchell, A Navajo Woman.* Albuquerque: University of New Mexico Press.

Iverson, Peter. 2002. *Diné: A History of the Navajos.* Albuquerque: University of New Mexico Press.

Kelley, Matt. 1999. "American Indian Boarding Schools: 'That hurt never goes away.'" *Canoe: Your Internet Network News*, Wednesday, April 28. http://www.canoe.ca/CNEWSFeatures9904/28_indians.html.

Krauss, Clifford. 2004. "Native Canadians Reveal Legacy of Abuse," *New York Times*, Section 1, CLIII, 52, 781.

Levchuck, Bernice. 1997. "Leaving Home for Carlisle Indian School." In *Reinventing the Enemy's Language: Contemporary Native Women's Writings of North America*. Joy Harjo and Gloria Bird, eds. New York: W.W. Norton, 175–186.

Lomawaima, K. Tsianina. 1994. *They Called It Prairie Light: The Story of Chilocco Indian School.* Lincoln: University of Nebraska Press.

Acknowledgments

Thirty-six years ago, the book *Miracle Hill* came off the press at the University of Oklahoma Press, in the late fall of 1967. It was a joyful moment! Then somewhere between then and now, when life became so busy in the fast-lane, ever-changing world of American dreams of industrialization, capitalism, and economic boom, the book ceased to exist. But a handful of good-hearted people didn't seem to tire of the book and its creator!

To make the story short, during my fifty-eighth year, I was teaching at a state school in a rural area of the Navajo Reservation in northern Arizona. I was at the podium, and my class was in full swing when a tall, *Last-of-the-Mohicans*–looking Indian man knocked on my classroom door. He had a shaved head, save for a roach of dark hair tied neatly back, and he was wearing buckskin and calico. He entered, followed by a group of students, who outnumbered my students ten to one.

The tall man had a slight grin as he stared at us, and I saw his twinkling and sparkling light blue eyes. He stood at attention and finally spoke. "Are you Emerson Blackhorse Barney Mitchell? The man who wrote this book?" he questioned as he held out my book!

"I'm the same man who wrote the book many years ago," I responded.

"I always wanted to meet the man himself for years! By the way, I went to the Institute of American Indian Arts after you left, and since then I've heard so much about you—that you were the first Native American writer who broke the ice for all the Native American writers of today!"

With that, I would like to express my gratitude to Mr. Barney Bush, a writer and composer himself, who pulled me out of the hidden shadows and who truly believed that this book should always be there for my Native people as an "ice breaker." I will also express my deepest blessing thanks to Dr. Paul Zolbrod, a friend who believed that the book had a great potential for Native Americans "with strong beliefs in literary writings and that nothing is impossible when [you] put your mind to it!"

I owe a great thanks to my cousin Luci Tapahonso, who has been using my book for years and, as a writer herself, has a great interest in it. Great thanks also to my dear friends and colleagues Laura Tohe, Simon Ortiz, Scott Momaday, Gayla Schumatz, Anna Lee Walters, Rex Lee Jim, Diane Erwin, and a handful of other artists in the world of writers! Not to forget my dear Austrian friends—Alexander (Shash) Stipsits and Thomas Steiner—who also had a strong influence in making all things possible!

I would also like to acknowledge Dr. Rose Marie Smith, a professor of theater at Arizona State University, who wrote a stage storytelling performance of *Miracle Hill* that premiered March 14, 1970, at Many Farms, Arizona, where Diné College was first established.

I could not have made it without the help of the University of Arizona Press and its dependable staff, especially acquiring editor Patti Hartmann.

With wishes for many blessings ahead of you, behind you, beneath you, above you, and all around you. In blessings it is finished!

MIRACLE HILL

"I Do Have a Name"

IT WAS IN THE YEAR OF 1943 on a cold morning, the fifth day, in the month of March. A little boy was born as the wind blew against the hogan with bitter colds and the stars were disappearing into the heaven.

The little puff of smoke was gradually floating skyward. The floor of the earth was hard as ever with a few stripes of white snow still frozen to the grey colored ground. With a queer squeaking, the baby awakes. His eyes were as dark as the colors of the ashes. His face is pink.

Following year, it was May and the bright sun shines in the land of enchantment close to the Four Corners, which was about thirty miles away. Four Corners is where the four states meets. They are New Mexico, Arizona, Utah, and Colorado.

The boy stood on his two little fat legs. Part of the time he crawl, but mostly he walks against chairs and his grandmother's loom. Very many lambs jumps and plays near the tent. The boy sometimes play with the lambs and goats. They smell like a wet dry dirt and the smell of corral.

But life was hard. Year after year the boy, his Grandmother, and Grandfather moved to various part of the reservation area. The boy was four now and begins to wonder, as he looks in the yonder valley and in the afar distance. With his sharp, dark brown eyes he would stand against the tree-shade house and look.

Day by day and step by step he learns different things. Very often Grandfather would say, "My beloved child, when you grow big, I got a surprise for you, Little One."

The boy would smile and sits on his Grandfather's lap.

But still, the boy would go to the hill and look into the distance, wondering when will he ever be there to see the place. The days were long, and, as he herd his flock of sheeps, he began to think about things that were around him.

As the summer has gone by suddenly, they moved back to the Mesa where during winter it is warm and partly cold. The winter slowly passes. When the boy herd sheep, he would play with the shepherd dogs and sometimes his pet lamb. Still yet he hasn't learn much, but he knew every tree and mountain passage through the great forest.

Very often when he herd sheep he would play bareback on the branch of a springy cedar branch which would throw him off. When he feel like playing, he would make his own toys out of clay. They were yellow, grey, orange, and blue. These were the color of his toys which are made by his own five fingers.

Many times he hunted rabbit and animals, carrying his four-feet bow and arrow. It belonged to his Grandfather who had given it to him for a birthday present. First, he learned how to shoot the flying arrow. It was taught by his Grandfather. He was very skill at shooting the arrow.

Since the boy is too small, he would sit and put his bow at the front of his feet and stretch the bowstring to shoot the arrow. Surely enough, the arrow flies like a diving eagle bound to catch a rabbit.

With his practice of shooting arrow, it gave him more and more ideas. While herding sheep he would shoot trees, imagining it as a huge lion, bear, and such. With his ability of learning, he quickly learn how to jump from rock to rock. He could run like an antelope when he runs into rocky hills and forest and down the rocky hillside.

When the boy was six years old, of what he has learn, he never forgets. But he has never seen yet much of a white man's ways.

Then one day he came home, carry a loads of rabbit in his bag made of buckskin.

Grandmother stood outside the hogan. "How many rabbit did you kill?" she asked, grinning.

"Oh, I kill six."

Then in English she spoke. "Oh, six."

The boy dropped the bag and put down his arrow bag and bow against the hogan. "Grandmother! What's that word mean?"

"What word?" said Grandmother.

"The word 'ce-e-ex,' " said the boy.

Then she laugh as though the whole mountainside crushing. She dance around a little bit and sang an old song, saying, "Oh twinle, twinle, little star."

"Grandmother, are you going nuts or something?" the boy asked, "or is it you feeling happy because Grandfather's coming home today?"

"No, Little One," she said.

Then the boy stand up against the hogan. He didn't know that his grandmother had been a student once. Now, Grandmother never spoke none of a white man's tongue. "Grandmother," he said.

"Quiet, Little One. Go get some water from the spring. Then I'll answer your question," she said.

The boy pick up the bag and runs down the hill into the forest with a white water bag made of goatskin. With his skill, he has no problem of running swiftly and no problem of falling. It was a mile and a half.

At the spring he filled up his water bag and started walking up the hill. He saw his Grandfather riding his horse through the canyon in the yonder hills.

The boy thought of an idea that he would have a race with him. So, with a quick jerk, he put the bag on the shoulder and jumps on the rock. Like he always did, he made the short cut, doing nothing but jumping from rock to rock. When he got home, Grandmother was preparing a meal outside the hogan.

She turns around with her hands on her waist, holding a big silver spoon. "What did you do," she said, "fly or something?"

"No, I ran," he said.

"Impossible," she said.

The boy sits on the log of an old cedar, his pants all dirty and shirt sleeves torn off on both sides, and wearing a white headband with a black eagle feather. He laughs at his grandmother.

"What is it?" she said.

"Oh, nothing," he said, "it just that, I didn't know you can speak a white tongue! So now would you tell me what the word 'six' mean?"

"It means six rabbit," she said. "Six mean six." She picks up a stick and writes figures in the sandy dust—1, 2, 3, 4, 5, 6—counting as she writes.

"One," the boy said, and "six." Then, "What do you call this?"

"That's a bucket," she said. "Now enough of that."

"Ooh, my Grandfather coming," the boy said.

"Where?"

"See, there he is down yonder."

She is stirring up the mutton soup, and on her left hand she holds a dough in a form of a ball. The soup smelled with vegetable, and the smell of fried bread made the boy grow hungrier than ever as she stack the brownish bread in a white plate. She was putting another stick and more in the fireplace to burn.

"Little One, get me the broom and I'll teach your Grandfather a lesson that he'll never forgets," she said. "He never thinks of us. He's always going."

The boy went back into the hogan and closed the door. As he peep through an opening of the door, Grandfather got knock off the horse, and Grandmother quickly grabs the broom and hits Grandfather again. Then she throws the rubbery dough into Grandfather's face.

"Take that," she said.

The boy just laugh in the hogan and suddenly Grandmother said, "Time to eat."

6

While they were eating, Grandfather said, "We're moving to summer home."

"Where we used to live in a tent?" the boy asked.

"No," Grandfather said. "We are leaving tomorrow noon, and your uncle is coming on the pickup to haul our blankets, dishes, and few lambs that are small."

Yes, surely enough, it was the next morning. As Grandmother and Grandfather packed the bundle of blankets and suitcases, clothes, putting and setting boxes in place.

It was a good day for traveling.

"Little One, take the sheep out of the corral and get a head start," said Grandfather.

As he opened the gate to let the sheep out, the boy look up the valley and down the steep canyon. He wondered as he stands there, wearing his white shirt, carry a big bow in his hand. The arrow were kind of heavy, but he was used to carrying it all the time. He kept saying the word 'six,' and 'one' and 'bucket' as he stroll after the sheeps down the grassland.

It looked like a green pasture with a stream of water. Only the prairie dogs barked in the far distance at the edge of the woods where there is an open sight. The boy didn't like prairie dogs. The crows flew across the blue sky as the white cloud are moving eastward like a big white sheep in the grazing land.

Down into the canyon he walks and jumps from rocks to rocks as he's going after the flock of sheep. He would ask himself, "What will I do when I'm seven years old next year?"

He wanted to speak English, but how would he learn? He would say, "When I was young, which was two years ago, I used to wondered about that rock down yonder. I have been there a few times now. Surely, there is a way," he said to himself.

Finally he brought his sheep to the edge of the mesa. It was around about three o'clock now. All this time he didn't know he has gone many miles with the sheep. The dust of clouds were up in the air like a dust storm. He didn't mind walking in it. Many times he rested.

Then finally it was getting dark as he arrive with his sheep at the next spring which has a bitter taste. It's good only for sheep so the poor boy has to thirst until Grandmother and Grandfather arrive. He waited and waited until late. He heard horse hoofs beating against the hard floor of the earth. The sheep rested quietly and the dogs barked. And the big yellow moon shined as the stars twinkle above.

The rumbling sound grew louder and louder. The owl hoot in the brushes. There were bushes and tall grass. Soon the boy saw them approach. It was Grandmother and Grandfather riding horses along the road. Then they turn off the road and headed towards the spring. As they watered their horses they joined with the boy.

"We'll make it tonight," said Grandfather, "but first, you must eat."

Grandmother built a fire and putted the sandwich aside for the boy to eat. There were roast mutton, baked potatoes and biscuit. Now it was around nine o'clock.

As soon as they had eaten, they started off for another journey which will surely take until the morning. The sheep knew their pack so they were going single file along the road.

The boy fell asleep sitting behind his Grandfather. Part of the time he would almost fall off, his head goes this way and that way. He didn't know that he was asleep until he wake up in a tent where he has never been before, or nor seen the place.

It was morning. Grandfather snores while Grandmother was outside making coffee and tortillas.

The boy went out to see the place, to see what it is like. As for him, he'd never seen a water tower, or big building, and real green trees. As he runs to the top of the hill, he could now see distance away. For many years he had seen Shiprock stand, but had never looked what was below and beyond. It was for the first time he is seeing buildings and towns. There were smokes going up in the air. In about four miles there runs a river. He could heard many ducks and various kind of sounds by the river.

8

He rushes back to Grandmother and asks, "What are the building and great tower like a ball in the air?"

Grandmother said, "They are town, and many people live there, and your mother lives there at the farm."

"My mother?" said the boy. "I don't know her."

Then Grandmother calls to Grandfather, "Get up and tell the Little One about his mother."

"Come, Little One, let's go up the hill and let me tell you more about the place," Grandfather said.

The boy and Grandfather first had a cup of coffee, as Grandmother sweeps the hard earth floor outside under the shade house. Grandfather stretch himself and then gets hold of the boy's hand, and went up the hill.

At the top, the boy again looks across the hills. Grandfather sat down with his leg crossed. The boy sit besides his Grandfather like a pet dog.

"Your aunt is coming on horseback before noon," said Grandfather, "and she's bringing watermelons and fresh green corns, and a few vegetables."

At that moment, the boy sees his aunt riding in a distance. His Grandfather said, "How do you know it's her?"

"Because I know it's her by the color of the horse." The horse was black and walks like he's about ready to take off on a race track. The boy turns and looks at his Grandfather with his eyes twinkling. "Grandfather?" he said, "tell me about my mother."

"Oh, yes," Grandfather said, smiling at him. "Sit down and let me tell you."

The boy sit against a brush.

"Your mother Emma has left you when you were eleven month old. She only went and took your brother with her."

"I had a brother?" said the boy. "I have a brother," he repeated it several times. "Then Grandmother isn't my mother," he said, "and you aren't, aren't my father."

"Your father was killed," he said, "during World War II in over sea."

9

"My father was killed." The boy quiet down and looked at his Grandfather.

Then Grandfather looked up and said, "Your father was a very kind man. Before he left, he made many plans, but he was killed." He wipe his tears.

The boy got up and looked below the foot of the hill. There were four kids playing. "Grandfather, let's go back to the tent," he said, "and see my aunt."

Grandfather gets up and hold the boy's hand. Grandfather didn't feel too well.

When they reached the house, Aunt Amy greet her father. "Oh father, I was late coming 'cause I was irrigating and plowing the field, and I had planted more corns," she said.

Grandmother was fixing a loom with yarn of colored strings to weave another rug.

The boy stood against a post which was there to hold up the shade house. He wondered why his Grandfather didn't told him more about his mother, or where she is now. Nor he didn't know he had a cousin too until his aunt told him that she had a daughter and she has no father too.

The boy asked, "What has happen to her father?"

Aunt Amy said, "My husband was the brother of your father. He has gone four years ago, and never came back."

"What's her name?"

"Her name is Annie," Aunt Amy said. "And she's coming to see us tomorrow and live here with her Grandmother too."

Later Amy was preparing meal as the sheep were in the green grassland over yonder on the tiny hills. By now it was getting hot, and the ground is getting hotter too. On the north side of the tent there were blooming flowers, colors were red and pink. Very often Grandmother would go out and get the blooming flowers and chop them into tiny bites and cook it and when it's cooled, she would serve it for dessert. It tasted sweet and part sour.

"Aunt Amy," the boy said.

"What is it?" she said.

"Why do they call me Little One?"

"I don't know. I suppose because you're small," she replied.

"Why don't I have a name?" asked the boy as he look at his aunt making a vegetable soup. She didn't stop. She went ahead and continue about her work. And Grandmother was busy rolling up more strings. She was ready to weave. Grandfather sleeps and snores.

"Do I have a name?" the boy said slowly as he looked down at his moccasins.

"Yes," she said.

"I do have a name," he said as he smile shyly.

Amy turned around and grinned. Then she said, "You were named after a colt that was born on the same day you were born. So your Grandfather named you Broneco."

"Broneco," the boy said and giggle with his hand over his mouth.

· II ·

Hello, World

I T WAS A WEEK LATER. Broneco was hunting rabbits in a deep
wash where there were tall weeds and bushes and, among the
bushes, were tall, red salt trees. As he walks through the red salt
trees, it looked almost like being in a forest, except there were
millions and millions of mosquitoes in it. They would bite and suck
blood. Broneco tries to slap them away, but he was carrying his
load of arrows and his big bow.

When he came to an open place, he saw a jack rabbit ready to
run. Broneco jumps back on his seat and puts the long, white arrow
in the bow. When he stretch the bow and the tough leather string,
he heard crushes of sound from behind.

He quickly jumps up. Quickly he put his arrow back into the
buckskin arrow bag. He sees a horseman, he sees another one, and
another one.

He looked southward where he sees a little opening in the salt
tree. It was a few step away. So he rushes into the opening.

The horsemen turned their horses toward south.

Broneco made his way through with a terrible scrape across his
face. The blood runs down his face like a reddish colored of a wine.
Quickly he tear off his sleeves and wipe his face with it. He stopped
for a minute. Then he looked back. The horsemen came up on the
left side of the wash and headed towards him.

Broneco throws down his sleeve. He thought for another half

12

a minute, then he took off his arrow bag and bow. He throw this into a hole. Now he's got nothing to worry about. He stood there for a while like a prairie dog. Then he looked west.

The horsemen whipped their horses just as hard as they could.

Broneco just knew exactly where to lead them. He started to walk like a quarter horse. He smile then started to run. He runned like a roadrunner. Soon he came to the hilly place, and then across the wide wash. As he looked back, he saw only the hills and bushes.

He was tired now, but still he run part of the way back home. When he approach home he saw a young girl carrying a basket full of corn.

"A visitor," Broneco said. Oh, no. Coming home with a scrape on the head!

Broneco sets down on a wild prairie grass.

The girl saw him, and stoods there.

The sun began to set when Broneco saw that the sheep were just approaching home too.

The girl just dropped the basket and calls her mother.

"It is Amy, Broneco," his aunt called. "Come here."

Then Broneco gets up and walks slowly back to the tent.

"Oh, poor child, what happen to you?" Aunt Amy said.

"The horsemen chased me."

"Where's your weapon?"

"I left it," he said sadly.

"Where?" Aunt said.

"A couple of miles from here. I throw them in the fox's hole."

"I suppose no one gets it, so don't worry," she said.

Then the girl walk slowly out of the door strangely, her hair dark as night and her face real light colored pink.

As she stood there Aunt Amy turned around. "Come here, Annie, this is your cousin, Broneco," she said.

Then the girl smile and said, "Hello. I been hearing about you when Grandfather comes home to see me."

Broneco shakingly shakes her hands. Then Aunt takes them by their hands and takes Annie and Broneco to the small handmade coffee table.

13

Broneco looks in the tent and out. He only saw his big fat cat sleeping on the bed. "Where's Grandfather and Grandmother?" he asked.

"They went to the farm for a couple of days," Amy said.

After supper, Aunt Amy tell a story of The Mesa Verde. It was quite a long story which put both Broneco and Annie to sleep.

The next day Broneco waked up. Annie was still asleep and Aunt chops the woods. Broneco opens the corral gate for the sheep to graze in the meadow of the yonder hill where they spend their day as usual. Broneco called his Aunt that he wasn't hungry so he ran down the hill and across the wash just fast be he could until he came to where he hide his bow and arrow.

It was still there as he left it yesterday. He picked it up and mounted his buckskin bag on his back and putted the bow across his chest. Now he looks like a real Indian ready to fight his enemy. He walked a little ways. He saw the horse's footprint which was yesterday.

He turned around and headed back for home. About halfway back he spotted a fox, sitting on top of a boxlike rock. And over at the foot of that hill, Broneco sees his lamb eating away as though nothing is going to catch her.

The fox didn't see Broneco. The fox creep down the narrow ditches made by the water when it rain.

Broneco knew that the fox is real clever at catching a fat lamb. So he hurries up the side of the hills. When he comes to the top of the hill, he saw the fox made a leap at the lamb. Broneco yells just as hard as he could.

The fox jumps up and runs. The lamb just shook his head and runs too.

Without thinking another minute, Broneco grabs his arrow like a real warrior. He lifts the bow and the arrow high up in the air above his head. Then Broneco bring the bow and arrow down and aims. As the arrow flew across the small hill, he only shoots the hind legs. The fox falls and gets up again. Quickly Broneco grabs another arrow. He lifts it a little way up and quickly lets the arrow go, while the fox was making circle like a whirlwind. The arrow flies with a speed and strucks the fox on the neck.

Broneco didn't know the horsemen has again arrive. This time there was one. Broneco turned around and sees the stranger on the horseback coming close. Quickly he grabs an arrow. It was too late for him to run. Broneco had his arrow and bow across his waist line, ready to aim.

The stranger kept coming, smiling. "Are you going to shoot me too?" he said.

Broneco just stood there. "Stay away from me," Broneco said, "or I'll get this arrow through your throat."

"Wait a minute. Don't let the arrow go until I get through talking and, for heaven's sake, put that arrow down. I come here in friendly turn," he said. "My name is Little White Horse."

Broneco laughed. "My name is Broneco," he said.

Little White Horse got off the horse and look down a little ways. "That fox, its fur is blue-grey, and I like it," he said. "We use it in ceremonial dance, in the fall when it get colder."

"A ceremonial dance?" Broneco said. "I never seen one. What is it like?"

"Well, it's a long story, but I'll make it just as short as I can, and give you a brief idea of what it's like," said Little White Horse.

Broneco looked at White Horse sharply with his eyes wide. He prink his eyes as he listen.

Then White Horse reached for his bag on the side of the saddle. He reach inside the bag as Broneco stares. White Horse opens his bag and picked two turquoise rings. They were alike.

"Here, you can have the rings, and I take the furry fox," he said.

Broneco slowly reached for the rings. "No, I can't take it," Broneco said. He turns and walks a little ways.

White Horse calls, "Broneco, please take it."

Broneco strides back slowly and picks up the rings. "Thanks," said Broneco. "Tell me. Why were some horsemen after me yesterday?"

White Horse laugh softly and said, "Don't be afraid. They were my three sons who were hunting fox."

"They were?" Broneco said. "Why do they chase me then?"

"I suppose you were real young."

"Young," said Broneco with a miserable look.

"Now I pick up my furry fox," the man said as he mount his horse. "Good day, Little One," he said, waving at Broneco.

"Little One," said Broneco, smiling as he swings his bow.

Broneco went on his way back to the foot of the hills, and there were all the sheeps quietly chewing their grass. Broneco went on. He strolled back home. It was almost noon now.

Amy and Annie were sitting under the shade house. "What took you so long?" said Amy.

Broneco explains and give the rings to his aunt.

"Oh, they're beautiful," she said.

Broneco didn't care about the ring, so he gave it to his aunt.

Now the week has gone by. The days went as the same routine. Then one day Aunt said she was going to the store.

Broneco wanted to know what it was like to go to town. He asked his aunt many times that he would like to see white's civilization.

Finally, Amy said, "O.K." Then Amy looked at Broneco. "Are you going in that dirty clothes?" she said, as she puts on a red, bright colored squaw dress with a white lace at the edge of her dress which made her look handsome. She was young and she wore an earring made of plain silver and a turquoise necklace. "Change your shirt and pants."

"What for?" Broneco said.

"All right, you go like that," she said. Aunt knew that Broneco would be embarrassed, but she understands that although Broneco has seen cars, he has never been to town. She didn't want to say no more.

It was five miles from where they live. So Broneco and his aunt walked for five miles when they came to the edge of the town street.

Broneco saw white kids, and they were dress up. They weren't dirty as he was. Broneco stop and said, "Amy, I'll wait here for you."

"All right. Don't you ran all the way back home, 'cause you going to help me carry some grocery," she said.

Broneco stood there alone. Right near a house there was a yard and green grass, and besides the house there stood a tall tree. He looked down the road as Aunt enter the trading post. He walked up to the tree and sat on the green, cool grass. Nearby a water sprinkle turns in a clockwise. As he watches the sprinkle, a white boy came out of the house slowly.

Broneco didn't look anywhere except watching the sprinkle.

The white kid step slowly down the steps. Then he reached the gate and slowly opened it. Then he snick around the white fence and stand there a yard away.

Broneco looked up and jerk back.

Then the boy said, "Hello!"

Broneco looked straight at the boy as he wore a white shirt and a blue jeans. Then Broneco got up and bowed instead of saying hello. The boy understood. Broneco smiled as the boy grinned.

Broneco stood there as the boy stands too. Broneco thought for a while to show some expression to tell him that he's waiting for his aunt. Then Broneco point his finger to himself and said, "Broneco."

The white boy smiles, then he pointed to himself and said, "Dale."

As Broneco and Dale communicate, they both learn quite a bit in the next four hours. By now, Broneco knew a little. Then he would repeat them again to Dale. Dale was the teacher. Broneco by now learned that "hello" mean to greet.

When his aunt returns he said, "Hello," to his aunt.

The white boy smile, waving him good-by.

When they got home, Broneco would say the words to himself. His ambition was to learn to speak English. By now, Broneco knew a little about white man's way. When another week went by, he has changed.

He learned to keep his clothes clean. He kept himself out of dirt. Broneco knew the way to Dale's house. So he went there on his second visit.

Broneco stood outside the fence. A man open the door and said a few words.

Broneco didn't understand so he said, "Dale."

The man smiled and shaked his head and left the door open.

Broneco stood there for a while, then Dale came out and said, "Oh, hello there."

Then Broneco repeats the words and smiles.

Now Broneco was clean, but his hair was still long. Dale holds Broneco by the hand and leads him into the house. Inside the house there were colored carpets, and various size of rooms, and different kinds and shapes of chairs.

A woman looks from the next room as Dale's father walk up and said, "I'm Mr. Curley and that Mrs. Curley," as he points to the woman who was in the kitchen with her apron on.

She was slim and short as her lips was red and had a long curly hair. Mrs. Curley hair was blond.

"You need a haircut," Mr. Curley said to Broneco, but he didn't understand at all. So Mr. Curley points. Then Broneco would understand.

So Broneco gets a haircut at the Curley residence. They washed Broneco's hair and putted some hair oil on it. Although Broneco didn't have any socks, so Dale gave him a pair. It was white.

Now Broneco looked like a real American boy with his short haircut and his white socks. He learned many more things while he spent his day at Dale's house. Dale's family were nice.

So, at the end of the day, Broneco said, "Good-by," in English, as he waved his hand and left.

It didn't take long for Broneco to get home. While on his way home, he reached the hill where he spent his day before. When he came to the top of the hill, he looked up towards the heaven as though an angel would appear. The wind blew gently and whispering in his ear.

Then he looked at his home—only a tent and a tree-shaded house, and the sheeps are now moving into the corral. Broneco stood for another minute and said to himself, "Surely there is a way for me to learn."

As he approach home, his cousin Annie walk outside the tent and said, "Broneco, your Grandmother come home and she was mad because you went to town to see your white friend. And my mother went back to the farm to help my Grandfather and I'm going back with you and Grandmother said we're moving back to Salt Water Canyon tomorrow. And Grandmother has got through packing."

Broneco sat down on a log sadly as his head hung down like a tired dog.

"You better go inside the tent before Grandmother comes out with that long stringlike metal bar," she said. "I'm scare too."

Broneco didn't say a single word as Annie left and walked back into the tent sadly. Broneco got up and stride and kicked a can and stepped into the tent.

Grandmother looked up like a mad bull. Like Annie said—"a metal bar"—Broneco got hit in the head with a bar. Then a broomstick over his back. Broneco's head was now bleeding.

Annie cried out loud and said, "Please, Grandmother, don't hurt him anymore."

Broneco half fainted as he fall against the bed, but he can still hear Grandmother's mad voice.

"That should teach you not to run off from your work at home, and you knew that there's a wood to chop and sheep to take care of," Grandmother said. "From now on, don't you dare ever run off again." She throw the metal bar outside. Then she stepped through the door and is gone.

Annie rushed from her corner bed over to Broneco. "Oh, Brother," she said, as she weep and holds Broneco's bleeding head over her lap.

At that moment Broneco recovers and opens his eyes and hug his cousin. "Oh, little Sister," he said, wiping his tears as Annie's tears runs down her light pink cheek.

The moon has rose high up in the sky as the stars twinkle. Then Broneco gets up and peeps through an opening of the tent. He only saw his Grandmother sleeping on a furry sheepskin.

Broneco turned around and said, "Annie, please go to sleep,

for tomorrow it is again my long journey with my flock of sheep in a dust of cloud."

Annie covered herself with a woven rug.

But Broneco didn't go to sleep. He kept thinking and wondering when will he ever be happy again. Thinking, all his life he had never been happy, as he recalls his past time, and thinking of the future. Thinking, will he ever reach it? He didn't know.

· III ·

Grandfather's Surprise Comes True

IT WAS DAWN BY NOW as the star were disappearing. At that moment, Annie wake up and gets up fast. "Brother! Brother!" she said.

"What is it?" Broneco said, slowly like if he had a cold.

"We'll leave to my mother's place, right now," she said.

"No, Annie. I can't do that. Surely this time I'll get my throat cut," Broneco said. "I'll go and open the gate for the sheep and start before Grandmother get angry again." Broneco kiss his cousin on the forehead and quickly opens the tent's entrance. Grandmother was still asleep and snoring. Broneco runs for the gate and opens it.

Quickly he gets the sheep out of the corral. Since all the lambs and goats are big now, there's nothing to worry about. As he followed the sheep over the first small hill, he remembers that he had left his bow and arrow. So he has to pick it up before Grandmother awakes.

He runs back and reached the tent. As he rushed in, he didn't see Annie, but he didn't think about it. The next moment he grab his bow and arrow bag. He quickly rushes back out and hide behind tent, and his Grandmother didn't notice him as she wakes up.

"Broneco, get up and get a head start," Grandmother said, but no sound came from the tent, nor she didn't hear any dogs barked. "Annie," she said. Still there was no sound as she combed her hair with brush made of grass weed. Then she looked toward the corral and she didn't see a single sheep. "Oh!" she said and gets up and opens the tent entrance and looks around. Surely now, Broneco's throat is going to be cut! She walks around in circle.

Now the sun is up and it was quiet. Only the roadrunner peek in a distance. As for Annie, she was gone. While Grandmother look in tent, Broneco run to catch up with the sheep and struggle along after them. The water spring was five miles away.

Finally, around about eight o'clock, Broneco reached the spring. Annie waited there with a bag hanging over her back. She had a blue jar in her hand as she stood among the wash.

Broneco rubbed his eyes and looked. "Annie! What are you doing here?" he said. "And how did you get here?"

"I made the short-cut," she said.

Broneco didn't say another words. He only turned around and sat down.

"What's wrong," Annie said.

"Oh, nothing, Annie."

"Are you sure?"

"Of course," Broneco said.

"You want some water?" Annie said.

"No."

Then Annie sat besides Broneco while the sheep rested, then struggling slowly up the hill.

Broneco gets up and Annie followed. They didn't speak or spoke another words until they come upon a steep hillside.

As the sheeps rushes down, jumping and turning, Annie said, "I'm tired."

Broneco stops and looks at Annie. "We got to make it, or else we'll have to spend a night and sleep on the cold ground," he said.

Then Annie stop. "Look," she said, "there, down yonder."

"Those are horses," Broneco said.

"Perhaps we could ride one," Annie said smiling.

Broneco grins. "Perhaps," he said as he look at Annie again.

"But there's no rope," and he look around for a while. "Oh, what's the use!" he said, tearing his both sleeves off.

Then Annie reached into her bag and had a two-by-three foot white cloth. Then they tear it into a narrow stripes and made a woven laced rope.

"Maybe that white mare is tame," Broneco said.

It was tame all right, but lazy. With her is a gray colt. When Broneco looked to the right he saw a fat stud, the color of his fur was shiny black gold. He stood up and stamp his feet and bowing his head.

"Whoa, boy," Broneco said, smiling-looking at Annie.

"Whoa," said Annie as she walks slowly with her hand out, and in her hand she had a pure fresh green grass. The horse just shaked his head again when Annie started to walk forward slowly, step by step.

"No, Annie, come back here," said Broneco.

"Sh-sh, quiet," she said.

The horse just stood still as Annie walks right up to him and gives him the green grass. Then she puts the woven rope around the horse's neck. Then Annie puts her head against the horse's head. "He's amicable," she said, grinning like if she's ready to cry.

Broneco had his mouth open standing at his position. Then he walked over. "Do you think we can ride him?" he asked. "I'll try first. If it bucks me off, it'll be O.K."

Then Annie gave the woven rope to Broneco.

Broneco pats the horse and examines it. By now the sheep has gone farther, and the mare horse neighs as her young colt gets up from behind the tall sage brush.

"I'll put this rope around his nose and tie it here," said Broneco.

But Broneco was too small to climb on the horse's back. So he swings himself on the neck, grabbing a hold of the shiny, long hair. He made it to the top as Annie steps backward away from the horse. There was no worry for Broneco because he was skillful at it. He turns the horse around and kicks him a little and the horse moves like a springy bed as he steps.

"Aren't you going to buck me off, black stallion?"

He neighs and shakes his head.

"Come on, Annie. We'll be riding for the day," said Broneco, laughing. "Swing yourself behind me. O.K?"

"I'll try," Annie replied. She made her first swing, but fell back off. Then she tries again and again when finally Broneco gets off and helped his sister, Annie, up the horse's back. The horse just stand high and great.

Then Broneco swings again on the horse's neck and grabs the long hair and kicks his leg over the shoulder of the horse. Then they were both on the horse with a rope around the horse's nose.

Broneco and Annie has been riding bare horseback before, so it didn't matter to them how hard is the horse's spine, although it wasn't bony. The horse was quite smooth and shaped.

"Well, what are we waiting for?" said Broneco as he smile and look back at his sister. "Are you ready?"

"Yes," she said, holding onto her brother.

It was late now. The sheep has now disappeared into the distance, only the dust of cloud is in the air. The white mare and the grey colt followed up, and Broneco now kicks the black stallion. As he moves, he walks like if he was marching in a parade, and his head shake like a pigeon is walking.

"Faster," said Annie, "so we can catch up the sheeps."

"Oh," Broneco said as he kicks the horse. He had his arrow bag and bow. Annie had a bag on her back which contained food and a glass bottle full of water which is only a quart size.

The horse speeds up and runs like a running deer. Over the hills and pasture they rode as the white mare and her colt followed along behind. That was the stallion's mother and brother.

Then they came to the hillside and now they could see the whole flocks of sheep down below. Since they were only concentrating on riding, as they looked ahead they didn't know they were now entering the Mesa. The horse walked on swiftly while followed by his mother and brother.

Finally they reached the herd of sheeps all moving on along the hot dry road. One coughs. Another spring is now one mile ahead.

"We'll rest at the next spring and for sure we'll eat and let the sheeps rest too. We'll start again when it gets cooler," Broneco said.

"What'll we do with this horse?" said Annie.

"Don't worry about the horses. They know their ways," he said, looking ahead.

When they reached the water spring, the sheeps just rushed into the water and so did the stallion and his family. The dogs were swimming in the center of the cold pooled water, and the spring twinkle down the side of the rock which was there against the side of another rocks and gravel.

"Let's get off the horse and rest under that tall weed brush," said Broneco, "and we'll eat."

The water tasted part of salt, but not very.

Annie didn't speak much. She was a very quiet girl. She opens her bag and puts out four rolls of biscuit and a roast mutton.

"Where did you get the mutton?" asked Broneco.

Annie look up with a strange look. "I took it out of Grandmother's oven," she said.

"You did?"

Then Annie looked down and smiled. "That's all right. She's got a lot of muttons. How far is Salt Water Canyon?" she said.

"Do you see that grey rock in the canyon?" said Broneco. "That where it is."

The sheeps didn't rest. They move on again. So Annie and Broneco decided to move on too.

The black-gold stallion stood under the shade when Annie got a hold of him again so they could ride. Like they did before, Annie and Broneco climbed and jump on the horse's back. It didn't take very long for Broneco, Annie, the sheep to reach the Canyon.

When they came upon Salt Water Canyon, it looked like a river as the water rushes like a stream of water running in an irrigation ditches, many salt trees and green as ever. The breezes of the wind became cool. The birds flew about.

So Broneco and Annie got off the horse and takes the rope off his nose.

25

"You can go now," said Broneco, "and we'll see you again real soon."

Annie groaned as she walked a little ways, carrying her bag. Then Annie sits down on a rock as Broneco followed and also sit on a rock too.

Annie and Broneco didn't know that their Grandfather was watching from the top of the canyon. Quickly he whip his horse and rides down the steep side of the rocky canyon, along an old road made by the ancestors. He rides through the salt trees and salt water.

"Grandfather coming," said Annie. She gets up and stands there.

Broneco just sat there and didn't say a word.

Grandfather jump off the horse and rushes over to Annie "Oh, sweet darling, are you hurt?" he said.

"No," said Annie. "Why?"

"That horse you were riding is Bronka."

Broneco turns around and looks with an amazement.

Grandfather breathing heavily and said, "Don't you know that horse, Bronka, has never been ridden before?"

"Never?" said Broneco, with his eyes wide open.

Annie turned around and looked at Bronka stands on a rock.

"That's my horse, and the mare too," said Grandfather, "and you were named after him."

"Broneco," said Broneco, looking at Bronka who neighs again.

"I sure can't believe it," said Grandfather as he smile.

Then Grandfather sat back on his horse. Then Annie climbs up on the back. Broneco walked on and the sheep moved on through the canyon.

The salty water streams twinkle as it flows down its path. The sun began to set by now. It is getting colder, except only the echo vibrates through the canyon, and the smell of cedar trees made a scent of tasty delicious corn bread.

At the top of the canyon, Grandmother waits on a grey donkey with a white muzzle and around the eyes were dark black. With its long ear it points skyward as he sees the sheep approach. Then Grandmother whips the donkey gently and the donkey moves on.

Then she approach Grandfather and Annie. "Oh, I was so worry about you kids," she said.

As for Broneco didn't look or turned around. He just walked on with his bursted head on the side. Since Broneco was wearing a large headband, Grandfather didn't see it. Broneco know, if Grandfather finds out, surely Grandmother would get whip like a small child and they would just fight like a rooster and a hen fighting.

Broneco didn't look like a real Indian 'cause of his haircut. But he didn't worry about it. He knew it would grow back before too long.

The next morning, just as soon as Broneco woke up, he washed his face with cold water. Then he stretch his arms out and yawned. Then he took a deep breath, filling his chest with fresh air. He looked at the hill and looked toward the mountain where he usually played and jumped.

He stood against the post. The puff of smoke smelled strongly. He wondered of Bronka and the grey colt which he seen yesterday, and it was Grandfather's horses.

Then he said to himself, "I'll see you again, Bronka, and ride you again."

Then he turned to his hogan and stepped back inside. Grandfather sat there with a red cup in his hand, and on his left hand a fork. Annie poured a hot coffee for Broneco and Grandmother. Broneco sat on the hard beaten-down earth, while Annie, Grandmother, and Grandfather sat on a woolly sheepskin.

After the breakfast, Annie sweeps the dirt floor. Broneco ran to the corral and opened the gate like he usually do. He almost forgot his bow and arrow, so he walked back to the hogan and picked it up.

Then Annie speaks and said, "Broneco, may I go too?"

"To herd sheep?"

"Yes," she said.

Broneco just ignore her, but Annie didn't pay no attention to Broneco as she followed. When they got to the hillside, Broneco ask if Annie could run like a scared jack rabbit.

Annie just stood there with an annoyance, as she looked like hiding her side of the face. Then Annie said, "Let me see you run like a scared jack rabbit first."

Broneco laughed hard.

Annie was now embarrassed. Her face became red. "All right, I'll race you down the hill and to that next forest," she said with her hands on her waist.

"Are you sure you can run that far?" asked Broneco.

"Of course I can. I used to race with Johnnie," she said.

"Who's Johnnie?"

"He's my cousin," she said.

Broneco started asking her question that soon he forgot to race with Annie.

Then Annie said, "Broneco, can you teach me how to shoot an arrow?"

Across the small valley the sheep grazing where the green grass is. "Your arms are too short," Broneco said as he pull one arrow out of his arrow bag.

"Just let me try," she said.

Broneco give the bow and arrow to Annie. "Put the arrow in between the bow."

Annie followed the instruction. Then she lifted the bow in the air as she stood and pulled the string.

"Downward."

Then she pulled downward and letted the string go. The arrow struck the side of a cedar tree as it bounces in an angle toward Broneco.

"Oh!" she said.

Broneco was struck with an arrow. Gladly he was skinny. It only struck his shirt which was kind of big for him. "I'm shot," he said, "and it doesn't hurt, Annie."

"What did I do now?" she said as she started to cry.

Broneco just stood silently against the old stump which was still standing.

"Just tell your Grandmother that I shot myself with an arrow," Broneco said slowly.

28

Then Annie rushed to Broneco and grabbed the arrow and Broneco moved sideways as his shirt ripped.

"It didn't struck you," Annie said. "It only miss the side of your bony ribs."

Broneco just laughed while Annie wiped her tears with her sleeves. She was embarrassed because Broneco keeps laughing.

"Oh, shut up," said Annie.

Broneco stopped laughing. Then he picked up the bow and arrow and looked at Annie. Broneco held the arrow in his hand. "This arrow is evil," he said.

Annie sat on the stump of a cedar. "What are you going to do with it?"

"I'm going to break it," he said. Broneco lifted the arrow horizontally in the air above his head and looked up towards the blue heaven while Annie only smiled.

Then Broneco broke the arrow. "No harm will come to us," he said. Broneco gave the bow and a new arrow to Annie again.

"You shoot first," she said gently.

Again, of what his Grandfather taught him, he lift the bow and arrow in its place, and lifted it above his head in the air. Then he brought it down slowly and made the arrow flying, and struck the tall cedar tree down in the yonder hill. "Now, it's your turn," he said as he gave it to Annie.

Annie has been watching Broneco carefully. Then Annie puts the arrow in the bow and slowly, as her eyes twinkle, she pressed her lips together and stretch the bow with the arrow in its side. Then slowly she lifted it in the air as the wind blew while her shiny long black hair waves.

Annie shut her eyes and slowly brought the arrow down. In the distance, the crow crowed, and Broneco with a watchful eyes just stood silently and never said no words. Finally Annie letted her arrow go. The arrow flew soundly then struck the cedar tree near the next tree which Broneco shot.

"It's very good," Broneco said. "I'll teach you more and I want you to practice every day here," he said.

29

Sure enough, day after day, Annie learns how to shoot arrow and how to aim. Broneco taught his cousin just as much as he can. It was winter now and it was in the month of March which was the third day.

"I'm staying home today," said Annie.

"All right," said Broneco as he turned around slowly that morning.

Grandmother turned around and smiled at Broneco as she was making Navaho corn ice cream. Annie sat down to make berry pudding. And Grandfather putted more sticks in the adobe oven.

Broneco stepped outside with his woven coat and his neck scarf. Grandfather step outside after him.

"Your Aunt is coming today," Grandfather said.

Broneco only grinned and picked up his bow and arrow and walked off towards the corral. Broneco felt different that day as he strolled to the corral and open the gate for the sheeps to graze. The dogs jumped him and wanted to play as usual.

Grandfather stared at Broneco as he is jumping and laughing, playing with his dog, Pinky and Yellow. "All of a suddenly my boy, Broneco, has changed," Broneco hears Grandfather whisper.

Then Annie step out from the hogan and putted her arms around Grandfather's neck. "Is there something wrong?" she said, looking at her grandfather charmfully.

"No, Annie," he said and smiled, kissing her on the cheek. "Now go help your Grandmother," he said.

Annie skipped back into the hogan.

Then, back in the edge of the woods, Aunt Amy came riding the horse. On her side there hung a big bundle of goods. Broneco still playing with his dog when finally she reached the hogan and got off the horse as she spoke. "Whoa! Steady, Blacky."

Annie peeped out of the small window. "Grandmother, my mother is here," she said.

"Sh! Quiet down, Annie, and stir up your berry pudding, and put more sticks into the oven, and see if the yeast bread is now done," Grandmother said.

In the next moment, Amy knock on the door.

"Come in," call Grandmother, sitting on her woolly goatskin. Annie got up and rushed up to her mother and hug her.

"Where's your Grandfather?" Amy ask.

"He was outside," Annie said as she step out the door and looked, but there was no sign of Grandfather. She rushed back to the door. "He isn't outside," she said.

"He's probably out after the horse, Pinto," said Grandmother.

"What Pinto?" Annie asked her Grandmother.

"Oh, it's the son of Bronka," she said.

"Bronka?" Annie again asked.

"It's your Grandfather's wild stallion," said Amy as she describe the color and what color his mate is.

Annie thought about it. "That's the horse I and Broneco rode once," she said.

"You rode Bronka?" said Annie's mother strangely.

Grandmother dropped her dipper and looked at Annie. "I can't believe it," she said gently.

"It's true. Grandfather saw us," Annie replied.

Broneco went jumping and running after the sheep.

It is late in the afternoon when Broneco gets back and Amy opened the door. Broneco is tired and stepped into the hogan and saw that the food was really prepared. Annie smile as she leaned against her Grandfather.

After dinner, Grandfather said to Broneco, "Remember the time you use to sit on my lap, when I use to mention that I had a surprise for you which is approximately two years ago. It is now out there in the corral."

Broneco didn't know it was his birthday. He looked at Grandfather with a surprise and rushed out the door. Then he looked toward the corral. There he saw a young horse. The color of the horse was black and at its feet it looked like he has been in a snow. At the neck there is a white spot.

Annie walked outside, swinging her feet as she walk. "That's Pinto," she said, "the colt that followed us with his white mother."

At that moment Broneco saw Bronka and the white mare in the other corral having a tasty hay.

Pinto just stood there as Broneco walked up to him.

"Pinto," said Broneco as he moved slowly to touch his nose.

Pinto didn't move a bit.

Annie smile while standing behind the fence.

Broneco spoke to his given horse and said, "My dear horse, Pinto. I'll teach you every trick."

·IV·

There Is a Way!

I T WAS IN THE SPRING NOW. The sun shined and it started getting hotter day by day. The cheerful birds sings as Broneco continue with his training Pinto.

Pinto was like Broneco. He was learning tricks quicker than Broneco though. Annie would come and ride Pinto while learning his various trick. At last, Pinto was taught to jump over five-foot fence. It was very hard. So he was started off with one foot, then two, and etc. Sometimes Pinto would just runned into the fence.

Day after day, while herding sheep, Pinto learns more and more. While, on the other hand, Annie was learning to do what Broneco used to do such as shooting arrow, riding down the rocky hillside, and riding horse and roping. At the end of May, Grandmother said to Broneco that it is time to move to summer camp to the usual place.

The next morning when it was early dawn, Broneco got up and started to bundle up the blanket. Annie putted the coffee in the open fire outside while Grandmother putting dishes into the boxes.

"Broneco, find Bronka and the mare, and Tellie too," she said.

"Oh, Tellie is mean," said Broneco. "Why are they always like that?"

"It's because they are ass, that's why."

Broneco picked up the rope from behind the bed roll and started on his way.

At the corral, he got the bridle and putted it on Pinto. Quickly he open the entrance and mounted his horse and gallop away. Pinto is now a real swift horse. Like an antelope he went over the bushes and over the ditches made by the rain. When he came to the hill, Broneco stopped Pinto, but Pinto couldn't kept still.

Broneco looked that way and that way, but no signs of Bronka nor Tellie or the mare. Then Broneco turns Pinto east and rode on down the hill into the forest of cedar. Then along the road to the spring, when Broneco saw Bronka standing.

Broneco whistle at Bronka. He turn and wave his tail and calls to white mare and Tellie. At Bronka's command, Tellie has to follow.

When the sun raise atop the mountain, Broneco trailing in after Bronka and others. Grandmother and Annie were having a coffee break, sitting together on the small bench. Broneco ride in and got off Pinto.

"Just tie Pinto to the post and Annie will feed him some wheat," said Grandmother. "We're all riding together today."

"We are?" said Broneco. "And we have to pack on the horses?"

"Yes," she said, pouring another hot coffee as the little steam float from the coffee.

In the fireplace there was a dry meat ready to fry. The smell of the meat was tasteless with grease. And the burning of the woods smelled cedar. Pinky and Yellow came for their usual chow in the morning, while the big black cat lick his paw pointing southward.

Meanwhile Grandmother started packing while Broneco get the horse and Tellie ready for the long journey. As the things were prepared, Grandmother and Annie started packing food and bedding on the mare's back and on Bronka including Tellie. Bronka once was wild, but now he is well trained by Grandfather.

Annie runned to corral and opened the gate for the sheep while Broneco and Grandmother still packing. The hot sun begin to shine. Only few white cottonlike clouds were in the air. As the sheep were on their way, the dry earth made dust. While Grandmother riding the white mare, Annie riding Bronka, and Broneco riding Pinto. They all started out together while Tellie tailing.

Down the green pasture, over the small hill, and down the side of the hill and into the canyon they followed slowly after the sheep. While riding, Grandmother whistle along as the echo sounds through the steep canyon.

It was now noon. The sky began to darken while the clouds moving in together. When they got to the open plain away from the mesa, it began to rain. It only dropped there and here. The wind started blowing.

Grandmother said, "Hurry up the sheep. If it rains heavy we are going have to stay here, so let's hurry before the yonder wash would fill up with rain water and never make it across."

Then Broneco whipped his horse, Pinto, and chased the sheep together. While Annie was getting the big black cat under her plastic raincoat.

In the next moment it started to rain then heavily and now the ground was wet and begun to soak. Finally they reached the wash, when the thunder roars like a hungry lion roaring in the forest ready to catch a deer. When they made it across, they slowed down. Now it was nothing to worry about.

Grandmother didn't care about getting wet, and so did Annie and Broneco. So they move on. In the late evening, finally, they made it to the summer camp.

Annie was about to fall off the horse when they came to the place where they lived the year before. Grandmother with an A-h-h sound she got off the horse too. Broneco just grinned and got off Pinto. He didn't feel pain because he had done much riding.

"My legs are stiff," said Annie while rubbing her Grandmother's back.

Now Broneco has to unload and get the bundle off the horse and put the several things under the shade house which stood there for a year. Quickly he cutted the tallest weeds, and sweeped the hard dirt and pile up some sticks and build fire so he can have a hot coffee and eat.

Grandmother fixed the place to sleep while Broneco ties the horse's front feet together so that they won't be far the next morning. Annie was real tired so she fall asleep with her cat.

Broneco and his Grandmother chatters, sitting in front of the fire watching the horses move over the hill, and the sheep are in corral going to sleep too. The stars began to twinkle and the cool air blew from the wet ground as it smell cool. Grandmother and Broneco went to sleep late at night. There was no more sound except the wind whisper.

The next day, the sun rise brightly and the grass has already turned green. Grandmother, Broneco, and Annie were still asleep when Grandfather came. He stack the fire kindling wood and build a fire and put on a hot coffee and prepared the breakfast. He knew that his family were tired. When he opened the gate for the sheep, then Grandmother wake up.

"Oh dear," she said, "your Grandfather is here." She got up slowly and move on her knees towards the fire.

Broneco and Annie were just waking up now.

When they were all awake, they put up the tent and started to move bedding in. It was a real tough job to unpack and wash dishes and even blankets. Grandmother and Annie cleaned the place all day. And Broneco was tired too, making holes to put poles in it and to make a new corral for Bronka, the mare, and Pinto. And Tellie can stay outside.

Things started like the year before, but there were little changes. As the days goes by, different things happen. Then one day when Broneco looked in the mirror, he saw that his hair was grown long again, and he was still wearing the designed headband.

Broneco went to Annie while she was sewing her dress which was torn by a branch while riding in the salt trees. And Grandmother is weaving like she always did.

"Annie," said Broneco, "will you cut my hair?"

Annie looked at her Grandmother, then she said, "Come inside the tent and I'll cut the longest hair."

Broneco stepped inside the tent, and Annie started cutting here and there. Then he comb it. It looked short, but still it was big.

When Broneco stepped outside and said, "I'm going hunting," he lied to his Grandmother.

He runned over the hill and across the small wash. Then sud-

36

denly he struggle to the edge of a group of trees and stood there. I'll sure surprise Dale, he said to himself. But it wasn't that way.

Dale was playing basketball outside when Broneco walked slowly up to him. But Dale just stepped backward and said, "Who are you?"

Broneco then said, "Broneco."

"You dirty rat, beat it," said the boy, "and don't come back."

Broneco struggled away sadly and never did look back. It wasn't Dale, but where's Dale!

Broneco didn't know that they had moved away to another place. So Broneco has to go back home without a haircut.

When Broneco approach home, he saw Grandmother still weaving. The sheep are in the yonder hills, also the horse too. Broneco felt like running away from home, but where would be go? There was no place for him like summer camp, he thought, walking toward the tent.

Annie walk out from the tent and stood there looking at Broneco. "What happen?" ask Annie.

"The pale-face didn't want me," he said.

Annie only stare at Broneco while holding a piece of material. Broneco just smile and put his hand upon Annie's head and walked on into the shade house. Grandmother still weaving, crushing the yarn of colored strings, changing the string on the loom and beating it down with a rhythm. She hums while unwinding yarns and cutting.

Broneco again began to wonder of speaking the white man's way. It continue in his mind day after day. Until one day in the month of August, Broneco's Uncle John come with his wife, Vera, to visit.

His wife smile and shook hands gently with her soft hands. John talked to his mother outside the tent for a minute. While Grandmother speaks softly with disagreements, Broneco sneaks out of the tent. He knew something was wrong, but he didn't know what it was.

Broneco stood behind the tent looking sad, but he felt happy. The sun shined and the day seems to be cool.

37

"Broneco," said John with a yell.

Broneco looked up while sitting behind the tent. Then he got up and slowly walked back into the shade house which is all covered with branches of leaves.

He didn't know that Grandfather was still sitting in the blue pickup outside. Grandfather opened the door and step out and walked slowly towards the tent with a cane in his hand.

"Yes," said Broneco to John.

He turned around and smiled. "You are leaving for school tomorrow," John said. "So today my wife is going to give you a haircut!"

John's wife smile and took Broneco by the hand. She picks up a red stool and picked up a small box and opened it. In the box there lay a silver plow that was a clipper. She picked it up and putted some oil on it and then pressed the handles together. Then she pick up the scissor and snip it together.

Then Broneco sat in the stool and putted a white nylon jacket on. John's wife slowly walk up and started snipping the long hair away. Then she used the clipper. When she got through, she said, "There."

Broneco looked up at the leaves and then at his feet, then got up and went into the tent. Annie and her Grandfather were playing a hand game.

Annie looked up with a surprise. "Broneco, I didn't know you were that handsome," she said, while she puts her arms around Grandfather's neck.

"Broneco," yelled John.

Broneco replied, "Yes."

"Come out here."

Broneco strolled back out of the tent and grinned.

"Remember, tomorrow at eight, you must be ready to go. Your mother is coming to see you also. She brought you a suitcase and clothing."

"My mother?" said Broneco with excitement, but Grandmother turns around and ignored Broneco.

Grandmother didn't like the idea of sending Broneco away to

school. John wanted Broneco to go to school, and so did Grandfather, but still Grandmother didn't want Broneco to go.

Again, John and his mother had to argue. Finally, it was settled when John and his wife went home.

When Broneco and Annie started to wash his clothes, Grandmother stepped up and putted her hands on her waist and said, "What do you think you are doing?"

Broneco stopped washing. Then she kicked the pan over. The splashing of the water dropped into Broneco's eyes with soap suds.

Annie rushed to Grandfather and told what happen outside.

"You will not go to school," Grandmother said harshly.

Now Grandfather was mad. "I'll teach her who's the boss around here," he said, as he throws his cane in the corner of the tent. Then he gets up.

Outside the tent Grandmother still argue. Grandfather steps outside the tent.

Broneco only wiped his eyes with a wash cloth.

Grandfather stood there with his rope in his hand. "You either straighten out or I'll whip you like the old times," said Grandfather angrily.

"Oh, you!" she said, holding a washboard in her right hand. "Since when did you whip me?" Grandmother said. "Whip me, my foot!"

"Now listen here, gooney bird, I'll whip you like I did one month after we got married," Grandfather said.

Broneco crawled under the small bed and watched, while Annie peek through the small hole made by a nail inside the tent.

"How dare you call me a gooney bird," Grandmother said and swing the washboard and throws it at Grandfather.

Grandfather drops the rope and grabbed a bucket full of water. While Grandmother was looking for another object to throw, Grandfather splashes the bucket of water in Grandmother's face. "Now, cool off, will you?" he said.

"I will not say yes," she said. "Now get out of my way and let me prepare supper."

Then Broneco crawls back out from under the bed. He didn't

know what to do. He only looked at his clothes laying on the wet earth and it smell like it had rain for the day.

As Grandmother prepares the evening supper, while sitting at the fireplace patting on her bread, Broneco many times wanted to ask Grandmother to let him go to school, but he refused himself.

Broneco didn't eat his supper. He only thought of going to school.

Annie and Grandfather enjoyed theirself besides the fire, eating and drinking hot tea and a fried potatoes. It smell with sweet, tasty butter.

Broneco couldn't go to sleep. He kept thinking of tomorrow. While Grandmother, Grandfather, and Annie all snoring, Broneco got out of bed and creep outside the tent.

Like it always has been, the stars twinkle and the big yellow moon shines. Broneco stood besides the pole and leaned against it. He wondered if his Grandmother would ever make up her mind by morning. Will she whip me, he thought. It was very hard to say. Only the owl hoot in the valley. Broneco could hear the water rushing swiftly down the San Juan River and hear the duck quack while the frog croak and squeal.

Broneco step back away from the pole and sat on a chair. He made himself comfortable and picked up the blanket and wrap himself. The cool air blew against Broneco. The night is still and quiet, only the bells that hung on the sheeps' neck jingle. Broneco fell asleep.

It is now early dawn. Everything began waking up, even Broneco, as Grandmother walks out of the tent half asleep.

She took a handful of water and splashed on her face to wake her up. When she turns around she saw Broneco. He looks like he is sleeping on the old chair, though he is awake enough to hear her when she spoke softly with a fading word, "My poor child, why do they have to take you away from me?"

Broneco sneak a look to see her sad expression on her face. She looked at Broneco like if she is going to wept. She must saw that Broneco had a tear on his cheek.

He felt her wipe the tear off gently with the tip of her finger. For a minute she stood silently and reluctantly. Then she turn sadly and stacked the kindling woods. When she lighted the wood, Broneco heard a roaring sound. He could hear, too, the spinning gyration of the wheels down the valley.

"Now, they come to take Broneco," Grandmother said, mixing flour and water.

Broneco stay with his eyes shut like still sleeping.

The sun rose brightly, ready to make its diurnal cycle as usual. The dogs began barking when the blue pickup approach. It was John and his wife, Vera.

Grandmother looked inscrutable as she sat there by the fire, making a hot pan bread.

John stopped the car and look around and start pull out his whiskers.

Vera looked at her husband, John. "Well, what are you waiting for?" she said.

"I'm waiting for the little boy Broneco's mother to go first," said John. "I see that Broneco is sleeping on the old chair."

Grandmother just kept herself busy patting the dough in her hand.

Broneco's mother, Emma, stretch her red blouse as she gets up. "Come on, Ronnie," she said, holding her son's hand. "I want you to meet your small brother."

"How tall is my brother?" he said.

"You'll see. Come on," she said as she stepped out of the pickup. Ronnie follows his mother behind, holding onto his mother's white and red striped dress. The red stripe is lined on the middle of her dress.

John, while in the pickup, continue to pulling his whiskers while Vera is blowing her nose. Grandmother pay no attention when she saw her daughter, Emma, walking slowly towards her.

"Oh, no!" she said, putting another bread on the plate.

"Hello, mother," Emma said as she hug her mother.

Broneco is still pretending to be asleep.

"Where's father?" Emma said.

41

"He inside the tent with his granddaughter, still sleeping," said Grandmother. "I'll get them up."

Emma turns around and sees Broneco. When he peek at her, he think she wondering if that is her boy whom she left seven years ago only taking Ronnie with her to find and seek her new home where someday she would support her family and live together.

At that moment, Broneco opens his eyes wide as John walked slowly with his wife towards the tent.

"Get up. Your daughter, Emma, is here," said Grandmother in the tent, trying to wake Grandfather and Annie.

Annie, still half asleep jump up with a quick jerk, her eyes wide open. She said, "My mother. Oh, my mother." She rushed out the door, only the material cloth of the tent waved and twisted.

"Wait, not your mother," said Grandmother excitedly.

Annie didn't hear Grandmother spoke. "Oh mother," she said. as Annie puts her arms around Emma's waist.

Emma didn't move or push Annie out of the way. She only putted her hand on Annie's head and runned her fingers through Annie long, black hair. Emma knew it was her sister Amy's daughter.

John scratches his head and said, "What a mix-up family!"

So John walked up to Broneco.

Broneco looked up at John and Emma.

John held Broneco's hand and unwrapped him without saying a word. While inside the tent Grandfather and Grandmother help each other to fix the bed.

"My daughter," said Grandfather and he rushes out. "Just like my daughter Amy," he said.

Then John said to Broneco, "Broneco, this is your mother, Emma."

Broneco looked eastward and stared. Emma walked slowly and saw that tears runned down his cheek. He didn't say a word. He only sat and looked eastward while the sun glow, while the wild flowers waves as the wind blew.

Broneco wiped his tear and looked at his mother. She looked exactly like his Aunt Amy, and at her side there stood a young boy. That must be my brother, he thought. He just blink his eyes and looked downward.

Then Grandmother stepped up to Broneco. "You are going to school, my boy. First, you must eat," she said.

John smiled and kissed his mother and said, "Shall we all eat now?"

"I Am Lost"

B RONECO GRINNED and holded his mother's hand. Annie, wide
awake, gets a hold of Grandfather's hand.

"Oh, I was so busy this morning trying to get various things
done," said a mysterious voice behind the tent. "How's my little
girl, Annie?" Then Auntie walked to the open side with her sister-
in-law, Vera, chattering together.

Annie only ignore her mother while Grandfather smile, holding
his grandchild, Annie, by the hand.

Then John call. "Please, everyone eat and let's enjoy the happy
day," he said.

While the whole family were ready to eat the breakfast feast,
Broneco sneaked out of the shade house. He rushed to the hill
which he was always familiar with since he was small. He stood
at the foot of the hill and then walked up the hill marching, in his
left hand holding a small bag.

In the small bag, there is a yellow grain of corn pollen to worship
with—to the blessing of the mother earth and to the father of light,
the sun. After his going-away prayers of words, he strolled back
down the hill.

When he reached back to the house, Broneco happily started
packing his clothes, taking his time, but he forgot to say goodbye
to his pet lamb. So he quit packing, leaving half of the clothes
unpacked.

He went to the doorway of the tent and peeped through his favorite get away hole. Then he went out the front entrance again. He stood by the door and watched his beloved family, still enjoying talking and chewing a bit of this and that.

Broneco saw John sitting beside his mother talking, holding a cup filled with dark coffee. Grandfather and Annie sat together at the far end of the family, sitting on a very delicate sheepskin. Broneco stood by the entrance of the tent and smiled at his brother, but his brother blinked his eyes and then cuddled close to his mother.

Broneco then ran to the corral and, before he could reach the corral, there was his lamb right beside her mother still chewing her cud.

"Lamby," said Broneco.

Without any doubt of waiting, she looked up from behind her mother. "Ba-a-a," she said, as if she understands what Broneco is saying. She got on her four legs and standed there, waiting to be call again.

Then Broneco climbed over the main gate into the corral. "Oh, Lamby, I'll miss you. I hope you'll remember me by next spring when I return from the land of my friends, the white ones. I, Broneco, will then be the brother of the whites. I'll long for you, sweet Lamby, but I'll return," he said.

Broneco looked at his pet lamb again as she looked up at him. "Goodbye, Lamby," he said as he kissed her on her soft, furry cheek. The smell was like the smell of wet dirt mixed with corral scent. For Broneco, he loved the smell of his pet, for he knows that he'll miss the smell of it. Broneco again kissed her before he climbed back over the gate.

Then he stepped away from the fence and looked into the distance. He was thinking, "Now, I'll see the world. It has been a long time, wondering of those yonder hills and even the mountains, urging myself what is beyond those dark mountains. Many times I go up on the highest pointed rocks back in Salt Water Canyon among the mesa. I see lights and, during the day, I see the flashing mirrors shine into my eyes. Is it true that my grandmother says it's the glass windows of the white man's house and there are towns? But what is glass, or what is window?" he asked himself, not knowing what glass and window means in English.

Broneco was now impress with all the things he thinks of. Still dreaming, he got back to the tent. There he joined his family to eat his favorite breakfast, fried potatoes and hot goat milk. Broneco glance at everyone eating before he started chewing on his hot roll of fried bread.

"I never been so hungry before in all my lifetime," said John, taking another mouthful of hot coffee, then puffing at the hot coffee, trying to cool it off.

The day has begun with a sunny bright day, the wind would blow once in a while shaking the dried leafs off the dead branch, which were piled on the top of the shade house.

Broneco has now finished his plate and gone back into the tent to finish the rest of his packing. He closed his blue suitcase while half the socks still hanging out from in the suitcase. One shirt sleeve's out, when Auntie came in to see if Broneco has got through packing.

Everything was ready to be stacked in the back of the car which was parked out front. Broneco was still wearing his old clothes which he has been wearing for about a week.

"Broneco, are you going to leave for school wearing your old clothes?" she said, smiling.

Broneco looked at his pant and laugh. "I was too excited," he replied.

"I bet you are very anxious to be a student," said Auntie, leaving Broneco in the tent to change his clothes so he could be ready right away and not wasting any more time to keep big John waiting in the car.

When everything was in order, Auntie and Broneco's mother picked up the suitcases, carrying them into the back of the pickup.

John took Broneco by the arms. "Come on, Little One, we're leaving now," he said with a grin.

Broneco slowly walked to the pickup. He turned around and waved his hand at his grandmother, his mother, and the rest.

46

Happily he enter the car. It was time to go to the land of white man to learn the schooling. The purpose was to learn to speak a good English like the other students, those who are in school.

His grandmother didn't want for Broneco to go to the boarding school. She thought that, if Broneco goes to school far away, he will be spoiled in his behavior.

For Broneco his thought were different from the way his grandmother thinks of him. Broneco was only a small child, but he behaved like a normal being. Now Grandmother and Annie has to take care of the sheep until Broneco returns in the month of June sometimes. Broneco didn't worry about the home situations because his Uncle John has promise him that he would always look after his Grandmother while Broneco is away.

How anxious Broneco felt and how his shiny eyes twinkle as the car moved. John lighted the cigarette. In front of the tent, Annie and Grandfather stood, while under the shady side of the house everybody waved their hands. Broneco also waved his hand again to say farewell.

Slowly John step on the gas peddle and the pickup moved onto the old road. Broneco could hardly wait to see the place where he will spend throughout the whole cold winter. Broneco in his mind kept repeating few English words he learn from his grandmother. He remembered everything that his friend, Dale, taught him few years back when he just started experimenting with English words on his own. For Broneco it was fun for him to learn.

Before he knew, it was in the afternoon. They reached the nearest town which was Farmington. The town wasn't any bigger, but to Broneco it was very big town, since Broneco has never been to a town like this, but only to trading post on the reservation. While passing through town, Broneco saw many things that he never saw before in his life.

Vera asked Broneco if he would like to walk around town. Broneco's answer was, "No."

So they drove on, passing more windows with wonderful things in the windows along the two side of the pavement street. People walking into the various department stores. Broneco sat quiet between his uncle and his wife. He'd never seen so many people shopping and some walking across the street each time the green lights turns on. And when the red light turns on, the people would stop and the cars move on.

"Why would the people has to stop and then cross the street? It is foolish. If it was me, I would run across the street," Broneco said in his mind.

Riding along the country road, there were many more exciting things to see. Broneco glance here and there. He was more excited about the things and object that he has never seen before. Even the modern houses that are along the highway were very full of joyfulness. While traveling, Broneco had now seen different colors of cars, and the shape of the coming and going cars. The trees are contrasting from the way the trees used to look back home.

When they reached the Colorado state line, the wind from the big mountain about not more than ten miles away. It looked like a big white sheep lying down in the green pasture. In the deep, cool forest they travel. It wasn't warm like is used to be back in New Mexico. Broneco could now smell the pines trees that grow up in the cold mountain.

"I never seen such a huge tall standing tree like that before," said Broneco, pointing at a pine tree that stood near by the road. What a beautiful sight it was for Broneco, but not for Uncle John for he has been in Colorado several times before.

Some white people were standing.

"What are those black objects in the white man's hands?" Broneco asked.

"They are cameras," said John.

"What do they do with it?" Do they look through it like my grandfather's spectacle?"

"No, Broneco. Cameras are to take pictures with and they come out like it is realistic. Just like you see on many magazines," said John, explaining what camera does.

Broneco listened carefully, thinking that he might own one too one of these days in the future years when he learns enough. Soon Broneco fell asleep before they could reach the school.

"Broneco, wake up and see where we are," said Vera, "and we're about to turn off the highway to the school."

Broneco wake up and rubbed his eyes. Broneco didn't smile this time. Still half asleep, he looked curiously everywhere. Everything seems to looked queer. Besides, it was towards evening.

As they reached the school ground, slowed down the speed of the vehicle. Around the school road to the building, John stopped the pickup in front of the big building.

"You are at the school now, what you been wishing for," said John with tired smile on his face. "This is the dormitory."

Broneco didn't even said a single word.

Vera got out of the car first, then Broneco stepped out of the car and reached for his suitcase. When it was too heavy for Broneco to carry the suitcase, Vera and John then picked up the luggages.

Broneco walked up to the cement steps. He was afraid to enter the building, but Broneco try not to show that he was scare to go into the dormitory. Bravely he walked up and stepped into the doorway as Vera and her husband, John, followed.

There in the hallway, Broneco saw many small boys, big boys, and middle size kids. Some boys like Broneco, running down the hall as the housemother kept yelling at the small boys.

Broneco just stood against the wall and stared. The next minute a dark-haired woman came around the corner of the main floor hall. Broneco could see that she is very kind. Her eyes shines as the reflection from the lights up high on the ceiling shines on her pink cheek.

"I suppose you are a new student here this fall," she said. "I am Mrs. Martin."

Broneco only nodded his head, for he was shy to say an English word to say, "Yes."

"Come with me to the linen," she said, reaching for Broneco's hand. Then she held Broneco by the arm and led him into the sewing room to give his towels and to mark his clothes and put them in the box, number sixty.

Broneco didn't know that John and his wife, Vera, had left.

49

Standing in the room, everything that Broneco sees were odd looking. They looked strange.

Just then a young boy, the same age as Broneco, came in and sat on the chair and waited.

"Go with him. He'll show you where your room is. The room is number fourteen," Mrs. Martin said, blinking her eyes.

Broneco held his hands tight together and walked slowly after the boy. He followed him around the corner and then up the steps with rails. Now Broneco was all confused because there was so many turns he made before he made it to the top of the next floor.

Then turning to the right again, there was still another corner to make.

"This is where your room is," said the boy, opening the door for Broneco. He was nice, but kind of stubborn.

As Broneco stepped into the room, everything he sees, like before, were too clean. It wasn't like his home where he used to smell all sorts of odor. Broneco roamed in the room and sniffing each furniture, when someone twisted the doorknob. Broneco stepped away from the small desk. "Who could that be?" he thought, standing by the bed.

Slowly the door open. There stood Mrs. Martin, carrying the suitcases. "Here are your satchel, son," she said.

After she left the room, Broneco grabbed one of his suitcase. He decided to put them away somewhere to keep them out of sight. Instead of putting the traveling cases in the closet, he put the luggages under the bed like he would do at home.

The smell of the furniture made Broneco sicker than ever, but he has to get used to the smell of it. While in the room, he couldn't seem to think. He decided to look out the window, so he moved across the bed which he was sitting on. Gently he pulled the string as the curtain opens up.

"Where am I?" he whisper to himself.

As he look out the window, he couldn't see anything except the trees which were in the way to see any farther. Before are the green lawns and water sprinkler turning clockwise.

Broneco sat back on the bed and looked at the wall and the

50

shining floor that looked like an ice that is real slippery during the winter. It was amazing but he could even see himself in the wooden floor.

"I'm in the lost world," he thought. "It was my own fault that I wanted to come this far to school."

Broneco felt very lonely, wondering of what he used to do back home, but it was no use thinking of it. He soon just put his head against the pillow on the bed weeping. He lay there for a few minutes when all of a suddenly he fell asleep.

For about half an hour Broneco has slept on the soft bed. It was like sleeping on a woolly sheepskin for a while. Then he woke up. Things were quiet in the room, no mouse in the room either.

After being awake for another minute, Broneco felt that someone was watching him. He decided that he look to the right.

"Hi there, I see that you are awake," said a boy that sat on the chair. Then, laughing out loudly, "My name is Virgel," he said, playing with a marble, "and what's yours?"

Broneco looked down at his shoe and said, "Broneco."

"Ha, that sounds like one of the horse's name."

Broneco didn't look up. He sat there with his head low. The boy's feeling was hurt, when Broneco looked kind of mean. He now knew that he also hurted his feeling, too.

"I'm a Navaho, and what about you?" the boy added.

"I am too, a Na-av-va-hoo," said Broneco with a grin this time.

Then Virgel smile and started talking about the school, telling few lies and part true.

Soon Broneco had forgotten about everything, even his loneliness. Broneco and Virgel ate together that night at the dining room. In the chow hall they kept talking together and telling Broneco what to do after finish eating. Virgel was the instructor for the time being, until Broneco learns.

·VI·

A Miracle Thing

THE NEXT MORNING after the breakfast, everyone did assigned work duty. At nine o'clock, it was time to go to school.

Broneco walked outside the dormitory. He looked everywhere. It sure didn't look like his home where you can see nothing but plain arid country. Everywhere he looked, he only saw building, lawns, and tall trees.

It begin to rain. First, it dropped here and there. While Broneco stood there, still shaking from the cool drops of rain, he held onto a rail which was along the side of the concrete steps. Broneco looked at the school building again before he started on his way towards the school.

All the students had rushed to school, keeping themselves out of the rain. Broneco putted his both hands into his pocket to keep him from getting nervous. When he made it to the school building, he walked up the steps again, then opened the door. Slowly he closed the door behind him. Excited, he thought of creeping down the middle of the hall.

Broneco went to the first classroom door. "No, it isn't the right door," he said to himself like he always did before when he is alone.

Broneco couldn't figure out the numbers, whether it is the right number or not. He can fairly well tell, though, what the number are by the shape of the number sealed on the front of each door.

He went farther down the hall looking at each door. At the end

52

of the hall, at last he came to the room marked 1, just the way Grandmother scratch it with a stick. It was across from the little beginners' classroom door. There Broneco stood in front of the first grade class. Broneco knew if he didn't sneak into the first grade class, he'd be in the zero class.

He reached for the doorknob, but someone from the inside was opening the door. Broneco stepped back a little when the door opened. A young maiden walk out of the first grade class, carrying in her hand a slip of pure white paper with a few words written on it. She was easily holding it at the tip of her finger. Then she reached for the small silver box which hung on the wall.

Broneco sneak into the classroom. Luckily he found an empty desk in the front row. Broneco sat quickly and put his hands on the desk.

The teacher step back in, smiling. Then she walked back to her desk and looked around as she sat. She picked up her pencil and held it high above her chin with confusion.

"I don't think I counted you kids right," she said. "I guess I made a mistake counting you student."

Broneco didn't say a word or nor move. The teacher look puzzled when she again said, "I counted one extra now. Have one of you just came in while ago? No, it can't be. I was standing right by the doorway. I guess I miscounted the first time."

Just then the teacher looked towards Broneco, and stared at Broneco with a surprising face. Again she smile.

When Broneco looked up at the teacher, she blinked her right eye.

Broneco got nervous, so he looked straight at the wall.

She sat there for while, wanting for Broneco to look again, but Broneco wouldn't look the second time. Slowly she pushed her chair backward and stood up. Carefully she counted the students, recounting the rows. She checked her slip of paper on her third time when she spotted Broneco was the new student.

"You must be the new one," she said, while looking at Broneco.

Every boy and girls in the room look at Broneco. Still he didn't say a word.

Then the teacher strolled up to where Broneco was. "I'm Miss Merriam, and your name please?"

"Br-r-r-on-e-co," he said without pronouncing his name clearly.

"Oh, I beg your pardon. Would you repeat your name again?"

Broneco sat there, highstrung. Then Broneco looked around him and ignored every student in the classroom. The teacher smile again. Broneco was now squeezing his hands under the desk.

"Johnnie Benally," he said slowly.

"Oh," she said. "We already have one student here with us in the class name Johnnie Benally, too."

Broneco didn't want to repeat his name so he give the wrong name and it was somebody else's name. He thought the name he's giving wasn't anybody's name in the class, nor he wasn't expecting someone by the name of Johnnie Benally.

When Miss Merriam seated herself back at the desk, Broneco smile. He sat with his head high and back straight. He knew he could make it into the first grade class instead of beginners' class. Miss Merriam didn't know he was supposed to be in the beginners' class.

The weeks went by when one day Broneco's teacher, Miss Merriam, called him to the desk.

"Now what?" thought Broneco, as he amble between the rows of desk. It wasn't embarrassing since the classmate are all out for a recess during the afternoon.

The teacher looked at him without smiling of any sort.

"Sit down, Broneco. I've got something to tell you," she said, as if she was going to get mad about something. Then she got a few papers out of her drawer to show to Broneco, pointing her pencil like always.

"Broneco, why didn't you tell me you were suppose to be in the beginners' class when you first came into this room?"

"I'm sorry, Miss Merriam. I didn't mean to do that. I'm sorry," said Broneco.

"I'm sorry, too, young man."

"What do you mean?"

54

Miss Merriam pep up with a laugh then. Broneco didn't know what was going to happen.

"You are going to be in my first grade class. Since you have proven that you can do a first grade work, as well as the third grade work."

After hearing of this, Broneco felt strangely happy. It was a good news.

Broneco kept up with his homework, as the weeks went by slowly. The subject was getting harder and each day it was even more harder than the day before. Broneco try all the best he could to give his best effort to get the top grades. The harder Broneco worked, the better and the easier the subject was.

All through the year, since his first day in school, he kept everythings that he done in his mind. What he has accomplish throughout the year, these things he can remember them all.

When the month of May was here, Broneco didn't know that he was speaking English fairly well. He found that out later, talking to his favorite teacher, Miss Merriam. She, too, was proud of what Broneco has gain the first year. During the class time, Miss Merriam depended on Broneco for such little detail of paper work. Many times, Broneco would stay after school. Often he was teased as teacher's pet. Broneco didn't mind the other students calling him various names. He knew that they were only jealous. As far as he was concerned, the important thing was what he's learning.

Miss Merriam always understands that Broneco liked to get experience with more of the dictionary words. It was sort of funny to her, though, for such a small child wanting to know what some of the harder words mean. Miss Merriam has to explain every little items. She didn't mind to be ask a questions about English words. To her, it was amazing for a student who didn't know a single words of English, learned so much in his first year of schooling.

Broneco was very understanding of his school work, but he didn't get along so well with his classmates. Back at the dormitory he kept to himself so much that his own friend, Virgel, often wouldn't speak to him. Most of the time Broneco would spend his time in the room, doing various thing by himself—maybe pencil sketching and drawing on his own spare time.

One Saturday late in May, after the usual cleanup in the building, Virgel sat on his bed while Broneco, as usual, reading the first grade book which they often read during their class hours five days a week.

Virgel, putting on his dirty work clothes, doubted, looked at Broneco, then he said, "Broneco, let's go to the park today."

"Let's do, Virgel," Broneco replied with a little change in his conduct. He somehow finally decided to go along with Virgel. Maybe he felt sorry for his friend that he treated him cruelly.

Broneco and Virgel went out on the fire exit and slid down the slippery iron slide. Walking on the sidewalk, Virgel seems to be smiling with cheer. So was Broneco.

"I really didn't know that the trees were that green," said Broneco, looking up at the waving trees above him.

"It sure is," answered Virgel.

While walking on the sidewalk, Virgel kept talking and laughing of the time when he was home, before he came to school.

"Tell me what happen when you were back home."

"Well, I suppose it's all right with you," said Virgel.

"I love to hear the story."

"The year before," he started off with his story, "when I wasn't a student yet, my grandmother once lived with us in the southern part of Round Rock, Arizona. Between the real sandy hill covered with wild tea. She decided to take us to the sheep camp where my mother and her husband were on the mountain."

"Go on," said Broneco.

Virgel laughed again and begin his story where he left off. "My brother, Joe, didn't know how to ride horse then. So my grandmother decided to put him in the potato sack, so she did. Then put us behind the saddle and tied us there, hanging on the both side of the horse we used to call He-who-has-the-cricket-nose."

Broneco started laughing when he heard the horse's name.

Virgel picked up the sticks of branches, then breaking one in

56

half. Catching his breath, he started off again. "My grandmother thought it was all right. Anyway, we reached the mountain passage through a very thick acorn brushes. Somehow we're pick up by one of the branches. While our grandma rode on her way.

"While we were left behind, we thought that we're still riding with our grandmother. We're only swinging back and forth on the springing branches. When we found out that we're hanging, we started crying out loud like a wolf, but still it didn't help. And that was the first lesson when we next time had to learn to ride horse or else," he said, finishing the story.

Broneco became so interested in the story that they both forgotten what they had planned to do that day. Then Broneco told story about riding on the donkey bareback and the famous game that was ever played on a get together (a potato pull, sitting on the bare back of the donkey).

"I was ready to pull the sack of potato when the donkey jerk back. I flew straight for the grey greasewood that stood nearby. Boy, it was fun then," said Broneco, grinning as Virgel laughed.

"Broneco, you know so much, tell me how can you catch a prairie dog?"

"Simple, Virgel. You plug up the holes in the prairie dog town in the evening after the sun sets behind the mountain in the west. Then get up early just as you see the crack of dawn, around about four o'clock. Take with you a net and a club or just the net. When the prairie dogs are still rubbing their eyes, trying to wipe the dirt out of their eyes, you grab them by the neck and put them in the net bag or else you lose your fortune of games."

"Gee, you smart. How did you learn how to do these things?"

"I was taught all these sorts of things by my Grandfather," Broneco said. "Now, we better go eat our lunch, Virgel."

"Why not?"

Across the green grass they race to the dining hall, ready to be in line. Together they sat at the same table where they first sat during the beginning of the school year. It could bring back the remembrance—how they acted when they first ate together.

Broneco smile as he place his tray on the table.

"I'm glad I don't have to tell you what to do and to begin our lunch today," said Virgel.

Broneco laugh. "Virgil, tell me. How expert were you when you had your first meal here?"

"Perhaps you tell me, Broneco."

"No, really, I'm curious to know."

Virgel put his fork down on the side of the napkin and leaned forward, looking straight at Broneco. With a little sign of a grin he said, unconcerned, "You tell me, Broneco, how did you react when you first came into this dining room, not knowing how to use that fork you got in your hand right now? Broneco, I did the worst crime. I didn't know how to use that spoon you got."

"Well, that wasn't so bad, Virgel."

"I would say that, if I were you."

"Why?"

"Because, if I tell you this, you probably would laugh down the whole ceiling above us. Besides, you did better than I did. On the other hand, you probably would have used your hands like I did."

Broneco let his head low. Virgel seated himself back on his chair correctly. Just then he begin to smile.

Then Broneco laugh with tears in his eyes. "Using a hand in place of a white man's tool!" said Broneco, still laughing yet.

"Shall we eat our lunch instead you might die laughing?"

"I think we should. Besides, it's getting kind late already. I don't see why we can't spend our time eating, otherwise we're just not chewing the food right. That's why when a sheep graze for the whole day, he chews or she chews the food overnight," said Broneco, beginning to cut up his pot roast of beef.

Virgel didn't bother to answer or ask another question. He went right on eating.

"Virgel, what are you going to do this afternoon?"

"Silence, please," he said.

"Virgel, are you listening or you already half asleep like you always do when Miss Merriam tell us a story about the Three

Little Bears? Or is that you just don't want to listen to what I'm saying?"

Virgel then put his plate aside and wiped his lip.

"Now what would you like to know?"

Broneco then picked up his fork quietly and started eating. "Where are we going this afternoon?" he said.

"I don't know, Broneco. Shall we go for a long walk to give ourselves an exercise? I used to take a long walk before. All this winter, we went up that hill and slided all the way from the top to bottom. It was fun. We even used our own shoes, too."

Broneco was through eating his lunch. Broneco and Virgel took their tray to the counter where they usually clean the plates and all.

Along the walk they picked up different colored rocks. Virgel and Broneco's favorite hobby, part of the time, was to collect rocks. Broneco liked rocks of various color. Before he attended the public school, in the canyon wash Broneco would gather many rocks as the young boys and girls would do on the reservations. They used them as for drawing picture and scratches on the smooth side of the steep rocks. Mostly the boys would climbed way high on the rock to draw color abstract picture or some kind of blanket designs.

(Sometimes, you see shepherds carrying many bits of tiny colored rocks in their pocket, which soon will wear out the material as they rub against the cloth inside their pocket. So soon that they learn it was much better to carry them in a small handmade bag.)

This was why Broneco and Virgel were still interest in collecting rocks. But it was hard to keep many rocks in the room. So they would only take one or two.

After their walk, Broneco and Virgel went back to the building to rest for a while. Broneco in his room fell asleep, while Virgel stayed awake. Later, Virgel told Broneco what happen.

Virgel decided to see what's going on downstairs. So he haste along the hall. Turning to make the corner, Virgel heard some talking in the rest room: "Are you going to the Bear Dance today?" This Virgel wondered about as he push the door open.

59

"What is Bear Dance? I never heard of it before," he thought. So he ranned across the main hall and went up the opposite stairs. He entered the room and waked Broneco up still half asleep.

"What? What's is going on?" Broneco said, barely waking up. Virgel keep on shaking Broneco.

Broneco grabbed his shirt and rushed to the door and tried to open the door, but he was in a hurry. Then he stood there, rubbing his eyes. "What happen, Virgel? I just got up without knowing where I'm going. Must be a nightmare."

"Oh, you scared me, Broneco. I thought you were going wild or something."

"I had a terrible dream. I dreamed that someone came in while I sleeping. Grabbing my throat like this," he said, grabbing Virgel by the throat.

Broneco still pretended like if he was still asleep. For waking up Broneco so quickly, he just wanted to scared Virgel so he won't do it again.

Late that afternoon, Broneco and Virgel walked down the east road and followed the dirt road across the river that flow down with spiral and waving motion. There, across the old wooden bridge, Broneco and Virgel saw smoke going up in the air. They could smell the scent of hot beef stew and fried bread.

"Just like back home at a squaw dance," said Virgel.

"Must be a squaw dance, all right."

Broneco and Virgel didn't know it was Ute annual ceremonial dance which is Bear Dance. Just then two small boys about the exact age came out of the tall brushes, carrying bucket of water which was too heavy for them to carry. Without saying a single greeting word, Broneco and Virgel helped the boys carry the water.

It wasn't hard to make friend when the boys are small. So it was. Broneco and Virgel founded themselves a friend. When they arrive at the farther down, there was a tepee. Still not a single word was said. When the mother of the two Ute boys saw that Broneco and Virgel had helped their sons, they let each choose what they like to eat inside the tepee.

After they ate, the two boys showed Broneco and Virgel around, making a sign language since the other two boys didn't know how to speak English. Broneco really understands the sign language for he has tried before. It was fun seeing the Bear Dance, too.

Across the scene, big fat women and right on down to skinny type, grabbing boys and older gentlemen. Some didn't want to dance, but since the women are stronger than men, they either be dragged out to the dancing position or accept the offer from the women.

Holding onto the men's belt, down toward the dusty earth with mighty weight of force, the women would start pushing back the men. Then the men, with his arms around the woman's waist, he would also in a run type drive the woman back as far as he could force her back, keeping to the rhythm of the sound of rasping stick.

Broneco and his Ute friend stand close together. The Ute boy wore a black hat with a long feather attach to the side of his hat. Broneco begin to smile when a Ute girl held him by the arm, wanting to dance with him.

The Ute boy saw him and then said something in Ute language until Broneco was release. Then the girl swinged her blanket shawl, slashing the boy with her designed blanket she asked him for a dance. The Ute boy smiled and walked out into the open.

Broneco and Virgel looked at each other and decided to leave.

It was a week later, Broneco and Virgel met on the hallway in the school building. Broneco carrying few pile of papers. Virgel stopped Broneco and shooked his hands. Then he reached into his pocket; give Broneco a ring which was placed [set] with real turquoise. Broneco put it on and stood there.

"Broneco, you have been so nice and the best friend of all through the year, even though you didn't speak to me almost all these months. But there was a reason for it, I guess. I will miss a friend like you. It is for this I give you this ring. I'll see you next fall when I return," he said.

"Virgel, you mean you are going home today? Why didn't you tell me soon?"

"I didn't know it myself until my folks came after me today."

Then Broneco shaked Virgel hands again. Broneco had no idea when he's leaving either. "Virgel, wait for me awhile, just let me put this away," said Broneco, entering the office rushing.

When he came out, Broneco didn't see Virgel anywhere waiting. He rushed out the main door. He only saw a red car just making the right turn.

Just then, Mrs. Flores walked up the porch steps. She smile. "I've got something to tell you that a boy told me to tell you—that you must wait for me here by the small garden next fall when you return."

Broneco smile and said, "I will be waiting there as you said. I will be there waiting, Virgel. I'll be there waiting." He repeat this several times, strolling back to the dormitory.

In his room, Broneco laid on the soft bed. He was thinking back on this year. He has learn one thing the first day—the first day in school was the hardest part of beginning school alone. First, no friend and not being able to know where to go.

Broneco smile when he thought of the day he first came to school and his starting of learning English.

"It was like a miracle thing," he whisper, lying on the soft bed against the wall of his room, looking straight out the window.

·VII·

A Gift for Grandmother

DURING THE SUMMER long in the month of June, Broneco came around the corner of the trading post where usually the people sell and buy goods. Broneco, tired-like, leaned against the adobe wall of the big trading post. He watched the strange looking being of his tribe and few white kids among them. The cars of various colors with roaring sounds speeding by.

Around the corner of the Trading Post four boys were sitting on the bench talking. Broneco moved, inch by inch, toward the boys, wanting to know what they were talking about. Broneco keep hearing the word "horse." He come nearer. Now he can hear what they were saying.

"During the horse race, prizes will be given to the first winner in all the contest," said the boy with the mad face. "Six races. Everybody will have a chance. A race for older people, younger, and small fries, and the same goes for the friends, too."

"What prizes?" another boy asked.

"Oh, turquoise necklace . . . rugs . . ."

Broneco eyes the boys and decided to ask more question while the boys still speaking of the contest. Broneco pulled his old worn-out hat a little lower. Then slowly he walked up to the four boys about the same age as him.

"What do you want?"

"Oh, I — I was just been friendly, that's all," said Broneco as he steps off into the entrance of the Trading Post. Broneco in his mind thought that he would ask a few questions. Instead, he wasn't welcome.

Broneco stayed in the store for a while, as he cooled himself off. He looked up at the clock. It was almost twelve o'clock. Broneco amble across the wide spaced floor. Along the side of the big counter there stood a young girl. She seems to smile as she wiggle herself when she step off away from the counter.

"Hi. May I help you?" she said.

"No, thank you," replied Broneco, walking straight ahead. The charming-faced girl smile, putting her arms across her chest.

"Bye-e," she said.

Broneco looked back, bounding to smile. "What a blast!" he said softly.

It was hot outside so Broneco tipped his hat sideways. Across the pavement street, there were some more teenagers, adults, and youngsters, playing in the old Boarding School yard. Broneco didn't pay any more attention. He strolled along the concrete walk, along the shady side of the trees.

Broneco walked along the street between the parallel trees until he came to the intersection of the road. Then he headed for home.

On the way home, he crossed the glistening water that rushed down the sunny side of the hill into San Juan River which flowed a mile away. Broneco ignored the frogs that made a terrible sound. They sounded like snoring of an old man sleeping comfortably.

Broneco was tired now. So he decided that he would rest for a few minutes under the tall tree. The wind was cooler than he had expected. He relaxed himself sitting under the shade. It was too bad, he thought, that he didn't find out anything about where the horse race will be held, nor when it'll be. Soundly he sat on the decayed log, trying to figure out a way to find out.

"What's the used finding out?" he thought, as he got up and stretched himself. Broneco looked up at the sun in the sky. It was time to be home and do some odd work around the house and tend the thirsty sheep to their usual watering area.

Since Broneco used to run for miles in his young days, he decided that he would race his shadow all the way home, over the hills and brushes. It give him exercise as he jump and making short turns, and etc.

While he was running along the sandy wash area, Annie rode upon the low rolling hill, trying to round up the sheep. She saw Broneco rushing down the side of the sandy hill. Annie watched her brother running like a scared rabbit.

Annie got an idea that she would use her skill that she once learned from her mother.

"Come on," she said to the horse she was riding.

Anxiously she kicked the horse with her legs. Down the steep hill she rides as the horse slides on his hind legs, she quickly reached the foot of the hill.

Broneco, without noting Annie riding after him, continued running. Just around the corner of the next rolling hill, Annie rode up behind Broneco. Then Broneco saw Annie.

"Grab," said Annie.

Broneco caught Annie's hands, as she expertly swinged Broneco behind her and rode on. Among the hills of tanned color they disappeared as the dust went floating high in the hot air.

On the other side of rough plateau, Broneco catching his tired breath, spoke. "Gee Annie, I didn't know you could do such a clabber [clever] things."

"You're learning fast," she said, knowing that her brother, Broneco, is going to find out that she knows several more secret tricks. "What's the big idea, you been running on a hot day like this? Don't you know it's bad for you to run?"

"Then what's the big idea you running your horse on a hot day like this?"

Annie stopped the horse so all of a suddenly Broneco almost fell off.

"I didn't mean for you to stop the horse that quick," said Broneco, climbing back upon the horse's back.

"I'm sorry," she answered, releasing the bridle lace. Then Annie asked, "What did you find out today?"

"Nothing much, except I wanted to find out where the horse

race is going to be held and didn't find out when. I just heard one of the bull-face kid mention it when I came around the corner of the trading post today."

"Ha! You should have asked me in the first place."

"Gee, I should have known that I guess. I - I - I didn't thought of it."

"Don't let that word get jammed up in your mouth. The horse race is a week from now and they are going to have it at the Salt Creek Wash."

"You mean—?"

"Yes, they aren't having it at the usual rodeo ground," she said, whipping the horse at the point of his shoulder gently. "Why?"

"I could win race and have beautiful necklace I can give to Grandmother for her birthday."

Reaching the aged road, Broneco and Annie saw the sheep moving into the shaded corral. Just then the dog started barking which made the lambs started prancing around, stamping their feet.

When they reached the corral, Broneco slided off the back of the horse's thigh. Then Annie got off the horse and lead him into the gate. Broneco crawled through the fence to get the horse a stroke of hay.

"Broneco and Annie, come get it," said Grandmother, shouting with a queer voice.

Annie raced her brother to the house, when Annie tripped and rolled over the prairie thorns. Broneco laughed, helping Annie on her feet.

The time was late in the afternoon. Broneco sewing his shirt button onto his hand sleeves, he had an idea which he thought it might work. Broneco threw his shirt aside and rushed to the corral. Quickly and nervous, he saddled Auntie's horse.

Broneco had made up his mind that he would find his horse, Pinto, in the Salt Water Canyon before the weekend. Broneco rides his aunt's horse to the canyon. It took a long while to find the horse's track. Along the salty water streams, he finally found the tracks of horses. His auntie's horse was sweating so he had to rest him for quite a while, and Broneco fell asleep.

While Broneco sleeping, the horse removed the bridle by scraping himself against the juniper tree branches. Broneco didn't notice the horse when he left, heading for home.

When Broneco wake up and grabbed the leather lace, he find out that the horse had left.

"What shall I do now?" he said, picking up the rope and bridle. Then he haste off into the greasewoods and came out on the opposite side of the salt water stream, carrying on his shoulder the rope and bridle.

Broneco came upon the small hill with nothing but large and small rocks. He looked in every directions, but couldn't see any moving object except on the steep side of the valley.

As he waited a while, he heard a sound. Then another one. The vibration of the sound echo through the canyon. Broneco looked toward the great rocky hilltop. There, where he can barely see the sight of the object, stands a horse. Broneco smiled and whistled putting his fingers between his teeth.

The horse neighs again and started down the hill, leaving the rest of the horses. Broneco met his horse, Pinto, at the foot of the hills.

"Now, you're going home with me," he said, as Pinto pushed him around for a minute before Broneco mounting him.

The sun was already setting. Broneco was lucky that he saw Pinto in time. If he hadn't, he could have slept on the dirt overnight. Now, he was happy. The night had approach when they made it over the mesa to the short cut.

Auntie's horse had arrive home. When Annie saw him trying to open the gate to the corral. "What on earth has happen to Broneco?" said Annie.

Without telling her mother, she rushed to the corral. She opened the gate with a queer smile, knowing that Broneco would find Pinto in time for his next ride. As she looked west, it was time to do her usual odd work around the house.

While walking back to the house, she counted her fingers. "Only six more days," she said, wiggling her small finger. "How will Broneco's race come out? Is he going to win?" she kept thinking as she shuffled along the usual walking pattern trail.

Grandmother was, as usual, fighting Tellie because he didn't want to enter the corral. Tellie kept rebelling for some reason, maybe it was that the corral was too small for two horses. Besides, he wanted to be outside where he likes to roll himself over the fresh dirt of another kind. So Grandmother had to let Tellie stay outside for the night.

When the sun set behind the big blue mountain in the west, Broneco approach a distance away, riding Pinto, the spotted one, as he was called. Behind him leaving the dust of clouds in the air. When the shepherd dogs heard the sound of horse's hoof on the hard beaten-down earth, they all started barking as if they had never seen Broneco and his horse.

The dogs kept barking. Broneco turned his horse around and chased Pinky, then Blacky around the sheep corral twice. When Blacky made a quick turn, so did Pinto. Broneco flew straight off his back. Into the smelling corral he fall and landed flat before the mean old ram. Pinto also jumped the fence after Blacky.

Grandmother glanced and glanced again. "The sheep!" she shout, and race for the corral, and Auntie did too.

"What's all the commotions, what!" said Annie, rushing through the gate with excitement. The piece of sharp-edged wire pointed out in a spiral shape caught Annie's apron. Like if someone behind the corner of a building caught her.

Broneco, Auntie, and Grandmother all watched Annie tears her apron off the wire. They couldn't see very well since it was quite dark. The moon has rose high as the stripes of clouds move slowly across the front of the yellow moon. Broneco got hold of the bridle string and then guided his horse out the gate.

As the days passed, Broneco and Annie would go out on the side of the hill, training his horse. Annie would run the horse every morning and evening until the day for the race comes. Luckily, the day, when it finally came, was cloudy and few drops of cold rain kept falling. Broneco saddled his horse around ten o'clock.

"Broneco, I hope you win the race so we would give the most beautiful gift to Grandmother on her birthday tomorrow afternoon," said Annie.

"I hope so too, Annie," he said, tightening the saddle strap. Then Broneco blinked his eyes and snapped his fingers together. "Well, sis, I'm ready," he said, smiling, "but first I must put on my old headband I used to wear, including my moccasin."

"Why all of that?"

"So that the bull-faced fellows I've met a week ago won't know me until I show them who's going to win that race."

"What makes you so sure that you'll win that race?"

"Simple. It only takes brain."

"Smarty, you better get going."

Broneco laughed and mounted his horse, Pinto. Annie smiling securely.

"Ey-le," he shouted as Pinto steps off on his left feet wildly.

Annie climbed upon the fence to watch Broneco ride away into the distance. The wind kept blowing heavy with cool breezes. Annie wanted to watch the horse race, but she had to herd the sheep for the day.

Before long, Broneco rode upon the next hill. He stopped his horse and took a deep breath. About a mile away, Broneco could see the group of riders on their horseback and some few of them were on foot and, besides the point, there were even wagons covered with canvas. Since the day was cloudy, they too were probably expecting a rain.

Broneco looked here and there as the horses moved in between the two hills. It looked like a cavalcade. Pinto wanted to run, but Broneco wouldn't let him. He wanted his pony to save his energy until the race starts. So Broneco rides on, slowly taking his time.

Broneco reached the wash when it began to rain. "How about that?" he whisper to himself. The rain made Pinto wanted to run. For Broneco it made him chill a little.

Along the wash area, it was real soft so that the horse's hoof wouldn't get hurt in case if one falls. Broneco looked to the side of the rolling hills. There were many more people still moving in to see the horse race. Some riders were on the top of the hills and some below. They all waited to see the race start. Broneco was nervous, glancing south and north, riding between the rows of horses and women on horseback. The sounds of horses neighing every inch of the whole sandy wash area.

The wash was also grown up with greasewoods and thick weeds. Broneco had never seen so many gathering before in his life. It was exciting to see. He stopped his horse and dismounted Pinto at the end of the crowded area.

"Whoa-a-a, boy," he said, standing in front of Pinto.

"Who's that poor kid in front of that spotted horse?" said a husky-looking boy, holding onto his horse too.

"Must be that shepherd boy who live across the gray hill," said another boy.

Broneco heard the boys talking about him. He just pretend like he didn't hear a single sound. He stood, still not bothering to look in any directions. Just then he heard another sound.

"Silence. Silence, please," said an old man, raising his right arm high up in the air. In his left hand, holding a woven rug, a genuine nickel-plated silver, and a necklace. Slowly he lift the item high as the cheers of voice proceeds.

That necklace! It was silver squash blossom with turquoise nuggets. It was exactly what Broneco wanted to give to his grandmother. He had to win it!

The old man raised his hand again to quiet down the roaring sounds of the guests. Then he spoke, half laughing. "First race will be the grownups, then secondly it will be the older, and then thirdly will be the young ones," he said.

The older people started moving into the starting position, when one of the boys among the crowded area rode out. Broneco seated himself under one of the greasewood that stood by.

The boy rode up to Broneco. "Hi there! I see that you got a good pony, and it looks just like my horse at home. I suppose you're

going to be in the race," he said, smiling with dimple on his cheek.
"Oh yes, I am," replied Broneco.

The boy stared at Broneco for a long time. Broneco too looked at the boy once in a while. "Are you in the racing contest?" he ask.

"No," the boy said, "this horse I'm riding is my father's horse."

While Broneco and the boy were still talking, there was the sound of the race starting. It sounded like as if the rain is just began pouring down all of a suddenly. Between the greasewoods the horse race on.

Broneco watched the riders ride behind the valley. Along the wash, the people waving their hat and scarfs.

The race was a mile long. It didn't take long when the first race was over. Now, it was the older age grownups turns to race.

Just the same as other race, it didn't take long for the race to be over.

Broneco took his horse to the end of the line. Pinto was very eager to compete with the other horse beside him. Pinto can't keep still. He kept prancing up and down. So did the other horses.

Broneco looked to the right of him and saw chestnut, black, spotted, and gray horses kept prancing, stepping out of the position. Broneco's horse, Pinto, prancing up and down and looking to the left at a palomino horse, a white stallion, and a freckle pinto.

A minute passed. Then the white flag waved. The minute the flag went down, the race was off on their way. Broneco started off behind. Half shaking, he whipped his horse real gently. Around the corner of the yonder hill, Pinto just now passed the fifth horse in the mile race. Then across the plain to the opposite side of the next small low land wash. It was about only half a mile to go when Pinto tripped over a small prairie grass which was harden with sands of different colors.

Pinto fall on Broneco and roll over twice.

Broneco laid still for a while and got up real quickly and grabbed Pinto, wasting no time. Half hurt and half full of doubtness of winning, he again got on the horse to catch up. It was almost late to catch up. Broneco was now worried.

"We must win, Pinto," he said to his horse softly.

Pinto wanted to run in the first place. So now he was regaining to catch up with the others.

Broneco's eyes feared. He was thinking that it was no used trying, and ready to give it up.

Then Pinto gain more and passed the white stallion and then the leading black horse. It was amazing when they were about to reach the finishing line.

Pinto passed another horse which was still in the lead. Broneco rode on and past the waving hands.

Broneco was gifted with the turquoise necklace with silver squash blossom.

It was mysterious to the crowds because no one knew his name. As he turned his horse around, smiling, wearing dirty clothes, he heard one said, "I wonder who could that poor boy be."

On his way home, it really began to rain. Broneco didn't mind the rain for he has won the horse race and rewarded with a prize. Now Broneco and Annie has something to give to Grandmother on her birthday. Broneco could see how happy Annie will be as he rode toward the hill.

·VIII·

"These Things I Can't Forget"

Broneco's second grade year started differently. He room where he room with his friend Virgel, but now his roommate was real rude and he was always mad about something. This Broneco didn't quite understand.

While in the room, Broneco always does nothing but reading books. Everyday, going to school, he didn't want to speak to any of his classmate. Some wanted to be friendly with him. This soon made him shy and soon it became greatly affected. In the schoolroom he didn't mind talking to his teacher, Mrs. Watson—she was the second grade teacher. She wondered why he didn't like to speak to any of his class student.

Broneco only knew what was wrong with him, but still he wouldn't tell no one about it. He kept all these things to himself. His dormitory attendant knew that someday Broneco is going to change and be a man. Many times he would say that Broneco is going to be someone, a great man. He would say this to his other instructor.

Broneco wasn't afraid to speak to the adult and older people. This continue throughout the year. By spring, he seems to be friendly but not quite that way. Soon it was school out again.

"Broneco, are you going to be back this fall?" said Mr. Smith, grinning, holding Broneco's suitcase.

"I sure am. I'll be a third grade by then. I wish I could stay here for the summer," said Broneco.

"Have a good time and make the best of your summer vacation," said Mr. Smith, waving a hand.

Broneco glance back and walk off the sidewalk. Then he step into the car. Slowly he closed the door as if he didn't wanted to go home.

Broneco's relative uncle—a very quiet man he was—sat still on the driver's seat. Without saying a word or two, he put his foot on the gas peddle.

"He's sort of stupid, ever since the day I saw him," thought Broneco, looking straight out the front.

Later that afternoon, they finally pull in back at the summer home where once there was a tent and a shade house to rest beneath during the summer when it gets real hot. Broneco's face was getting red already. Quickly he opened the car door. Broneco was sort of mad because his uncle was too. For some reason his uncle didn't seem to like him too well, but his other uncle, John—he's always nice to his sister's son.

Grandmother stood by the doorway of the new house that was built recently. It was quite a change—the new home.

Broneco didn't smile about anything. He was really different. His grandmother notice him when he first returned from school. She didn't mention this to his grandfather, nor to anybody.

Broneco rushed up to his grandmother and then went into the house and there was Annie, making a curtain for the new house.

"Hello, big brother. Since you are back now, together we'll have to keep the house in good condition, and herd sheep, of course."

"You bet we will, and don't you forget I've got a job for you too."

"What could that be, I wonder?" she said.

"You would be surprise. I mean you going to learn from me English."

Annie laughed, then she looked down at her knee. She was a little embarrass. Grandmother started fixing up some food for Broneco to eat.

"What would you like to teach me in the first place? You said you will teach me, so why not start right now? Besides, I will be going to school too."

"When?"

"I'll be by this fall when you are returning to school. Aren't you surprise?"

"Annie has learned a lot from me this year," said Grandmother, mixing up the flour with warm water. "I didn't think it was fair for only one of my family to learn English."

Broneco sat there frowning when his uncle drove off without saying that he was going. Grandmother didn't bother to say a word of him. She just went on making her rolls of dough and placing them on the small oven pan that she always used.

The week went by. Broneco and Annie herded sheep together. Sometimes they would race the horses together by the Salt Creek Wash along the side of shadows. Annie was getting more skills out of this than Broneco. There, every afternoon, they would run the horses.

One day again they went to the same place to run their horse. There were some boys whom they discovered it was a good place to train horses for entering horse races. Broneco and Annie rode by not knowing that they were going to get chase that day.

The boys saw Annie riding down the trail when Broneco rode above the deep side of the sandy hill. Broneco saw an approach of one of the boys behind the tall salt trees.

"Annie, there is someone behind that red salt tree, waiting for us perhaps. What do you think of it? Shall we go ahead and race the horses along the side of the shadows farther up?"

"I don't know. Make friends with them, I suppose," she said.

"But Annie, how do you know they are friendly?"

Annie looked down farther and there were two more boys just around the corner. Broneco and Annie stopped their horse and waited for a while, hoping that nothing will occur when they reach the track.

The horse started prancing right then. Annie try not let her

75

horse prance, so she whipped her horse and rode down the middle of the wash.

Just then, five boys took their horses out of the salt trees.

"Oh, no!" said Broneco. Then he kicked his horse, Pinto, and took off to the opposite side of the hill to make a short cut to join Annie and have all the fun of being chase along the creek wash.

Broneco waited while Annie still riding around the corner of the next hill. Annie rode straight into tall brushes, while Broneco waited a hundred yards away. Then he went behind one tall greasewood that stood in the way. The boys spotted Broneco so he was chased again.

For the next half an hour, Annie and Broneco was just having fun. Until the other horses were tired. So was Annie and Broneco's horse so it was time to quit.

Broneco's main interest back home was horse racing. Like the Indians used to do back a long time back before Broneco was born, his interest was still here.

The time when Broneco was born, the family he live with, they begin to live more civilize than they were before. He had listened to many legends and tales. The most he was more familiar with was the story of the future. This he was most impress with in his mind. From time to time, he would wonder of his future life that is ahead of him. So many times he tells these things of what he had in mind to Annie.

Annie wasn't pretty smart, but she was excellent in making jokes all the time. It wasn't only Broneco that has a great problems, but there was Annie too. They both knew much about living on the reservation. They knew every sections of the land mountain passage, but still they haven't learn much about the white man's way of living. Since Broneco went to school he knew a little about white man's way. Annie and Broneco were just a beginner, learning the outside world which is unknown to them.

Together as a team they did various and obvious things all through the summer. When the month of August was here, early in the morning they sat outside the house with their grandmother patting on her rubber-like dough. Even the dogs would sometimes sit around the fire since it was getting colder every morning and even at night it was cold. During the day it was warm in the afternoon.

Then the day came for Annie and Broneco to be ready to go. Returning back to school was fun. For Annie it was her first experience to be in school, but what her grandmother told of being in school was a good reference to keep in mind, since it was going to be useful.

Broneco and Annie were in school now. On their first day, they ate together. Soon, when Annie begin to know more girl friends, she forgot all about Broneco. For Broneco, he doesn't seem to see Annie, during the school hour or between classes. All through the year they went to school as normal school kids would.

While Broneco attending school he learned quickly. It wasn't hard. Since he worked in every class, he passed the fourth grade soon. For the way he did all the work and no late papers, he skip the three grade that year. As for Annie, she was really tagging along behind. She was two year behind, but she was going real fine.

Broneco was very proud that year, since he had passed to his fourth grade. Then one day Annie met Broneco outside the school building.

She laid her books on the concrete step. "I've got a letter today, and I didn't understand it very well. Perhaps you'll understand more than I do," she explained.

Broneco didn't know what was wrong that day. He seems to sense something, but he didn't know what. He was about ready to smile for the first time when he read, "Your grandfather has suffer a great deal of illness. On Tuesday he passed away." This he read across the page and his face became red.

Annie, standing besides Broneco, notice his red face. She waited for an answer. So she waited, but then she asked, "Broneco, what's the matter?"

"Oh, nothing is wrong, Annie," he said. "It's that I was still thinking about the homework that I'm suppose to do tonight. And it says that everything are just going well and fine back home."

Annie smile and took the letter and put it in her pocket.

Broneco didn't tell everything about what happen to his grandfather that they loved so much. Annie would get a big shock if she was told, so Broneco kept the tears back deep in his throat.

When Broneco got off the bus back at the dormitory, he just rush off into the front entrance. This made Broneco coudn't smile any more worse than ever. Broneco was now filled with loneliness.

Broneco kept back all the tears for the whole year round. He didn't say word about it whenever Annie met him. In the month of May, while returning on the bus, Broneco wanted to tell Annie about it, but still he can't seem to say it.

Approaching home, Broneco fainted on the hill where he used to sit with his grandfather.

Annie quickly grabbed her brother, and shake him a bit. "Broneco, speak. Say something," she said, worried nervously.

Annie was ready to run for the house when Broneco recover. "Annie, Annie, are you here?" he said.

"Broneco, what's the matter? Are you sick?"

"No, Annie. It's just . . . that . . . "

"That what? Broneco, please tell me what the matter."

"Annie, I used to sit here with my grandfather on this hill since I was small. These things I can't forget. You know I mean? It's been a long time I wanted to mention it to you. I'm sorry I made you waited too long to answer your first question you once asked me on your first letter from home which you let me read it. At that time, I . . . I wanted to tell you."

Annie sat down on her knees. The tears ran down her cheek.

Broneco standed up and looked up the hill, as it seems to glow. Half frighten, he reached for Annie's hand and walked away from the hill.

Things went a little better after that. Annie had forgotten unhappiness. Like always, she was proud with joy. Keeping her grandmother happy made a lot of difference around home. Annie's mother has stay with Grandmother after all. But for Broneco, he was different. Everything went well that summer.

Again returning to school that August on the usual date,

Broneco and Annie said good-by and carry their suitcase into the
car that waited in front of the corral.

Every year it was the same until Broneco in his seven year and
Annie fifth year. Broneco still worked like the old days and past
year. After all these years, Broneco had no interest in various
recreational activity.

It was in the month of March third, nineteen hundred and
fifty-nine. Broneco in his room stood by the window and watched
the small kids playing outside the building. Then they all went
inside.

Broneco slowly walked to the closet and opened the door and
looked through the different color shirts. He reached for the black
and white shirt, and the black socks to match the color.

Broneco, for the first time, seems to smile to himself, looking at
himself in the mirror. It was almost time for school so he quickly
changed his clothes. While looking at the calendar, he hum a little,
buttoning up his shirt. Then he combed his delicate, dark hair.
Broneco's hair neatly wave, so many would say many times, just
to tease, "Mexican." They know it Broneco wouldn't like that, so
many times he would just ignore them.

Just in time, Broneco stepped out on the porch of the boys' dorm.
Then slowly, step by step, he walked down the concrete steps,
carrying in his right hand a pile of papers and a notebook. There
was a math book, science, and world history book. The day was
bright, except the wind kept blowing dust on every student's
dress-up clothes that day.

Broneco can hear the wind whisper in the trees that have no
leaf or two. And everyone was sort of happy and full of gay.

When Broneco made his last step, he stood there to take a deep
breath of an fresh air to brighten up his lungs inside. He was
watching the freshmen and seniors getting on the school bus.

"Come on. What are you waiting for?" said Steve. "You'll be
late for school."

Broneco looked at Steve, bounding to smile.

Steve almost smile.

79

When the bus was all loaded, they rushed onto the bus before they were late.

Broneco went to school as usual, but had come to the class with a change on his face, and with a different attitude towards others and to his classmate.

In the classroom, Rod, a charming young boy a year younger, always wanted to tease Broneco. He looked up from his desk when Broneco enter the room. The rest of the students didn't bother to look, for Broneco wouldn't dare make a single friendly smile at them.

Broneco setted his books on the first row desk which was third to the last desk where he was assigned to sit since the beginning of the school year. In a meanwhile, waiting for the teacher to come in and start off with the math problem which he was just explaining yesterday morning when the bell ring for the next class.

Someone spoke his name, third row behind.

"Who could that be—a girl or a boy?" Broneco asked himself this question several times, sitting still in his desk, waiting for another answer patiently.

There was another call. It's a boy's voice as Broneco can tell.

Then he turned his head towards the back to see who's calling his name. "Oh, it's Rod. He's always got something to say," he thought, but anyway he straight out his books that were unneatly piled on his desk. Then, taking up a deep breath, Broneco walked in front of the desk and down the lines of desks to where Rod was sitting.

"What do you want, and don't talk about what you think," he said.

"Why?"

"Because that won't do you any good, asking me about why I'm the most queer thing you ever saw in life."

Rod sat there and laughed. "That wasn't the question, my friend, Broneco. I just wanted to ask if you would help figure out this problem for me, if you please," he said without teasing this time.

Broneco was ready to do the problem when he glance across the room. There he saw a face that he never seen before. "Gosh, who could that be I never saw before?" he thought, trying to remember if he had seen this person.

"What's the matter? Can't you figure out this math problem that I thought you had solve yesterday morning?"

"Just give me time. Let me think about a little," said Broneco as he pick up the pencil and started figuring the circumference of a circle that Rod couldn't get.

Rod, like many other teenagers, he liked to mess around with various girl and calling them that it's his girls. On the other hand, the girls do like him and admired him.

"I see you are smiling," said Rod with a tease as he would always tease Broneco.

"Am I?" replied Broneco, ignoring Rod with a side glance. Broneco had now forgot all about the stranger by the doorway in the front of his classroom.

"Broneco, come on and smile, will you?"

"Will you cut that out! I don't feel like laughing as the way you would, each time the building bound to tremble, making a tiny bits of cracks in the walls of this high school," said Broneco with a hot temper.

"Are you going to the game tonight?" asked Rod.

"No, I'm not going," answered Broneco in loud-toned voice.

Broneco then went back to his desk when the teacher came in sight, ready to continue his problem of explaining the math since yesterday. He glance at the blackboard and started with his math problem that he was doing. With his pencil he figured problem real easily. The problems seem to be very simple in some way. When looked up at the clock on the wall of the classroom, he saw it's time to go. The bell rang.

Before Broneco knew it was time to eat. The bell rang again, getting ready for lunch. Walking down the hall of the school, Rod met Broneco on the way to the entrance.

"Well, so it's you again," Rod said.

"I suppose it's you again too," Broneco said, snapping his finger together.

Rod look at Broneco. "I think you'll make a nice vocalist, if you keep that up, you know."

"A vocalist, my foot!"

"At least you know how to start off with all that gesture in your body." Rod laugh again like he always does. He kept on talking and making jokes that Broneco would never smile nor laugh about.

"Rod, I think you are a very silly boy," Broneco said.

"Well, Broneco, once in a while a man has to laugh and say all kinds of things. Now come on and be like the rest."

Broneco didn't say a word for a while, thinking and trying to solve his problem like if he would do math or any other course of study. "Perhaps," he thought, "I should be more friendly with the rest of the students and try again."

So Broneco, for once again, made up his mind.

Rod didn't say another words. He just stroll by all the way to the dining room and followed Broneco down the line.

After they got their trays, they both sat at the farther end of the small table that only fitted four. There at the small table they sat when Rod's friend, Mike and Tom, seated themselves there also. As they all discussed problem of their school that day, Broneco watched the boys chatter together.

Broneco thought of the old days when he was with Virgel, eating their lunch together, discussing what they first did—the way Virgel said he ate the first day not knowing how to use the table tools.

Broneco could hear Virgel speaking in his ear so he answer: "It's been so many years since this happen, and it is starting again and I hope it'll be the happy one and, by the way, today is my birthday and I wonder what is my gift of this day," he thought. But Broneco whisper a little without knowing that he was speaking softly, smiling.

The boys watched him smile up a bit.

"Broneco, you're smiling," said Tom.

"Well, I'm not surprise either," said Mike, and they all look at each other.

"Don't be too surprise. I had to smile," Broneco replied. "Why? Well, it's like this. Today is my birthday and I wanted to be like the rest of the student from now on. I don't know why I acted so unfriendly, and now I wanted to forget about everything that happen in the past that doesn't even exist. Really, I wanted to be friendly, and that's the way I'm going to be ever after," said Broneco with his eyes rounded with twinkling tears.

"Oh, we all understand what you mean," said Tom, beginning to smile when Broneco smile with a great charm, like as if he was the happiest one and he was.

Before he knew that, everyone in the dining room saw what happened that day. What could be the next? It was impossible to guess what is going to be the next for Broneco. For the first time, he had shown a smile on his birthday.

Everyone begin to treat Broneco with friendship that following afternoon. It was quite amazing that only one smile did it all. What has been behind all of that, no one didn't know. It was a great secret that Broneco himself only knew and until later he mentioned it to his new friend that he later met. And these happen all at once. On the same day of his first smile was just to begin with.

Broneco, after school that day, walked out in front of the school building, waving his hands to Rod and his friends.

One boy stepped beside his friend and said, "Since Broneco, our unhappy classmate, give a cheerful smile this afternoon, he's right that minute became popular."

"What will be the next, I wonder," said another boy.

Still, the secret was that no one knew. That was the hardest question to know. What was all behind this?

· IX ·

Birthday Gift for Broneco

T HE DAY OF MARCH FIFTH, nineteen hundred and fifty-nine!
All day the wind was blowing and howl outside the school.

After school, Broneco raced Rod to the building. "I'll beat you,"
said Broneco, breathing heavily while Rod was too.

Happily Broneco rounded the living room corner into the main
hall. The floor shined like an aluminum polished. He made another
corner and went up the stairs. He stepped into the top hall and
made his turn to his left.

Broneco slowly twisted the doorknob to his room clockwise.
He walked into the room when he saw two beds, his and another
one. "Who could that be, after all this time rooming all by myself,
and someone has to room this late," he thought. Then he opened
the closet door without a sound. There were suitcases and more
clothes that were hanging neatly.

"Oh well, I forgot that I'm tired," he whisper and so he fall on
the small tan-colored couch and relaxed in the comfortable position on the soft couch. He heard a footstep down the hall as it
became louder and louder. Broneco knew that someone was walking down the hall, but not knowing that it could be to his room or
the next room.

He sat up with his arms across the back of the couch. He soon
became curious so he stood up and walked up to the drawer chest
that sat by. He picked up the clock that set on the desk. When the

84

roommate came in, Broneco stood still like if he was frighten. He dropped the clock that was in his hand.

Besides, the clock belonged to the new roommate that just entered the room. Broneco leaned back against the desk. The clock still tick after it hit the floor.

The boy then moved to where the clock laid. It was the stranger that Broneco saw in the classroom before. He picked the clock up and set it on the desk again right beside Broneco, except there were few broken pieces of glass. The new roommate walked up to Broneco and then, picking up the pieces of glass, held them in his hand.

"Broneco, must you be nervous?" said the boy, throwing the broken glasses into the trash can.

"Gee, I . . . I'm sorry," said Broneco.

The strange boy smile and moved right besides Broneco and gently held his arm on the both side. "Do you know who I am? I suppose you don't."

"I don't know you."

"My name is Johnnie Benally."

Broneco felt shock as he thought of the first day in school when he said his name was Johnnie Benally. "I see it must be the boy that I was told, when Miss Merriam said to me that very first day that there was one extra Johnnie Benally," he thought and recalled it.

"But Johnnie, honestly, I'm sorry," Broneco said.

"That's all right," he reply. Then released Broneco's arm and sat on the couch.

Broneco then sat quietly and pulled out the chair that sat besides the desk. "Where were you going to school all this time?"

"Here," Johnnie said, unbuttoning his shirt.

Johnnie was going to school there? All this time! It was quite funny that Broneco didn't know him. Broneco moved away from the desk and collapse on the bed.

"Broneco, what's the matter?"

"I don't know. I don't seem to remember anything at all. I don't remember," said Broneco, lying on the bed.

Since there had been more students all year round, Broneco never thought of Johnnie being around. Johnnie has been around since the day Broneco turned out to be different. Everything started way back, when Broneco's friend fooled him, saying that he would return and for Broneco to wait for him in the strawberry patch. It was his own fault that everything went the wrong way, and now he doesn't remember his classmate in the first grade and saying that he doesn't know who they are.

"I know you very well, my friend Broneco," Johnnie said. "I know too much about you, but don't let me embarrass you."

"I still don't understand."

"You know Rod very well, don't you? He's my best friend too. I'm in the class A group in the seventh grade."

Broneco rose up from the bed and sit on the other end of the couch. Bronceo, sitting there with Johnnie, started his forgotten years.

Starting off, "It was back many years, I'm lonely for all these years when I enter this school here. I was fine and in perfect condition. I had a friend. One told me he passed away and the others say they don't know, and the others say he went to another school. But I believed that he was dead. Since today I found out that he living, and going to school in the Intermountain Indian School. My heart almost broke because he was such a great friend. He gave a ring which I still have with me."

"I know what you mean," said Johnnie with a low tone in his gentle voice.

Broneco didn't know that it was his first friend to be with. Johnnie was a real happy boy, and he was very quiet roommate.

Broneco grin as he sat on the couch looking at Johnnie. "Will you join me with a Seven-up in the boy's lounge."

"Of course, I would like to."

Johnnie stood up to tuck in his shirt. Broneco too more excited again in the beginning of his friend, Virgel. He reached behind the suitcases. He picked out a large sack full of popcorn. Full of cheerfulness, they enjoyed the evening snacks together.

At nine, Broneco was tired watching television so he decided to go back to the room. So he did when Johnnie came a minute later.

"Come right in, stranger," said Broneco.

For Johnnie, he only smile.

Broneco sat up on the bed and wondered when Johnnie said, "What's the matter, Broneco?"

Broneco looked up and frown. "Oh, today was my birthday and lots of odd things happen in a miracle way," he replied.

"Why didn't you tell me that today was your birthday?"

"Sorry, Johnnie, I forgot all about it, but you shouldn't worry about it."

"Why?"

"Because we had such a wonderful time watching T.V. this evening, and besides, what more can I want? My birthday gifts were to smile and start a new way of living," said Broneco, taking off his shoes.

Johnnie grin, falling a little to the side on the couch and putting hands behind his head. "Broneco, how about tell me a story or reading a story for me, since you have a lot of paperback books."

"Sure, why not?" said Broneco, picking up a book from the bookcase below the desk.

Johnnie moved his bed close to Broneco bed and listened reading and explaining the story about The Spotted Heart, a story about the famous horse that was stolen from the Navaho during the war with the Utes.

Broneco took his time turning each page, since he read the story many times over. He didn't need to read the whole story—all he had to do was tell Johnnie the main parts and the interesting part. When Johnnie fell asleep, Broneco went on, thinking that Johnnie is still awake. Then Broneco all of a suddenly dropped the book out of his hand and turned his head sideways.

Johnnie didn't cover himself. He went to sleep with his school clothes on. And for Broneco, he was very tired too, so he too slept with his street clothes.

About an half an hour later, Mr. Ray came around checking each room to see if the boys are in bed and making sure that none of his boys has run away or went AWOL. He was a very intelligent man. Being a night attendant, he understands almost every boy in the dormitory. His manner, very casual and gentle, for he was brought up poorly like some of the students.

Mr. Ray, soundless, opened the door and walked into Broneco's room. He saw Johnnie and Broneco sleeping one on the couch and the other with a book on the chest fast asleep. Carrying his bright, shining flashlight, he looked at the two boys sleeping. Leaving the room, Mr. Ray nodded his head and shut the door, then went on checking the room. Later Mr. Ray tell Broneco all this.

Saturday morning Johnnie and Broneco wake up. The day seems to be clear, except the wind still blowing. The first thing for Johnnie to do was to wash up and clean up the room. Broneco too has to do his detail first thing before he would help Johnnie clean the room. Broneco had finished his work rapidly so he could help Johnnie.

When Broneco reached the room, Johnnie had finished his work. "I'm through working, Broneco."

"Why being in such a rush?" Broneco stood with his hands over his chest against the closet door. "You did the fastest job I ever seen. How did you do it?" Broneco smile, waiting for an answer.

"Oh, it's real simple, and would you like to know?"

Broneco looked up towards the ceiling and putting his feet behind the other feet said, "Oh yes, I would like to know."

Johnnie then put the bucket full of water on the floor. "All you have to do is wax the floor over the dirty floor that you have waxed last week, and it really shines up without scrubbing so hard."

"What on earth are you trying to teach me?"

"It's instant, you know," said Johnnie.

While all this time Mr. Williams, the attendant, was listening to Broneco and Johnnie about how to clean up the floor like it was really scrub. Then Mr. Williams opened the door and look at Johnnie across the room.

"Johnnie, will you report to my office soon as possible?"

Johnnie fell on the bed when Broneco trip over the bucket of hot water. "Oh, no! I had to go to the office and you have to do more cleaning in the room here. I suppose Mr. Williams heard us discussing how I cleaned the room floor so quickly," said Johnnie.

After Johnnie left the room, Broneco wondered what's going to happen to Johnnie. Will he be spanked or just a few shakes?

In the advisor's office, Johnnie was frighten. He also thought he was to be spanked or punished.

"Have a seat, my boy," Mr. Williams said, searching through the desk drawer and then looking and glancing over a slip of paper. "I have a small note, saying that you're to go home Monday. It has been requested by your parents."

Johnnie was beginning to sweat, but when he was told that he was to go home, he felt better. When Johnnie left the office, he went to Rod's room, an old friend. Johnnie knocked on the door before he entered the room.

Rod opened the door before Johnnie did. "Well, hello there, Johnnie old pal, I haven't seen you for quite a while."

"Oh, now you cut that out, saying you haven't seen me for a long time. It was only yesterday that I moved up to Broneco's room. And I think he's real nice in some way."

Johnnie walked around the room then pulled a chair to sit on. Then got up and moved to the window.

"Johnnie, what you so nervous about?"

"Well, it's just . . ." said Johnnie as he stood by the window, looking out the front. While he was looking out the window, at that minute Broneco walked out of the entrance of the building. Then Johnnie turned around, facing Rod, and said, "Rod, what would you do if you was to leave a very good friend of yours?"

"I would tell him my reason and why."

"Is that all?"

"Yes, and he would understand, depends on whom you talking to," said Rod, dusting the dresser tops.

Johnnie standed there for awhile and reached for the doorknob. "Thanks," said Johnnie as he went out the door with a rush. I wonder what will Broneco say, Johnnie thought. Broneco know Johnnie's thoughts.

During that afternoon, Broneco and Johnnie went to town and it was a wonderful day. Broneco and Johnnie went down to the cafe and eat there for a great pleasure. Together they had a joyful supper. That evening they went to the movie and Broneco was real overjoyed so that night he went to bed again without putting on his p-jay.

Johnnie didn't tell a single thing about leaving Monday morning. Broneco knew it, but he didn't tell Johnnie. Sunday morning was a hot day. Like never before as the voices of gospel hours vibrating into Broneco's ear. Johnnie, with a charming smile, walked down the steps.

"Broneco, I wanted to tell you something before we enter the church."

"Go ahead and shoot," replied Broneco.

"I'm going home tomorrow and I will be back. I guess you understand anyway that I don't have to explain everything."

Broneco listened to Johnnie as he strolled along the tennis fence.

"A friend has to depart sometimes. You can't keep a friend forever beside you," said Broneco. While talking, he kept on kicking every small pebble that he sees on the sidewalk and, for Johnnie, snapping his finger together. This time, Broneco didn't seem to be disappointed.

The next morning Broneco stood by the stairway window on the north side of the interior of the dormitory. Broneco looked at his watch that he had. It was striking eight. He put his hands on the rail of the stairs. Broneco turned around again and saw Johnnie carrying his suitcase.

Johnnie looked for Broneco to say a few words again before he leaves, but he could not see Broneco anywhere in sight to wave at him.

While on the stairway from above Johnnie, there Broneco looked with a little smile. For he know how it is to depart from a friend you begin to know. Johnnie said that he will be back next year, if he tells the truth, thought Broneco as he picked up his book, ready to move.

It's been nice meeting you, my friend Johnnie, and see you

later perhaps. Your family needs you and I, Broneco, had to complete my seventh grade year. So, until we meet again, he said as he walked down the stairs with few of his pile of book that he studies each after school that he was carrying in his right hand.

Johnnie slowly taking his time went on and reached for the door handle. Without looking back, he entered the car.

That day again, it was like the day when Broneco had the great smile and met his friend. It was really turning different of various things that Broneco knew all through the year long. He watched almost everything he sees and know the difference it has. For the weather is cool and the wind kept on blowing and lots of dirts went up in the air each time the wind would blow, messing up the sharp-combed hairs of every students that are strolling along the walk. Some talking together and smaller kids running and racing together to see who's the fastest.

As Broneco walked behind the bigger students, he notice that the girls begin to smile each time he approach one. But for Broneco didn't seem to smile back but a little grin would do, so he did.

Broneco went to school with thought to it. A friend would come and tease Broneco once in a while, sitting at his assigned desk.

Suddenly and gradually the week passed and soon it was another week. Broneco forgot about counting the days left of the school year to end, and again take a three-months vacation which might give a big rest to every students that had been working hard all through the year. Some got their diploma and had planned their future years of school and various type of business which they desired.

"Someday I will be there on the stage, strolling toward what I been working for all these years and still I need five more years to complete with great struggle I will try," he said to himself as he sat there with another friends which they also had the same aim of thought too.

After graduation, Broneco walked out of the commencements hall and drinked a cool water where there was a water fountain which was newly built past few weeks. It was refreshing and so he stood there when one of the boys in a group came and greet with friendship.

"Broneco, are you going to stay for the dance that is going to be held here in the gym tonight?" asked one of the boys.

Broneco grinned for a while and looked straight at the next boy which stood there and smile a bit.

"Come on and stay, Broneco, that . . . that it is a lot of fun."

"Since you talk me into it, I'll stay," Broneco said.

"You sort of look lonely tonight. Come with us and let's have a few cups of punch. Then you might feel better."

"Maybe, it might help, perhaps," said Broneco again looking down at his shoes with a grin or any other face expression.

Broneco followed the boys around the corner of the table that sat there and one boy got a bottle from underneath the benches that were set along the gym floor. Upon the lighted stage four boys started playing their instruments with a slow beat of jazz music. It looked like being in a bar lounge downtown as Broneco had seen it few times as he passed it along the street once in awhile when he goes to town.

Then there a smell of wine from where the boys were. Broneco for a few minute sniffed a bit and sat still. Then one of the boys from the bunch came and sat by Broneco.

"Have some punch, Broneco, for you looked sort of tired from the day's work. Besides, you always worked so hard in school each day as I notice you doing all that work. You have a great mind, I suppose," said Danny who was sitting besides Broneco.

"Oh yes, I am so tired and right now I am thinking of my good old bed," said Broneco, taking the paper cupful of punch that was filled with wine.

Broneco, without thinking, the next minute took a deep breath and drinked the liquid without smelling or giving a little taste. When he drunk about halfway of the cup, he suddenly felt the difference of the taste that took place of the punch.

For a minute, Broneco didn't say a word. He just put the cup down on the bench without a sound. Broneco then glimpse across the floor to the other side and everybody were out there, holding each other tight and comfortable position dancing on the smooth, shining floor of the gym. On the stage, the music continue on with more jazz music.

How awful it tasted for Broneco! He shooked his head and looked at Danny. "Danny, why give me that nasty stuff? You said it was a punch."

"I didn't mean to give that stuff, but I thought it might do you good since you said that you were tired after all."

Broneco then leaned back against the back of the bench and watched everyone moving and some still on the floor dancing. For a while Broneco watched, and then slowly got up and walked to where the punch were on the table and picked one and then return to where he was.

"Broneco, you want some more?" asked one of the boys who were in the dark corner of the room.

"No, thank you."

"How do you feel?" said another one.

"How do you think I feel? I feel like giving each one of you a pair of dark eye, for one thing," replied Broneco, sitting still against the bench like he was before.

"Are you getting drunk?" asked Danny who was sitting near.

"No I don't, Danny. It's that I feel like throwing."

"Do you want to leave now. If so, I'll go back with you to the dormitory."

"Shall we?" Broneco said with understanding Danny's feeling of the taste of liquid that he had. He lick his lip on the account of dizziness, and blinking his eyes once in awhile. Broneco, for a while, watched Danny and finally he motioned him that he was ready to leave.

Broneco and Danny walked out the front entrance of the crowded area, but they didn't notice them and moved out without a smell.

The next day, during the school time, Broneco and Danny strolled to school, discussing what had happen last night.

"It was quite obvious," said Danny with a laughter.

"It wasn't funny besides the point."

Broneco noticed that the grass were green as ever by now since many recreational things were going on everyday. The trees were even waving their branches with tiny leafs fattening each time the wind blew in Colorado which was the state in which Broneco was in.

The next day Broneco stood there and imagine his friend pass by. "I'll wait and wait. Till the next coming fall and now I know how it is to be polite and be friendly. I must be ready to leave for I'll be heading west, toward where the sun sets," he said.

He smile and walked a little ways. "Johnnie, I know you'll come back this coming year, and for sure we'll both have something new to show to each other. I will never be sad and lonely anymore, for I know you will be back and, until then, goodbye, my friend Johnnie," he said to himself and walked away from the school building with a smile.

He headed for the red car that waited a few yards away for Broneco. "It's suppose to be tomorrow, but I had forgotten that I was a day ahead of myself," he said, walking on. Happily he amble and reached the car. Feeling great, he rode away.

·X·

The Shared Love

I T WAS IN THE MONTH OF AUGUST and Broneco had finished his tenth grade year at school. The sun was high in the blue heaven. No stars could be seen, except there was cotton-like clouds that stretched across the sky.

Broneco amble out of the south door at home, rubbing his eyes from the good night sleep.

"You're late for breakfast this morning," said Annie.

"Oh, I suppose I am."

"Where you're been last night?"

"I went to the dance at the Catholic Center," said Broneco, smiling with a wrinkle nose, "and where did you go?"

"Ha, oh my! How dare you ask me that question."

"All right, all right, I will not ask you any more questions."

Broneco, blinking his eyes, then entered the next house. The breakfast was ready for him to eat.

"Broneco, my boy, you are late getting up this morning," said Grandmother. "You did better haste a little with your breakfast this morning, for your cousin Parrie is going to be here to take you back to school. Annie, too. He could be here any time now."

Broneco washed his hands and then combed his hair. He quietly sat at the table without saying a word and started to eat. The breakfast was good and tasty. The black coffee didn't matter, so he didn't bother to pour the hot coffee. Instead, he poured himself a tall glassful of orange juice for drink.

Then he reached for the hot biscuit that smelled like a yeast bread. Grandmother has made the bread in the adobe oven the day before, but it was still fresh. Since she could reheat the bread again, it was hot.

The scent of spiral shaping clouds of the steaming puffs floated about his nose. The smell gave more appetite with a hungry feeling inside.

Annie in the other house. She combed her hair neatly as she has always done before. Took her suitcase outside and set the cases there. She waited there for a minute and then the wind begin to blow.

The cool, gentle wind kept blowing from the east to west. Her hair keep waving as of the glimmering water. Looking farther into the great distance, Annie could see the tall prairie grass with a few sagebrush. The smell of the fresh air, the hills with green sides, the mountains covered with greens everywhere she looks made the day seem different.

Annie forgot all about that her cousin Parrie was coming this morning. She stood there and listened. She heard the sound of the approaching car suddenly when the dogs started barking. They roared and growl, jumping over the corral. Annie tried to calm down the mean dogs, but there seems to be nothing she could do about the dogs. If she doesn't do something, one of the best shepherd would get run over with tremendous weight of the car. The dogs kept barking and ignore Annie.

Broneco inside the house was still eating when he heard the horrible roaring outside. He got so excited that he didn't look where he was going. Trip over a chair and then knocked the cups off the table.

Annie stand there, trying to think of something to quiet the dogs. Then she got an idea that she never thought of before. Annie reached for the woven whip that she used to use in the past. Since, it's been hanging on the old post for about a year. However, when

96

she was ready to shake the dust off the whip, Broneco banged the door open.

"Annie, will you . . . you—" Broneco didn't finish what he was going to say when Annie interrupt.

"I can't now. They are too far away to whip at least one."

"Then you help me pack?"

Broneco went into the house to get ready. Annie didn't say a word, but she followed Broneco into the house, closed the door behind her.

"I don't have time to fold at least one," said Broneco.

"One what?"

"My clothes, silly."

Annie laughed, folding one of the shirts that was on the bed in Broneco's room.

Broneco grabbed every shirt that hang in the closet and piled them right into the suitcase without folding another one neatly. "I'll have them iron just as soon as I get back to Ignacio," said Broneco. "I can hardly wait—wait to return back to school. Besides, Johnnie is coming back."

"How do you know?"

"My conscious tells me. That isn't all, however. I dream about it too."

Broneco was through packing now. Annie helped Broneco to carry the heavy loads of package outside. Then, when they were ready in the car, Broneco remember something he has forgotten.

"My suitcase," he shouted. "Stop! My suitcase, is still in the house yet. I almost forgot all about it."

"Well, what are those package?"

"They are my unfolded shirts and slacks."

Broneco got off the car and rushed back into the house to pick up the suitcase. It took him several minutes, but he came sooner than he thought he would.

Grandmother stood by the porch and wave goodbye. Now she has to take care of the place for nine months until Broneco and Annie returns sometime in the month of May. She didn't worry about the hardship. She knew that Annie's mother would come to help her again after she comes back from Delores, Colorado.

Since a woman was always first, Annie was the first one to get off by the girls' dormitory.

"I'm shaking," said Broneco.

"You must be catching cold."

"It's not a cold. I'm just afraid to enter the boys' dorm," said Broneco, putting on his black sweater.

Broneco has been that way when he returns to school. Parrie knew that Broneco soon will forget that he was a stranger for a while. Parrie smiled and drove to the corner of the dirt road pavement. Broneco waited for a while again before he got off the pickup.

"Oh yes, my friend is suppose to be back this year." He thought about it and then grin. Broneco unloaded his personal belonging on the side of the car. Then he took them across the road. There he stood, then wave a hand for Parrie to leave.

The truck left, and Broneco stood by the dormitory steps. Slowly he pick the luggage and went up the steps, taking a considerable amount of fresh air. Then a little smile.

"Broneco, why smile alone? How about me?"

"Johnnie, it's you!" said Broneco, putting the suitcase down on the steps.

"What were you thinking of?" asked Johnnie.

"I was just daydreaming, and didn't know I was smiling."

"I see. Won't you come in?" Johnnie opened the door for Broneco. Johnnie grabbed one side of the suitcase and walk into the office.

"Well, hello there. It's nice to see you back," said Mr. Williams, reaching out to shake hands with Broneco. "I see you got your partner, Johnnie, with you already."

"Must be the shared love."

"Perhaps," replied Broneco laughing.

Mr. Williams then give a ticket to Johnnie and blinked his right eye. "Show him where he room."

Johnnie grinned and picked one of Broneco's suitcase. Not a single word was spoken until he had reached the room. Broneco looked up at the clean-smelling ceiling on the hall. Gently Johnnie opened the door and then glance back with a smile.

Broneco followed Johnnie into the room and closed the door behind him. Broneco looked at the bed, the ceiling, window, and the last was the furnitures. Then he took off his sweater and lay it on the wooden chair covered with slick varnish—the texture very smooth.

"Johnnie, when did you come back?"

"This morning, around about nine o'clock."

"I couldn't believe that you're here, and I'm glad that I didn't have to wait in the strawberry patches," said Broneco, trying to pull the curtain to one side.

Outside, the green trees and grass kept waving. The smell of the floor, furnitures, desk, and chairs made Broneco felt awful. "Johnnie, I think I need a long rest. Do you mind if I use your bed?"

"No, Broneco, as you please. In case you wonder where I'll be, I will be in the boys' lounge, playing piano."

Broneco unbuttoned his shirt and crawled on the bed. Then he kicked off his shoes on the side of the bed. He put his head on the pillow where it suited him. Without another sound, he fell asleep.

When Broneco wake up in room four he whisper to himself, "Oh, my head is aching. I think I'll take couple of aspirin and cold glass of water."

Broneco got up and went to the clothing room. "Mrs. Brown, would you give me couple of aspirin? I have a terrible headache."

"It's right there in the cabinet," she said with a mean, harsh look. She got her needle and started sewing again.

Broneco, without reading the label written on the bottle that set next to the aspirin bottle, he took the wrong pills. Broneco took six pills, then he went back into his room. There, in the room, he poured the water from the pitcher full of water into the glass.

Instead of taking one, he took them all but one. The sour taste made his jaw jerk a little. However, Broneco wanted a quick relief so he didn't mind the taste. Broneco carefully poured the cold water from pitcher again and took another cupful of water.

"I think I needed more sleep, for I'm getting sort of dizzy," he said, drinking another glass of water. He sat on the leather-covered chair and watched some small kids playing whooping Indians outside on the lawn. Then Broneco fell asleep again without knowing it.

Broneco's head turned sideways. His chin touched his chest. Fifteen minutes pass, when Johnnie returned to the room to see if Broneco was awake by now.

Johnnie opened the door hastenly. "Broneco, what . . . what are you doing sleeping on the chair?"

"M - m - m - m," said Broneco with his eyes narrowed.

"What's the big idea?"

"Oh - oh!"

"Broneco, if you asleep, why aren't you in bed?"

"No - o - o."

Johnnie stared at Broneco and waited to see if he was going to answer. Broneco sat there on the leather covered chair as if he had a couple of whisky. Johnnie was now worried. "Broneco, are you ever going to answer me?"

"Johnnie, I . . . I'm sleeping."

"You what?"

Johnnie walked up to where Broneco was sitting in the chair, shook him a little, then harder than before. Johnnie stand silent, trying to think of a way.

Broneco kept collapsing off the chair.

Finally Johnnie helped Broneco to his bed and Johnnie knew what happen now. Broneco was pointing at the one pill that was left on the table.

A week later, it was on Saturday night. Broneco was in another room, helping Ricky with primary colors on art. Johnnie waited for Broneco to return.

"Blue and yellow makes green, see?" said Broneco, sitting besides Ricky mixing colors. Ricky finally understood the mixing of the colors.

Broneco had forgotten that Johnnie said for him to return to the room soon as possible. "Ricky, I forgot that Johnnie said come back in about five minutes."

"Thanks a lot helping me with the colors."

On the way down, Broneco kept thinking of the English class. "The subject is getting harder and harder. I must get it done before there is too many things to do tomorrow," he thought. He returned to his room to picked up another book to study in the room eight. He was ready to leave when Johnnie stopped him.

"Broneco, do you have to go?" Johnnie asked.

"No, not exactly. Why?"

Johnnie smile and took the book out of Broneco's hand. Broneco looked curious, but he didn't say or asked a question why. He then seated himself, waited for an answer.

Suddenly Johnnie said, "Broneco, let's go to the dance tonight."

"Don't be ridiculous."

"I don't mean it that way. All I ask was if you would go to the dance with me and watch."

"Where's the dance at?" said Broneco, half laughing.

"Broneco, don't be so funny for this isn't a love bird."

Broneco stopped laughing. Broneco wasn't ready so he sat there, looking at himself from head to toe. Then he asked again, "Where is the dance tonight?"

"It's just across the tennis court. In the Junior High School gymnasium."

Broneco looked at himself again. "No, Johnnie, I can't go. I think I better stay home. Besides, I had to do some of my homework tonight so I don't have to do much tomorrow night. You can have all the fun with every girl without a friend with you. So I stay," said Broneco and then decided to leave the room.

"Oh, come on, just this Saturday," said Johnnie.

Broneco stood facing the door. His hand twisted the doorknob, but he didn't open the door. Broneco thought about it for a longer time, thinking, "Shall I stay or shall I go?"

Broneco decided that he would go, not because that he liked to go, it was that he didn't want to disappoint a friend. "O.K.. Johnnie, I'll go."

Broneco looked to where Johnnie was. He was lying on the bed with a little smile with his hands on the back of his head. Johnnie knew that Broneco wouldn't disappoint him, if he gives him time to think about it.

"You sure that you will go?"

"Of course I'm going."

Broneco and Johnnie dressed up for the dance an hour later. The clock that set on the dresser chest was now striking eight-thirty. Slowly it tick, but it was sure going faster than Broneco and Johnnie thought.

"Stop the clock," said Broneco.

"You think it'll help?"

"Perhaps, maybe not. Forget about it."

Another five minute has gone by. Broneco excitedly opened the door and was caught a loose nail in the woodwork on a door frame. Broneco's shirt ripped.

"My sleeves," he shouted.

Broneco rushed back into the room to change his shirt. It took him another ten minutes to select another shirt, when he forgot to polish his shoes.

"Wait a minute, Johnnie, I haven't polish my shoes yet. One moment, please," said Broneco, picking up a rag.

Finally, Broneco was through. Wasting no more time, they head for the gymnasium. With a clicking sound, they disappear into the darkness of the night. It was dark since the moon hasn't rose above the height of the mountains.

"I'm afraid to go into the doorway," said Broneco, following in behind Johnnie.

"They won't bite you."

The music sounded with tingling sound in different pitches. Then the beating of the drums. Broneco followed Johnnie down the main hall, then into the next room which was in the gym.

102

Broneco enter the dancing floor and looked straight ahead until they had reached the bleachers.

Johnnie leaned against the bleachers. "What's the name of the band, do you know?"

"I think it's The Pine River Boys, as I read it in the school paper yesterday," Broneco said. "The most brilliant thing about the stage."

"What about the band?"

"They play the most unusual melody that I rarely hear in the most orchestra."

"Broneco, tell me. How many times have you been to a dance?"

"Couple of times back home," said Broneco when Johnnie glimpse across the floor and saw a girl stand up and pause. Picked up her purse, sweater, and her white gloves. Then she started on her way across the shining, wooden floor.

Johnnie wanted to tell Broneco, but he was still talking— Broneco was so excited about the band on the stage.

Then she stood before Johnnie. "May I join you two gentlemen?" she asked.

Broneco didn't even notice her standing. He thought it was Johnnie who was talking. So he said, "Certainly, you may suit yourself and keep quiet."

"Thank you," she said.

Johnnie didn't know what to say. He looked around to think of a way to tell Broneco that the girl is sitting with them.

"My name is Bernie," said the girl, introducing herself.

"I'm Johnnie and that's my friend, Broneco."

Broneco still admiring the band on the stage. "Just look at that boy with a saxophone. I wish I could play like him. Look at the way he fingers the keys with a speed. Wow-gee, the way he moves with a step!" Broneco still haven't discover the girl with a charming smile next to him.

"Your friend must be so excited," Bernie said to Johnnie.

"No, he's talking to himself," reply Johnnie.

Broneco heard Johnnie this time so he turned his head to see who was Johnnie talking to. Broneco was froze when he saw the girl all dressed in white. "Must be an angel or something," said Broneco.

"May I have this dance?" she asked.

"You asking me or him?"

The girl looked at Johnnie and then Broneco. "You," she said, pointing at Broneco.

"I don't know how to dance. Him . . . dance with him better," said Broneco nervously.

"Proceed," said Johnnie, making an offer girl's hand and then escort her into Broneco's hand.

Broneco then unbutton his shirt near to the throat. "I'm choking," said Broneco.

"Shall we all go out and sniff the fresh air?" the girl asked.

"Thank you," Broneco said, still nervous.

Bernie held Broneco's arm and on the left was Johnnie. She also held his arm. Broneco and Johnnie had no idea of any sort. For the girl it was a big bet. So she was trying all she could to make the two boys on the go.

Outside, the air was blowing with cool breezes from the forest. Broneco and Johnnie sat on the rail, and for Bernie, she sat right on the corner of the rail. There was a little whistling sound as the wind blew through the trees. Broneco notice that the moon has risen by now.

"Shall we have some punch?" asked Broneco.

"Please," said Bernie smiling again. "The dance is about over, isn't it?"

"Would you like to dance?" Johnnie asked her.

"No, Johnnie. Until your friend returns, then you two can take me home with a stroll," she said with an interrupt.

Just then Broneco returned with three paper cups of punch. The punch taste with sour-lemon luxurious taste.

Gently Bernie held the cup in her hand. Then put the cup down the concrete step. "Next Saturday, let's have a juicy steak in town together," she said.

Broneco and Johnnie agreed without delay this time.

"Shall we go home now?" she asked.

Then they all went down the exit step, Bernie walking in the middle of the two boys. Around the corner of the gym they stroll as Bernie request it the first time. Now the music sound with echo as if escorting a bride to her wedding. Broneco and Johnnie were no longer nervous now. They had all forgotten all about timidity.

The weeks went by slowly. Broneco and Johnnie continue school as they were before. There was always a happy weekends. Bernie would walk with Broneco and Johnnie in the evening after supper each day. Sometimes they would all go to town and spend their time in the cafe, drinking coke and etc.

Soon it was April, the leafs on the tree begin to sprout again. Broneco didn't know it was April. Then one day he sat by the window when his young memories came back. Looking through the trees with tiny leafs, Broneco lowered his pencil and dropped it to the floor and stared out the window.

"I will return soon. It will end. I will return very soon," Broneco whisper, sitting by the window.

Johnnie doing his homework heard Broneco. He stop wiggling his pencil and asked himself a question—What does he mean? Johnnie sat still and with a strange fear ran up his spine with chills. "Broneco, are you all right?"

"Oh sure, I'm all right. Why?"

"I just wondered."

Broneco moved away from the window and closed the curtain. He walked up to where Johnnie was and stood before him.

"Who were you talking to?" Johnnie asked.

"Johnnie, you'll never understand," said Broneco still standing, "till someday you'll know what I'm talking about. That will be at the end of my Miracle Hill."

"What about the Miracle Hill?"

"It's too soon to know."

Johnnie still didn't understand. For Broneco, he knew what he was talking about.

Then the month of May came. Broneco knew it was Johnnie's

birthday. Broneco and Bernie were very busy all day, baking a cake. Johnnie's cake had sixteen candles.

Broneco sang "Sixteen Candles" that night. It was for Johnnie.

It was nearly school out again. Broneco was sitting in the room eight where there was a piano. He, gently holding a piece of rag, dusted the dirt off the bench and the keys.

Just then Johnnie came in. With a smile, walked up to the piano.

"Someday, Broneco, I hope that you'll remember me by this tune and the song. I myself like this song. I guess there is a reason for that. The chord starts with C."

"What's the name of the song?"

"Matilda," he said.

Broneco looked out the window and listened to the tune that Johnnie played. The tune itself was romantic. Then Broneco walked away from the window and walked down the hall. Now the music was quiet. Broneco walked away from the room because he knew that he wasn't coming back to school. There were lots of problems that rang in Broneco's head.

During the last day of school, Broneco and Johnnie joined Bernie on the sidewalk. Broneco was happy like never before. Johnnie notice that too. Bernie laughing with a little giggle, they all shuffle hand-in-hand down the road.

"I won't be seeing you anymore," said Bernie.

"Why?" said Broneco and Johnnie all at once.

"Please don't ask me any more questions, for I have a surprise for you."

"What kind of surprise?" said Johnnie, anxiously waiting.

"You sure you won't disappoint me?" she asked.

"No, we won't if you tell us now," said Broneco.

"You promise now?"

"Oh, sure," said Johnnie and Broneco with their arms around Bernie.

She looked at Broneco and then Johnnie. She was smiling with a twinkle in the eyes. Then she reached for Johnnie's neck.

Broneco released his arms away from Bernie.

"Now both of you shut your eyes," she said.

"Now what's this all about?" asked Johnnie.

"It's the shared love, remember?" she whisper, running her fingers through Johnnie's delicate smooth and wavy hair.

Broneco opened his eyes and saw Bernie's lip depart from Johnnie. Then she release herself from Johnnie, whispering again. Then she turned facing Broneco as his heart begin to beat louder than before.

"Come now, don't run away from me," she said, embracing Broneco's neck. Shutting her eyes, she made her lips into the shape of a heart.

Broneco, moderately in slow movement, pull back away, fearing, as his heart beated faster than before. As her rose-colored lip came nearer, the bright daylight begin to fade away from the view of Broneco's eyes, then the surrounding objects, the lovelier they were, now whirl into a spin of darkness, then it stopped.

"Bernie . . . Bernie . . . Bernie . . . ," said Broneco, recovering from the fainting spell of Bernie's distasteful lip. "If it had been sweet as the rosie lip look, it could have been all right," thought Broneco smiling, then slowly open his eyes.

Johnnie, seeing the incident take place, he laugh in a gentle mood of casual. Standing with his hand placed on the waist hip, nodding his head.

"Broneco, I didn't touch your lip," said Bernie, still holding onto Broneco's weakling neck which, in the matter of minute, would fall from the lack of blood running through his veins. She smiled as she gave more pressure on Broneco's neck.

Broneco's eyes again begin to blur as the view of Bernie's face seems to transform within the wave of the moving air. "I think . . ." said Broneco, in that second of spoken word he was interrupted and look away into nature's clear and pure current of the flowing air.

"Broneco, not again. Come on, it's all right. Now, stand on your feet. She's leaving now," said Johnnie, holding Broneco by the arms, keeping him on his feet.

There she stood, smiling as she put her weight to the side, upheld by the smooth figure against the clear month-of-May sky.

"What's the matter, boy?" asked Johnnie, laughing again.

Broneco seeing Bernie giggle. She wave her hands and walked down the road. Her long black hair fluttered about the cool air, she stopped and wave again, laughing, as the gleaming white teeth showed together with her rosie lips. Bernie showed that she was thrill with gladness above all her present moments.

Broneco meant to ask a question, but he waited a moment later before he asked, "Who was she, Johnnie?"

Johnnie laugh again along with Broneco, and they walked away in the opposite direction of Bernie's destination.

·XI·

Home for Christmas

HOME FROM SCHOOL during the month of December, 1962, Broneco wake in the morning, remembering that he had planned to go shopping in Farmington before it was Christmas. It was the day before Christmas.

Broneco, still lying in bed, thought of all the wonderful things that he was going to get. He could see all the gifts that he could afford. Then he rubbed his eyes and arms to get the chills off.

He looked at the clock on top of the bureau was just now striking five. He got up and looked around. First, he put on his everyday shirt. It was cold that morning so he put on his jacket on top of his shirt.

Grandmother, Auntie, and Annie still in their deep sleep. Annie in another room all curled up in her homemade blanket, in her right arm was her favorite teddy bear. It was given to her for her birthday.

Broneco went into the kitchen to fry himself two eggs with bases, and three slices of bacon, toast also. Carefully he lighted the fire to the butane burners. Then, the pieces of logs that was already set to fire in the fireplace. He put a little bit of kerosene on the wood before he lighted it. Broneco inspired the vapor from the rising odor. It made him sniffle for a second before he lighted the twenty-four inch cottonwoods, and the circumference approximately eight inches. The flames of smoke went up the chimney.

109

Then Broneco setted the frying pan on the burners. Then set the water heater afterward. Broneco's teeth was about to make the jingling sound when there were few embers in the fireplace.

Broneco picked up the chair and seated himself besides the fire. The heat blazing and making sizzling intonations of pitch. The variation of the wood as it burn, making colors of creamy blue, red, yellowish form of colors. Broneco soon took off his jacket and hung it over the rail of the chair.

The water on the butane burner was now whistling its tooting sound. Broneco dipped a cup of hot water from the water heater. Then into the washpan, adding a little more of cold water made it just right. He splash a handful of warm water on his face.

Broneco repeated this several times, using soap, then clear with plain water. After washing, he slowly placed the bacon in the frying pan which also gave off the smell of vapor. Broneco, wrinkling his nose, breaked the two eggs into a small bowl.

While in the back room, in Annie's apartment, Annie snuggle in her twin bed, all of a sudden sniffed the scent of breakfast in her room. She opened her eyes. "I must be dreaming yet," she thought, so she cuddle into a comfortable position and closed her eyes again.

For Broneco, he was washing all the dirty dishes that needed washing while waiting for the bacon to fry. He wiping each cup after washing. Broneco picked up another cup which he held in his hand. Then he remembered.

It was a small ivory-colored cup. Still holding it in his hand, he thought of his grandfather and when he got the cup. Broneco was still half-wild then.

Grandfather went to Durango, Colorado with Grandmother during an annual Spanish Trail Fiesta. Broneco smiled when he remembered what Grandfather said also.

He said, "Your grandmother and I are going on a Gray Dog from Shiprock depot, and on our returning, white eagle bring us back to Nataani Nez on the seventh day of the week."

This Broneco thought about it, and finally knew what Grandfather once mentioned. Now, it made itself clear in his mind. Broneco giggle in the kitchen holding the white cup.

Yes, it was on the seventh day of the week which was Sunday they came home with this pure glossy goblet. That wasn't all. Also there was a gift for Annie. Grandmother and Grandfather each had a beautifully designed covering on the small package for Annie.

With a surprising sign of smile, Annie opened the boxes. It was a pearl necklace and a small ring with one turquoise stone set in the middle on the ring.

This Broneco thought of as he was washing the dishes. He didn't know he was daydreaming early in the morning. Then he put the drinking cup next to the tall glass. The gildering of the fire in the fireplace made the glass sort of twinkling.

Broneco had forgotten all about frying bacon. What he saw was only the carbons left in the frying skillet. He inhaled the strong odor and then lifted the pan from the burner and set the heavy stewing pan on the platter. Broneco, with a repelling eyes, skimmed the drifting bacon from the grease, using a fork.

The strong smell from the burned bacon woke Annie. She pushed her head-resting cushion aside and slowly walked into the kitchen. She stood there in her robe, waiting for Broneco to turn his direction, facing the bedroom door.

Broneco went on separating the burned bacon and then drained the grease into the waste pan which was also used for paper basket.

"I see you trying to burn more bacons," said Annie, leaning against the casing of the door. She had a key chain in her right hand, tossing it around her first finger. Then she laugh as she put the key chain down on the coffee table.

Broneco then smile, setting the skillet on the burners again.

Annie kept staring at her brother preparing another slice of bacon in the kitchen.

Broneco dropped the slice of bacon on the floor. His face begin to turn its color from natural light complexion into dark red.

"What's the matter, Broneco? Knaves are suppose to be smarter than that."

"Will you stop staring at me?" said Broneco, nervously holding another melting bacon in his hand.

Annie didn't stop staring. She sat with her eyes set on Broneco.

Broneco stopped what he was doing and turned around to face Annie, but Annie didn't kept eyeing Broneco. "Annie, if you don't take your eyes off of me, I'm going to throw this bacon right in your face."

"I'm sorry. I was just wondering."

"What?"

"Today is the day before Christmas. I could hear the bell ringing, even the joyable sounds of the season's greeting. I wonder what will it be for me?" said Annie with her chin on her hands.

Broneco then put the bacon in the frying pan. This time he didn't make mistake.

Annie helped Broneco to set the table by the fireplace. Then it was time for breakfast when Grandmother and Auntie joined Broneco and Annie at the table to eat.

Broneco poured the hot coffee for Grandmother and Auntie. Annie with a smile helped herself with burned toast. Annie used to get up in the morning and do the cooking. This time she was late getting up so Broneco prepared the burned breakfast.

After breakfast, Broneco put on his neat clothes. Then he put his jacket on last. Smiling, he went to the mirror and patiently fixed his winter tie. The color of the tie was red. Broneco went to the window and drew the curtain apart. He looked out the window and stand.

The strip of hard frozen snow patched here and there along the side of the dirt road. The wind blew against the window and made a lonely sound of music. The sky was clear, except it was cold outside. Broneco waited there by the window and listened to the queer noise made by the wind. Then he stroll across the bedroom and reached for the door handle, twisted the knob from east to west. He waited there. Looked at Grandmother, Auntie, and Annie before he opened the door.

"Goodbye and I'll be back before four o'clock this evening with my presents," he said.

"Where are you going to shop this Christmas eve?" asked Auntie.

"I'm going to Farmington to shop."

"We are going to Durango to shop."

Broneco stood there for a while and then nodded his head and closed the door behind him. The wind blew wildly, bending the prairie grass that are left from the summer month. There was no dust whirling about since the soil of the earth was widely froze.

Broneco headed down the road. The air was cold but he didn't mind it. He thought of all the presents, gifts, and his donation of packages to be put under the Christmas tree. There was no Christmas tree yet, but surely there would be one. Annie had said that they will get one tree from the mountain.

It was four miles to the Continental bus depot. Broneco hurried himself along the dirt road. He looked at his wrist watch and it was almost nine o'clock. Broneco thought of Johnnie while walking towards the streets of pavement. The signs of happy Christmas were along the side of some houses. There were colored lights in the village.

Just then Broneco saw the bus just arriving from Gallup. So he hurried. He made it in time for the takeoff. There were many riders in the bus. Broneco found himself a seat when a girl entered the bus.

She seems to smile, carrying her overnight suitcase along with her black purse. She sat right besides Broneco and setted her things down. Her face spot with a little scars. Broneco looked out the window.

Broneco looked at her when she isn't looking at him. In return, she would look when Broneco isn't looking at her.

Broneco decided to look again, but this time they both turned their face, facing each other.

The girl didn't know what to say, and so was Broneco. He decided to say hello, when they both said, "Hello."

"Excuse me, I mean hi," said Broneco.

"That's all right," she said with a clear voice. Then she put her purse besides her. She smile again before she asked a question.

"My name is Bernie."

"Mine is Broneco."

"You what?"

Broneco sat silent, then he remembered. It was Johnnie and

113

Broneco's shared love. All those days are gone now, but Broneco remember what happened all that forgotten time.

Bernie didn't know it was Broneco who she was talking to. Broneco turn sideway and smiled. Then he looked at Bernie.

"Bernie, it's you. Still remember me or have you forgotten?"

Bernie stared at Broneco with her twinkling eyes, as the sun shined on her eyes. Her long wavy hair tremble with a flowing motions. The tears almost was shown in her glowing, watering eyes before she answered.

"I . . . I thought you were someone I didn't know. You looked so familiar when I first saw you boarding this Trailway, but I wasn't too sure that it was you."

"I knew it was you after you said your name was Bernie."

"I'm all right now. I was sort of froze when you said that your name was Broneco. I'm sorry."

"That's all right."

Bernie reached into her purse and couldn't find what she was looking for. Broneco knew what she was looking for, so Broneco reached into his shirt pocket and pull the scarf and give it to Bernie to wipe her tears off. With a grin, she gently picked the pure bleached scarf.

"You haven't tell me where you're been all this time, Bernie, sweet girl."

Bernie blinked her eyes before she replied, "I was working in Window Rock, Arizona, and still I am working there until the first semester. Then I'll return back to school."

"Which school are you going to?"

"I had to go to California and finish my four years of Business College there."

"I have only one more year to receive my diploma," said Broneco.

"What are you going to do after you graduate, go on to college or some kind of vocational training?"

"Gee, Bernie, I really can't say."

"I was like you. I didn't know what to take until I talked and discussed it with my counselor before I graduated from Farmington High last year."

Broneco and Bernie went on, talking about various things, sitting together. They kept themselves busy discussing school problems and other activity that was to be held the next night. The bus approached the entrance of the first street where the bus stop on the red signal light.

How anxious they both were to get to town and do their shopping! As they pass through the street, there in the windows of the different department stores each had displays of toys, clothings, jewelries, decorations, and other donations of gifts. The bus finally came to a halt. Patiently Broneco and Bernie waited for the other travelers to clear.

Broneco and Bernie, taking their time, departed from the bus station. Bernie left her carrying case in the keeper's room in the depot until she returns. Broneco and Bernie walked along the side of the first block of the department store. People jamming on both side of the street. Broneco and Bernie were looking at the silverware in the window when they walked into another couple holding hands just around the street.

"Oh, excuse me," said Bernie.

"Why don't you watch where you're going?" said a girl with her hair brushed up like a tumbleweeds. Her face with plenty pale of makeup, and her lip as if she had drunken at least a cup of blood. The boy with a long hair kept blowing sideways as the wind blew, but did not answer.

Broneco stood there, waiting for the green light to flash. For Bernie, she amble by the couple. Then held Broneco's hand crossing the street. This time, Broneco and Bernie watched where they were going.

Broneco and Bernie did their shopping that day in Farmington. When the day passed, they head back for the bus station.

"It's been a wonderful day for me," she said. "I wouldn't have enjoyed myself being here alone. Besides, we are both riding west again tonight," she said, carrying loads of presents, and so was

Broneco. "And I really enjoyed the lunch this afternoon and this evening. What more can a Miss want?"

Broneco didn't answer. Instead, he went right up to the ticket counter and bought two tickets to Shiprock. Broneco gave one to Bernie.

She was tired so she seated herself on the long waiting room bench. Broneco sat besides her, helped her with her overcoat. Then she button it up and leaned back against the back of the bench.

Broneco was tired too. Quietly they sat together. Bernie went to sleep with her head touching his chest. Broneco listen to the bells ringing in the street. The roaring of the cars, siren sounding, and the music of Christmas everywhere, made the merry evening. "Tomorrow is Christmas night. What will it be for me, that package under the evergreen tree? What could it be? Who knows? Only whom that may be that put the present there underneath the tree for me," he thought, holding Bernie's hand, squeezing each finger.

It was 6:30 when the bus from Durango arrive. Broneco enfolded Bernie's hand to wake her up when she did.

"The bus here?" she asked.

"Yes, Bernie, better get your personal belonging in order or else you'll leave one."

"Help me with this," she said, holding her carrying case in her right hand. Then she picked up the heavy sack and set it on the bench.

Broneco put his junk on the benches too. Then decided that he would leave his paper sack full of present there until Bernie's in the bus with her things.

Broneco carried Bernie's things into the bus first before he went back to the bench and brought his stuff.

"At last, we're heading for home," said Bernie.

"Why don't you have some sleep? You looked very tired."

"You looked tired, too."

Broneco only smile and undone his tie to release the throat choking after a hard day's shopping in Farmington. He looked out the window and saw the twinkling stars in the sky.

The bus then started on its way through the street, heading

116

straight through the main street, passing two green lights, then it was out of town. Looking back, many shades of different colors shone in the populated area of Farmington. The lights with numerous of shapes, some flashing, blinking, and others as though they are clicking.

Bernie put her head against Broneco's chest. Broneco kept looking out the window of the bus, roaring along the highway with the speed of sixty mile per hour. At a time the bus would rattle a little as it crosses the roughness of the road. Some cars passing with tremendous speed that Broneco could even hear the sounds of the wheels giving its expanding tar.

Broneco kept thinking of tomorrow. It gave him the tingling feeling that run up his back spine with chills of colds. Then the bus slowing itself down to a halt when an old lady entered with a wrinkle face. The old lady toil down the aisle of the rows of seat and seated herself four row down.

Bernie was wide awake by now, and for Broneco, he was now fall asleep. Before Broneco went to sleep, the bus came to a stop by the depot.

Bernie stood up to investigate, knowing that her relatives are waiting out there. Then she glance to where she was sitting.

"Oh, Broneco, I have to leave you here now. When will I see you again?"

"Maybe tomorrow."

"Where would that be?"

"Catholic Center, and don't forget. I'll be there."

Broneco smile and grabbed his belonging and moved on down the center aisle after Bernie. Departing from an old friend was difficult after a hard day shopping together.

Bernie turned around and walked away.

Broneco waited and then stroll along the side of the dark street into the alley of the neatly rowed houses. He walked across another street, when he came to a bridge made of wood. The bridge was like a ladder. He almost slipped crossing it.

It was late at night when Broneco came creeping home. The dogs didn't bark because they were not around at the summer camp

117

without the sheep, usually at this time on Christmas it would get too cold. Broneco notice something when he looked into the sky. The stars were hidden behind the dark moving objects. He stood before the door waiting for Grandmother to open the door.

The wind was blowing harder than it was. The dark shadow of the clouds making images of various shape here and there. It gave fear as the shadows move. Broneco's hand were freezing, his teeth begin to chatter with a tapping sound. His knee shaking like a rabbit that is ready to be caught by a hound.

Broneco waited and waited, when suddenly there in the house a warm of bright light appear by the window in the kitchen. Then the sound of a twisting doorknob was heard with a chill of spook.

"You must be cold. Come right into the kitchen," she said.

Broneco, without saying a word, entered. There by the fireplace was Annie and Auntie sorting out bags of peanuts, separating them into the small sacks.

Annie looked up and said, "Good evening, big brother. We thought you'd come home sooner."

"That's all right. I been shopping all day long and I had such a wonderful time in town today. Oh, there were many, many people in Farmington."

"Fantastic, wasn't it?" asked Annie.

"Much more than that," said Auntie. "Broneco, who was that girl you were with right around the corner of the Karl's Shoe Store across from Avery Hotel?"

"Tell us. Who is she?" ask Grandmother.

Broneco, facing the fireplace, cracking peanuts and casting shell into the fire as it blaze, bending his head to the side with his hands crossing each other crushing another nuts, didn't seem to help a bit with nervousment. Still, he had to answer the question.

"He . . . he was, I mean she . . . she was just ask . . . asking me if I knew where Johnnie was, if I had seen him."

"Where she's from?" said Auntie, smiling.

"Oh, that's Johnnie's sister."

"Johnnie's sister. Then I suppose you tell us what's her name."

Broneco looked at his hand quiver. Then he reached into his pocket. He turned about face and smiled. "Her name is Bernie. You know her don't you, Annie?"

"Oh yes, I do, but she's not Johnnie's sister," she said. Annie laughed, knowing that her brother had nothing to say.

Broneco and Annie like to tease each other very often. Her mother would ignore her when she start teasing her brother. She was very religious about it.

Grandmother lighted the butane burners. For Auntie, she was wrapping presents in the bedroom. Annie and Broneco joined together in her bedroom, also wrapping gifts for tomorrow's Christmas night. Annie turned on the battery radio. Gradually she turned the dial to where it numbered sixteen.

In Broneco's hand he held a small box. Annie couldn't guess what was in it. Annie held up the box and felt the weight of it. Annie thought about it and wondered what was in it. It was to Grandmother.

"What could that be? Could it be a clock? Or it could be a small dutch oven." Still, Annie couldn't guess.

Broneco picked up the package and wrapped the box with a red paper decorated with the sign of Christmas on it. Annie would find out next day it was a cheese for Grandmother. Then Broneco wrapped another gift for Grandmother. Soon the presents were all ready for Christmas. Annie then brought the evergreen from the porch. Broneco pick the tree and set the pine-smelling evergreen by the fireplace.

After Broneco and Annie had completed the green tree with icicle, sparkling bulb, and the packages underneath the Christmas tree, there were more coming from Auntie and Grandmother.

The next morning, Grandmother preparing breakfast with Annie's mother. Grandmother almost forgot to bring in the corn ice cream. Just then Broneco and Annie wake up and both rushed into the kitchen. Annie got the first cut of the icy cold ice cream. After taking a few bite, Annie started shivering. For Broneco, he sit by the fireplace with his back facing the fire.

119

"Tonight we'll have our Christmas party late," said Grandmother, nibbling on the ice cream also. "It'll be around ten o'clock. Why? Because we are having some visitors coming."

"I'm going to the Christmas dance tonight, but I'll be back before the party starts," said Broneco.

"I'm going to the dance too," said Annie.

Annie's mother looked to where Broneco was sitting and then Annie. She had disapproval look as Broneco can tell. "Dance, dance, that's all they say nowdays," she said, repeating again, "Dance, dance!"

· XII ·

And New Year's Eve

ANNIE AND BRONECO that Christmas morning work around the house helping with certain labors. Washing every dishes needed. For Auntie, she was preparing to roast a whole heavy weighing pounds of turkey. Broneco could taste the undone rare turkey. "Tonight," he kept thinking.

Before long it was almost time to leave for the Christmas dance. Broneco, Annie dressed themselves up for the dance.

Annie put her long black coat on. "Is Bernie coming tonight to the dance?"

"Sh-sh, keep quiet, will you?"

"Excuse me. I forgot already."

"You bet she's coming."

Then they looked at each other and opened the door and head down the road. There was no car to ride. Broneco had a car once, when he went back to school that coming fall, his uncle wrecked the car. Broneco and Annie didn't mind walking. They were used to walking.

Annie and Broneco kept asking each other different questions about the night's dance, asking who were playing.

"I used to know him. He asked me one time if I still sing like I used to do."

"What's the name of the band?"

121

"The Shades."

"Oh, I heard of them, and you also told me about the Shades, but I haven't seen them yet. This will be my first time here at the dance. What kinds of music do they play?"

"They play all kinds of music."

Broneco and Annie stop on the corner of the intersection, waiting for the automobile to clear off the pavement. Then Annie and Broneco crossed the street. Anxiously they rounded the corner of the big yellow building. There they could hear the music full of joyfulness.

"I'm afraid to enter," said Annie.

"I am myself, but that's what we came for, so why wait? Let's go."

Broneco lead the way. Annie held onto Broneco's sweater. The admission charge was dollar and half. Then they went before the ticket desk. A girl with a wonderful smile, stamping each hand, stood there. Broneco reached into his back pocket to paid for the entry fees, when another boy that almost looked like Broneco stepped in front of him.

"Broneco and Annie are the Tails of The Shades, may they follow me without any charge of expense? If charge is available, charge it to The Shades," he said.

"Did you hear that?" said Broneco.

"Tell me, what's the meaning of this?"

"You heard the man. Follow me."

Broneco and Annie grin and followed their brother Ronnie farther down the rows of chair, close to where the orchestra were playing. When they reached the third row from where the Shades are playing, another boy pulled a chair for Annie. Broneco and his brother who interfere Broneco during their entering seated himself and then smiled.

"What's the matter, Broneco? It wasn't my idea," Ronnie said.

"Gee, Ronnie, do you have to do that?"

The boy who seated Annie said, "I'm Rusty and this is Frankie, my girl, that's Bernita, Delores, and the rest I'm sure you know them."

Rusty was Broneco's uncle's young boy, and the boy who lead

Broneco and Annie into the dance without paying of charge was Broneco's older brother. The girl with a reddish blond hair color, neatly brushed with waves, sat besides Ronnie. Broneco knew that was his brother's girl. Annie knew Frankie, Rusty's girl, fairly well. Frankie was very gentle and always ready to cheer up any of her friends.

Then there was Bernita. She was quite a girl—always ready, wanting to be ask for a dance. She like to dance as every other boys knew her. As she reached into her big buckskin purse that was on her lap, Broneco also notice something. The label it read, Seagram 7th, it says. Broneco smile when he saw that. Bernita giggle with a laugh when she knew that Broneco saw in her purse. Then she lighted her cigarette, expertly holding the match at the tip of her finger.

Broneco never dance with a twisting music before, but Annie she knew how. When everyone started twisting with the twist music there was Annie, Broneco, and Bernita sitting at the table watching. Then a boy came and escort Annie to the dancing floor. Then Broneco and Bernita were the only two sitting together.

Rusty and Broneco's brother Ronnie saw them and motioned Bernita to dance with Broneco.

"Shall we split the scene?" said Bernita, taking a little cupful of whisky.

"I - I don't know how to twist, Bernita."

"Come on. I'll show you how swing your hip."

Broneco smile again before he stood up. Bernita fixed her dress-up coat and layed it over the purse. Broneco, half-scare, slowly step off onto the dancing floor. Broneco tried, but he could seem to get the gesture.

"Like this," said Bernita, swinging her hip a little.

Broneco was about to laugh when it was over. Bernita laugh with a giggle, again seating herself. After that, Broneco only watched everyone doing the stroll. Bernita and Broneco sat together talking about The Shades, and Delores came over too.

"Rusty plays the lead guitar, and my cousin, from the left to the right, is Ervin, and so on down is Melvin," Bernita said. "The drummer is Ernest, Delores's brother. Tomorrow they are playing in Chinle, Arizona. Perhaps you would like to go with us."

"Not tomorrow," Delores correct her.

Bernita laugh. She was getting a little high since she was dranking. "Excuse me, boy. I mean next week."

Broneco laugh, when he saw Bernie standing before him. He didn't know what to tell Bernie. Then, she offer her hand and Broneco stood up. As they stroll out the entrance, she smile and departed from Broneco. There was another boy who stood there by the edge of the dark shadows.

Broneco blinked his eyes and walk on after Bernie. He joined Bernie around the corner.

"Broneco, sorry we didn't dance together tonight."

"That's all right, Bernie, it's all over."

Bernie held Broneco's hand instead of Broneco holding her hand. Then Broneco put his arms around Bernie.

She said, "I love you, Broneco, and I always had."

"I love you too, Bernie, but—"

Before Broneco could finish, Bernie interrupted again. "Yes, I still love him too. I really do," she said. "Walk me across the street. There someone is waiting for me whom I love too."

Broneco without delay walked her across the street and stood there by the edge of the dark shadow. Bernie waved her hand and walked into the dark street to where Broneco saw someone standing. The music with a brilliant tone echo through the air as they stroll away into the darkness of the night. Broneco waited by the tree.

Then, there was soft snow falling peacefully. Broneco saw a white shoe disappear among the dark shadow. He looked down at his shoe and wondered. Who could that be? Could it have been Johnnie or was it someone else she loved? Yes, it was my friend, Johnnie, he thought. Maybe it was. It was hard to say. Broneco never did find out, but he didn't see Bernie after that. It was on Christmas night it happen.

A week later, on December 31st, Broneco didn't feel so good after thinking of what took place last week. Broneco's thoughts was headaching. The wind wasn't blowing this time like last week the night before Christmas. Instead, it was warming outside. The frost on the ground begin to melt instantly. On the mountainside, the fattening clouds moving skyward over the mountain covered with glistering snow.

Broneco could see the LaPlata mountain in Colorado also white as the cotton sprouting in the meadow beyond during the month of August. The melting snow begin to ripple into rivulet stream of water. Now the sun was high above the eastern mesa. The tall standing rock far in the distant land along the plateau look as if a company boat sailing in an open sea.

"I'll go for a walk today and see the countryside. Maybe then I'll feel much better, maybe," Broneco thought. He was sitting besides the window in the interior of the house.

Annie, like she always has been—happy and full of pride—throwing another piece of cottonwood into the fire to burn. She waited by the fire, heating a pot full of water. She didn't bother to used the gas burner.

Broneco watched Annie and then walk over to where Annie was. "Annie, why don't you use the butane heater?" he asked.

"I wanted to make a real old style Mormon tea. Maybe, if you take a drink of my hot tea, you might feel better. Might even stand on your head," she said, stirring the warming tea with two long stick that was tie together.

Outside, on the south side of the house, Grandmother and Annie's mother were unyarning their spinned gray strings into form of balls. They then packed the balls of yarn in the paper box, getting ready to return to the winter camp the day after tomorrow. By then, Annie and Broneco will be on their way back to school. Broneco and Annie were only home for Christmas vacation.

Broneco and Annie sat at the table with hot tea filled their cup. The breakfast has been prepare by Grandmother and Auntie that morning.

Broneco, after tasting the tea, begin to eat. "What's today?"

"Today is December the thirty-first. Tonight is the New Year's night."

"New Year already?"

"Before we know, we'll be in school again three days from now. I haven't study for the semester test that is coming up after we return from here."

Broneco didn't answer any of these Annie mention. He took another sipping when remembered that he was going to take a long walk.

A minute later, Grandmother and Auntie carrying the load of yarns into the house. "What are you two up to now?" said Auntie.

"We're having a tea party this morning," answered Annie.

"Aren't you going to say 'Join us'?" said Grandmother, leaving her bundle of marble-like yarns on the floor.

At the table, Annie started talking about what happen a week ago at the dance. She kept giggling, telling about whom Broneco was with.

"Bernita unusual kind of girl," she said. "She kept falling backward on the dance floor, dancing with another boy that I didn't know. After, she was outside with us. Looking for Broneco, she fell in the snow twice before we saw you."

"We thought a girl might have hooked you or something," said Auntie with a tease.

"Annie said they all thought you were kidnapped or something. I thought you were kidnapped by one of those beautiful blonds," said Grandmother, sipping a cup of tea.

Broneco didn't say anything, but he only smile, biting his lip a little.

Then, leaving the table, he said, "I'm going for a . . . a long walk today in the warm heat of the sun."

Grandmother looked up and said, "Remember, don't run off with that dark-haired girl we saw you with in Farmington."

Broneco frown and went into the bedroom to change his shirt. Maybe this will be nice to wear in the warm sun, he thought, putting on his milky-colored sweater and underneath the sweater was black shirt. Then he was ready to go for a walk. He stepped outside and stretch his arms and stroll off the porch.

Broneco went over the first hill, kicking pebbles along the way,

126

didn't know he was about to reach the highway. He looked up and saw two cars passing. After crossing the pavement, he came to the next foothill. Then down the hillside. Below was the Salt Creek wash. When he crossed the wash, there up on the top of the flat land, Broneco saw a car parked on the side of the road. "Who could that be now?" Broneco asked himself a question.

He slowly climbed the hill. The blue-and-white tone color Ford roared its rodding sounds of pipe, skid right besides Broneco walking along the dirt road, and stopped. Broneco almost raced for the fence and head for the greasewood forest below, when someone he knew spoke.

"Say, daddio, how about stopping for a while?"

Broneco knew who it was so he laughed and nodded his head and answered, "I'm not your daddy."

"Hop in and we'll go for a ride this New Year's Eve. How about that?"

"There's no objections, isn't?" asked Broneco.

Broneco's brother Ronnie shift his gear and step on the gas. The dust of clouds form in the air with the rolling sound of the wheel spinning.

"Now, we'll be on our way for the New Year's Eve and to the rest of us," said Rusty, sitting in the back seat. "I mean, to the three of us," replied again Rusty.

Broneco looked in the back. There he saw base drum, guitars, and cases of instrument packed. He now knew what they were going to do. "Where are we going?"

"First, we are going to Gallup. Then tonight, we be heading for Chinle, Arizona."

"We'll have our New Year's night in Chinle, and after our paid, we will be heading back around about 2:30 in the morning," said Rusty.

Broneco looked about in the car. He looked back and, before he knew, he was out of town. "What's the use telling them that I don't want to go?" he thought. "What shall I tell my Grandmother and Auntie when I get back tomorrow?"

Rusty got his guitar and pluck on it, playing out his musical scale for that night. Broneco found himself that he was snapping his finger. It made Rusty play more of this best quality of music. Chording in different keys, playing melody—durations of strings vibrating as they last. Broneco watched his cousin play his tunes of vocal music equally arrange into beats of musical score.

During the afternoon, riding through the street of Gallup town, Broneco had never seen so many drinking people under the old bridge. "I heard of this bridge so many times in my life, I don't see what so special about this bridge—many Indians patched with dirts," said Broneco.

Rusty and Ronnie didn't answer.

Broneco watched crowded area. He was curious so he had to ask another question. "Tell me, what's the name of this place?"

"This place is Indian Community Center. The people of different tribes gather here almost everyday. Also, this where we played a lots of time."

Ronnie parked the Ford they called "Night Train" in the parking area. Rusty and Ronnie had gone into the Indian Community Center to wash and get ready for the day's travel for Chinle. Broneco decided to walk around. He looked up and it was about noon. Then he looked across the street and saw a long train, moving along its railroad track, making a clanging sounds.

He walked through where there were rows of automobiles parked. Some ladies selling apples, jewelries, Indian homemade breads, and other crafts of arts. Last of all, Broneco went right over to where Navahos were selling goods. When he was criticize by some Navaho girls sitting in the back of the pickup.

He smile a little when he heard the girls. He pretend that he didn't understand Navaho. Before long, he returned to the car and waited for Rusty and Ronnie.

Soon they return. Broneco sat in the back seat with silents. Rusty seated himself in the front seat, asked, "Broneco, would you like to ride by the rows of cars across the street? Might buy somethings, you know."

Broneco looked at Rusty and then answered, "No, thank you."

"Why not?"

"I was dishonor with words. Why do I have to face those chili crackers everywhere I go?"

Ronnie laugh and started the car on the move. Rusty, with a grin, looked across the street.

"Let's get moving then," he said.

Ronnie, Rusty, and Broneco has been driving all day towards Chinle. It was about nightfall when they reached the place. The place small, but it was populated. Ronnie and Rusty showed Broneco around the park. Broneco sat on the rock under the tall, leafless tree, breaking pieces of sticks in halves. It was getting cold and the wind blew with cold breezes through the tree tops.

"Let's go to the other dance first before we set up our instruments tonight. Besides our dance doesn't start until 9:30. Right now, it's quarter after eight," said Rusty.

"Where's the other dance at?" asked Broneco.

"About six blocks from where we are going to play."

An hour later in the Junior High gym, Broneco and the rest of the crew dancing. Everyone had their dates. Broneco sat with The Shades when Bernita entered. She was all dress up for the dance. Broneco watched The Enchanters fingering their keys of notes on the stage. When Broneco felt someone was looking at him from the side. He didn't look. He only looked straight ahead, watching The Enchanters.

Then Broneco looked. It was a girl with a short hair. Broneco looked the other way and saw Bernita heading straight for him. She laugh with a giggle as usual.

Broneco knew that she wanted to dance with him, so he got up and danced with a waltz until the last pluck of the guitar. Then Bernita went back across the floor to where her brother was.

The rest of the time Broneco sat alone. When Broneco and the girl sitting farther down the rows of chair give a glance. Broneco didn't know what to do when they stared eye-to-eye for a second. The music was over again rapidly. Delores and Ronnie seated themselves besides Broneco and asked if he would like to dance with Delores.

Broneco only answered, "No, thank you."

Then Delores asked, "What's the matter, Broneco?"

"Oh, I just don't feel right. I'm getting the headache that I can smell everyone in this unair-conditioned dance hall."

"Oh, Broneco, don't say it," said Delores.

Just then, Bernita return and wanted to dance with Broneco.

"Go on, and have all the dance you want," said Ronnie, when Bernita spilled almost the whole bottle of whisky on Delores's breast.

Broneco quietly grabbed the bottle and closed the top and put it back into Bernita's purse. "Gee, Bernita, must you drink so much?"

"Oh huck, no used," she said and pull out the whisky bottle from her purse again to take another drink of Seagram 7th.

Broneco reached for the bottle again when she hid it in her heavy coat.

Broneco and Bernita decided to do another waltz when she couldn't stand straight. Bernita was about to fell to the floor when suddenly the music stop. Then she reached into her coat pocket to taste another drink.

"Bernita, please stop, will you? Police are watching us from across the other end of the table. Will you put it back in your purse?"

Bernita was mad now. "Who's telling me what to do around here?" she said, embracing Broneco around the waist.

Broneco was embarrass by now when her big brother came and tried to calm her down before the police finds out she was drunk.

"Broneco, you cotton-picking loose trash, just take your hands off my hands," she said, throwing the whole bottle of whisky on the floor. Bernita's brother tried to stop her from getting mad, but she was angry. "Don't ever forget this," she said, slapping Broneco across the face.

Broneco was wearing dark sun glass. It slid all the way to where the girl was sitting alone. She was the one whom Broneco was glancing at when they faced each other eye-to-eye. Broneco didn't know where his glass went, so he forgot about it.

Bernita was caught and taken outside to cool off.

130

Broneco stood by one girl. She stood there and soon, they were standing together.

"May I have this dance?" said Broneco.

The girl only smile and offered her hands to Broneco. She didn't answered. Broneco felt little nervousment, but tried not to show it.

"Know how to twist?" she asked.

"Just a little."

"Are you one of The Shades?"

Broneco blinked his eye and then smile. The dance was almost over when Rusty and Ronnie passed by Broneco and placed their black spectacles on and Broneco knew it was time to leave. It was a signal of The Shades.

The girl looked at Broneco and held his hands. He had an extra dark sun glass in his pocket. He put the glass spectacle on and pressed the girl's hand as it make a little cracking sound from each of her fingers.

"I'll see you at the Chapter House thirty minutes from now. My name is Broneco. Be in the back stage for a while," he said, and left the charming young girl standing alone in the middle of the gym floor.

"I'll be there," she shouted.

Broneco disappear into the mob of the teenagers moving out. Rushing out of the crowded area, Broneco tripped over a chair in the hall. Grabbing onto anybody's clothes did a lot of help. Just in time, Broneco made to the car park on the dirt street.

Taking no time, Ronnie spinned his wheel and made it around the corner and then another before they made it to the Chapter House. Rusty rushed into the entrance of the doorway. The instruments were already set up. "Turn them on and give it a little juice and see everything's are all right," said Rusty.

Broneco turned on the switch, and went outside.

Everyone was present. Ronnie and Delores still in the Night Train, getting everything in order before the dance was over. The night was cold. Broneco could tell it was cold, since the car window was chilling up with frost. He walked back to the car when Frankie joined him.

131

"Who's that in the car smoking?"

"I don't know. Maybe it's Ronnie. He's always smoking."

The soil was hard-covered with icy water. Beyond the ruts, there in deep pile of snow, show no glistering in the nightfall. The moon rose, making fearless shadow everywhere from objects. Only few icicle hanging alongside of the Chapter House, showing its twinkling form in the moonlight. The lights of different colors around the Chinle area made it a merry night, filled with various colors of lights.

Frankie almost fell on her back when Broneco caught her back on her feet.

The watch on Broneco's left hand was now reading eleven-thirty. Broneco reached for the small button and wounded the wrist watch to keep it clicking for another twenty hours.

Frankie wearing her long furry coat in a milky white, gratifying by praise of chilly winds blowing from the west. Her shiny spectacle moisturing itself with misty frost covering.

Then she took it off and wiped it with her handkerchief. She said, "Shall we join the couple in the car till the dance starts?"

"Sure, if Rusty doesn't mind."

"I'll tell him you save me from first-degree bruise," she said, giving a grin.

Broneco looked down at the hard frozen mud and then looked up, blinked his eyes intensely with a smile.

"Don't spoil the good year for Rusty," said Broneco.

"He's intellectualize." She laugh. "Now, shall we join your brother and his date?"

Broneco walked behind Frankie to the car they call Night Train. Ronnie opened the door for Frankie to enter. Broneco sat in the back seat.

"Frankie, close the door quick. The cold blowing air gives me the tickling affection up my spine," said Delores.

Frankie closed the door behind her with the right of respect. Ronnie, with a little sipping of a sizzling sound, inhale another dose of tobacco leaves. Since Broneco didn't like the smell of the ciga-

132

rette, his nose keep jerking with an instinct of dislike. Broneco lowered the car window to freshen the interior of the car.

"I think I better go inside and watch every swing," said Broneco, reaching for the door handle. He made his way out of the car. Then he saw Tomi, the girl he met at the dance before. She stood there holding her winter coat neatly folded in her arm.

Broneco walked up to the girl and took the coat. The girl looked about with a mood. Then they walked into the Chapter House hand-in-hand.

"The Shades," said Bronceo to the ticket agent who was waiting for another green paperback to be deposited. The agent was a girl also stamping each hands with printed red, with the symbol C.

Broneco escort Tomi to the right of the refreshment stand. Not a word was spoken. The music was playing with rhythm of modern beats of tunes.

"Like a . . . or would you like a refreshment?"

She grin and took off her white gloves reluctantly. "Please," she answered finally.

Broneco glance to where the band were playing. Rusty plucking on his guitar, saying, "You're doing fine for first class, Broneco."

Broneco skim at his wrist watch again before he amble in front of the refreshment stand. Feeling obstacle, he reached for a decorated cookies folded with dinner napkin. Secondly, he took the overflowing artificial lemon flavor in a paper cup.

Time the dance was over, Broneco and Tomi were well in love affection, holding hands. Broneco with a merry smile stood up, picked up Tomi's winter coat. The coat flicker of variable tone in the shade of the room. Around the neck fashionable of raccoon hide, tan into delicate soft. It bristle as if it was alive. Broneco carefully slide the girl's outer covering. "You live far?" he asked.

"No, darling, . . . I - I mean, Broneco. I live across the street," she said, flustering of errors she made saying "darling."

Bronceo, biting his lip, standing with a heavy weight to the side. Then they head for the exit. The dark-haired girl with her arms

133

around Broneco's waist, they walked a little ways in the cold. Broneco, with his arms around the girl's neck, covering her face from the cold blowing air.

The girl held Broneco's hand then closer. He stared in refuse of attention and answered, "Tomi, not now. Until the wedding bell rings."

Tomi's tears shown in the moonlight glow as they disappear below the eyes. Then she swallow her tears. "I understand," she whisper softly, deciding to leave.

Broneco held her back by the arm. "Don't leave yet, Tomi," he said.

"All right, I'll wait," she said and smile.

"I don't have much time, Tomi. I must go. It - it," he said and didn't finish what he was going to say. He looked at his hand when he saw his ring shining in the moonlight. "I'll come back very soon. Will you wait?"

"I will," she said.

Broneco took off his class ring and give it to Tomi and place it on her third finger.

"Your ring," she cried in despair of his return.

"I love you," said Broneco, softly speaking.

The girl wave her hand weakly, beginning to smile.

Broneco disappear into the darkness among the still of the night, leaving the figure of shadow behind in the light of the moon. It was twelve o'clock, New Year, the blasting of cracking sound everywhere. Broneco looked back and saw none of the girl. Before Broneco and the rest of The Shades leave, a light across the street was turn off. Then it was quiet in the Chinle area.

"Have a wonderful time?" asked Frankie in her boy friend's arm all comfortably position in back seat of the car.

"It was such a night!" reply Broneco, closing the car door behind him as he entered.

Again Delores shouted, "Quick, quick, close the door, for my knees are shaking."

Ronnie waited for a while, then reached into his shirt pocket. Carefully shook the cigarette, expertly the rolled tobacco weeds released itself from the pack. Watchfully he placed the odoring refined commercial weeds cigarette in his mouth.

Broneco patiently remain in the seat. Waiting for a few minutes, the vehicle started to roll. Sniffing the floating elements of un-destroy mechanical carbon quivering through the capacity of the car, Broneco was getting the headache. He could feel the pebbles of rocks each time the car wheel itself over millions. The window was covered with decomposing of melting frost.

Once in awhile, Broneco's head dropped to the chest. Bending, his head was aching after waking up. For Ronnie, the road was getting blurry. Opening the window helped a little, but only enough to keep awake.

Early in the morning, Broneco was wide awake when he sighted an object that stood in a distance. The fog, changing by degree, barely lifting itself off the earth. In the mist, a tall, dark ocean liner it resemble. It was only Shiprock, standing with its long shadow reaching out towards the west.

It was six o'clock when Broneco, empty feeling with light weakness, almost tremble out the car door by the road.

The rest of the crew went on their way home. Broneco could hear everyone laughing, talking, variations of musics, the New Year sounding of the firecracker popping everywhere as he walk with a shuffle along the old forgotten dirt road. He rubbed his eyes.

When he looked at his hands, they looked in the color of black. Broneco knew then, he didn't have enough sleep. On the way home, he kept thinking of his soft bed that he always sleep on without any interruptions of any kind. A few hundred yards away was the house. Broneco fell and trip over a few prairie brush, but it didn't matter to him. All it amounts to was reaching the house and sleep silent.

There on the roof, the chimney showed, exhaling the puffs of gray smoke. The tree without its leafs showing no sign of spring stood by the house with stiff branches. Broneco, without knocking, twisted the knob hastily and pushed the door opened. Grandmother and Auntie was in the kitchen doing her morning duty of preparing breakfast for the family.

135

Broneco went into his own apartment and dropped dead on the bed. A little roaring sound of snores deeply increase. Once in a while, the cool air of New Mexico blew, making a tooting sound of musical hums through the holes of the window.

An hour later, Broneco was awaken by the banging sound of the dishpan in the kitchen. Opening one eye was the key to Broneco saying, "You still haven't have enough sleep," but he made himself get out of bed.

Broneco didn't know that Grandmother was watching, holding the broomstick, ready to sweep the floor standing before him. He rubbed his eyes again and looked about in the room when he spotted a shoe. Then he looked up, motionless from feet to head. "Good morning, Ma," he said in a ragged voice.

"Come into the kitchen and eat your breakfast," she said, smiling after seeing that Broneco was very tired.

Broneco went into the kitchen and washed his face with a splash of warm water.

"Where you're been?" asked Grandmother, pouring a hot coffee.

"I was with my brother Ronnie."

"Then where did you go—drinking, did you?"

Broneco looked up and smile. "No, Grandmother. I was kidnapped by a dark-haired girl this time, it wasn't blond."

Auntie was washing dishes when she dropped the plate and broke it. Then she looked to where Broneco was and blinked her right eye and laugh.

· XIII ·

Original Tea and the Dream

BRONECO was completing his eleventh year of schooling. It was early in the morning, the rooster crowing in the nearby barnyard. The glossy black bird wearing his donations of colors stretched his wing again when Broneco wake up. Broneco, lying on the bed, glance out the window. Blinking his eyes, he listened to the birds tweeting in the trees. The bed was double decker. Below him sleep Johnnie with a little snores.

Broneco layed in bed silently, his heart beating by the seconds of a minute. His head curl in the soft pillow, he kept thinking about different things. For him and Johnnie didn't get along in certain ways lately. He wondered about it more, until his head begin to ache with illusion of misleading thoughts early in the morning.

Shall I tell him, "I'm sorry for what I might have done to make you mad for so long"? he asked himself the questions.

Before the morning bell rings, Broneco was out of bed. Creaking around in the room still didn't help, trying not to disturb the others. The floor in some part keep squeaking as he made the step each time. It was quiet, could hear many more rumbling snores down the hall.

Broneco seated himself on the couch. On the nearby gleaming from the early dawn, the dresser coated with smooth varnish in

137

shade of dark brown showed its treasure of few jewelry, and much collections of pictures. Broneco looked at the pictures that were on the bureau.

Johnnie's picture seem to smile as Broneco watched, self-possessed of the photo itself. Then he picked up his towel, rubbing his eyes, yawning. Broneco stood before the door and looked about in the room again before he left.

As soon as Broneco returned he started folding his shirts and piling them in neat bundles side by side. Leaving the hanger in the closet vacant.

An hour later it was time for breakfast. Broneco walked down the main hall when he heard the music Johnnie used to play. How lonely it was! Broneco stood there listening awhile before he went on his way.

"Good morning, Broneco. How's the world treating you?" said Ricky, slapping Broneco on the back as he walk up from behind.

Broneco grin and said, "Just fine."

"Hey, you looked worried about something," said Ricky.

"I guess I am, but you shouldn't worry about it," said Broneco, strolling toward the main entrance of the dormitory.

Out in the front, sniffing the fresh air was a lot of help. On the lawn, neighbors' dogs were rolling, wrestling, and playing their domestic games of morning sports was enjoyable to see. Looking over to the other lawn, robin pulling on rubbery earth worms out of the damp clay in between the grasses.

The sun was now traveling on its way to make another day of light. Among the universe, the clouds were moving eastward over the rocky mountain. The wind blew once in awhile with cool summer breezes of whistling air against every object in the way. The grass, in some part with gloss of green, flatten themselves with waves in various directions. Among the villages across the road, rosebush bristle, changing its course with the winds also.

Approaching the dining hall, the scent of the kitchen gave a hungry smell. Broneco's mouth filled with saliva dribble in the depth of the tongue. As it grew more and more, there was more appetite.

138

Soon there was a long chow line. Students arguing and pushing each other out of place, banging from one side to the other. Broneco watched the band of boys and girls. Finally, the dining entrance was opened. The matron giving each and every one the smile as one passes by, greeting with the word: "Good morning, how are you?" And "My, you look fine this morning."

Again there was argument about who takes that seat and who goes there to sit at the table. Broneco patiently waited to find a spot where it suited him best and where there was no treacherous feeling of sitting with someone's girl friend. Then, Broneco saw his sister, Annie, with her friend, Eve, in the corner nearest to the window.

"Come and sit with us," Annie shouted, waving her hand high in the air.

Broneco looked about again before he took the seat. Many giggling girls was discouraging, making durations of pitches. It was no time to listen, since each and every other students chattering here and there, some screaming, others laughing as if the whole dining room is going to tremble with a sudden crash in the next couple of second.

"Who's coming after us today to pick us up?" asked Annie in a sharp tone of voice.

"Our big brother, I guess," Broneco answered, chewing the piece of bacon with a cracking sound.

"He's mean," said Annie, poking her girl friend with her elbow.

When Broneco heard, "Am I?" he said, cutting the piece of bacon in halves.

Then she giggle, laughing.

The girl that sit next to Annie looked horrible. Her hair fixed in shape of desert tumbleweeds, colored in shades of blond. Winking her eyes constantly in a moody possession of her face covered with sticky makeup in pale of ghastly look.

Broneco glance about in the dining as the kitchen smell of atmosphere increase into strong odor of a pig-pen smell. He took a swallow of milk then he decided to leave.

Broneco returned to the dormitory. He sat in the room, directing his eyes to make sure that he didn't forget anything. He spent most of this time in the room getting ready to leave. Gently taking the picture off the dresser, he thought, "The Shades." It was a picture of one of the guitar expert player. Carefully placing the photo in the traveling suitcase, Broneco then closing it, giving a weight of pressure to close the luggage.

Suddenly, there was a knock on the door. Broneco threw some of his clothes into the closet. Quickly he jumped on the double decker bed and placed a pillow under his head and answered, "Come in."

The door opened slowly.

Broneco had a magazine in his hand, pretending that he wasn't getting ready to leave.

"For heavens sake, aren't you ready to go home?" said a mysterious voice.

Broneco dropped the magazine on his chest and glance over his shoulder. "Oh, it's you, Ronnie."

"Are these your suitcases?" said Ronnie, pointing at the set of luggages on the floor.

"Yes, take them out front for me. I'll go and check out right away," said Broneco, grabbing the shirts he threw in the closet together, tying his shirts into a bundle.

Broneco waited in the office awhile before the attendant returned from his off-duty.

"I suppose you're waiting to check out for home," said Mr. Veldez, a man with light-complexioned skin, giving a sign of casual smile.

"It's a coincidence," said Broneco, laughing.

"Are your folks here?"

"Oh yes, they are over at the girls' dorm."

"Aren't you suppose to stay for the summer to work here for three months?" said Mr. Veldez.

"There must have been a mistake. I was . . . and . . . I mean, there wasn't no informations."

"Watch it! You on the wrong side of the road again."

"I mean, I was told nothing about," said Broneco.

Mr. Veldez laughed. "Well, I'll be darn." Turning with a little squeaking sound in the loose, lazy-man's chair, rocking it a little. "Is 'Bread' going home too?" he asked.

Always he was saying to Annie, when she going home, "Bring me some bread," and she make him adobe bread and always give to him back at school. He call her "Bread" and she calls him "Joker."

"You bet she's going home," said Broneco. "I can see her coming now."

"Coming back this fall?"

"Yes-no."

"There you go again."

"I'll let you know. Give me time to think about it," said Broneco, backing out the main door.

"I'll see you later."

"Bless your heart," said Broneco, rushing out the door.

Broneco stepped out the main entrance to the boys' dormitory. He looked about as he had done when he first came to school. It was his first day in school when he stood exactly where he's standing now. Blinking his eyes, glancing at the Junior High School building, years past made a great difference.

Broneco looked across the dirt road. The lawn more glorify than it was back in nineteen-fifty-one. Broneco walked down the concrete steps holding onto the rail. When he reached the sidewalk, there he stood for a while to breathe the cool blowing air.

Once Broneco entered the pickup that waited outside the front loading zone, he didn't bother to look back.

"What's the matter, Broneco?" asked Annie.

"I just gave it a little thought—leaving this place." Broneco looking out the front car window. "This like when I just started school and then leaving. I been here for eleven lonely years in that haunted house. I was a fool."

"Don't say it here. Tell me all about it when we get home," said Annie.

"I agree with Annie," said Ronnie, smiling.

Broneco laughed and glance to where his brother was aiming his eyes straight on the highway. It was exciting, seeing how much

141

improvement has taken place in that eleven years. Looking to the north, the glacier of icy snow on the big LaPlata Mountain. Again it reminded Broneco of a sheep grazing in the meadow, resting up. Broneco had too much to think about when he finally fell asleep from the awful headache that occurred of discouragement of thoughts.

The sun was halfway west. Broneco awaked, approaching home, crossing the wash in the bumpy area. "Where are we?"

"Almost home, silly," said Annie, still holding her books placed in her lap.

Broneco kept rubbing his eye to sober up from a deep, snoring sleep. "Why didn't you wake me up?"

"Thought you needed the sleep. Besides, you were talking to your lover in your dreams."

"What did I say?"

"You said, 'Oh, my Cupie Dollie, you have a sour nose,' " she said, "calling your own thumb a nose."

"Oh, forget it," said Broneco, looking as though he had just gotten off the stage, all exhausted from shaking his head, result of singing in high pitch of shout. Broneco yawning, step out of the car and seated himself in front of the porch. Tipped his chair and leaned against the side of the house, when something familiar happen.

Broneco looked toward the hill when it started to glow, giving off radiations. He blinked his eyes, then he saw none. He rubbed his eyes and looked again, but it didn't happen again.

Broneco, in fear, rushed into the house and grabbed Annie's hand. "Annie, lo-o-ok!"

Annie, wondering, Broneco almost drag her out of the house. "What is it?" she asked.

"Did you see that?"

"See what?"

"The hill glowed."

Annie looked at the hill in amusement. Then she said, "Broneco, I think you're crazy."

142

"Maybe I am," said Broneco, running his finger through his hair.

Annie giggle and went into the house while Broneco stared at the hill for another minute before he took his eyes off the hill.

In the house, Annie was unpacking her belongings and placing them in the drawer.

Broneco went into the kitchen and poured himself a cold, bittery taste coffee into a coffee cup. He didn't drink his coffee. He left it there and stood by the doorway. "I'm going to walk up there and see," he thought.

Then Annie asked, "Where are you going?"

"To that hill."

"Broneco, don't go. It might be something," said Annie.

All of a sudden, he was furious. Broneco only went as far as the corral and waited there, when he saw his Grandmother, distance away, riding her donkey. Annie's mother followed her behind.

Broneco got himself a job in Shiprock at odd chores for Fairchild Company and had forgotten all about that hill when a month passed. He tried again to go up that hill, but he refused the mysterious hill. Telling his Grandmother and aunt didn't help. They didn't believe him. They would only tell Broneco that he's crazy.

Then, one day Saturday, he made his final decision. Broneco strolled up the hill to the very top and looked every directions. He could see far into the great distance. He didn't find anything unusual except there a very attractive blooming desert tea, growing on the farther side, almost near the foot of the hill.

Broneco smile and walked off the top of the hill to where the wild tea was. He sniffed the green tea plant and break the branch off from the east. "I'll have this traditional Indian tea for tonight's supper," said Broneco, talking to himself.

Broneco came home and left the tea plant out in the hot blistering sun to dry.

Annie was waiting by the corral. "Is that what you found up there on the hill?" she asked, grinning.

"It's original tea," said Broneco.

"I never saw a tea brush so attractive."

"Sort of unusual, isn't it?" said Broneco. "Just you wait and see. You'll find that this tea is going to have a powerful taste."

Broneco was only joking, but, for Annie, she believed what Broneco just said deliberately.

Annie glance at the tea more than twice before feeling the texture. Feeling the smooth surface of the stem made her wonder about the tea plant. Annie breaked the bark off the plant, skeptically placed the bark in her mouth, testing the taste. Then she begin chewing it, when she discovered that it really had an unusual flavor.

"Broneco, come quick, hurry!" she shouted very excitedly.

Broneco was in the kitchen when he heard Annie calling his name. His chest filled with heavy pressure of air. He was struck in chills of deep fear, thinking about the tea sprouting into a beautiful blooming blossom. Broneco's eyes grew wide. In dreadful bemoved affections, he rushed through the bedroom out the door. Without thinking what to do next, he found himself standing before Annie.

"What's the matter?" she asked, giving a cheerful smile.

Broneco shaked his head. "I don't know. I just rushed out the front door. Why? Because you worried me so."

"Why?"

"I was thinking about the tea plant when you call, as if you seen something horrible."

"Forgive me, for I have been nasty. It was about the plant."

"What about the plant?"

"It was such a wonderful tasting flavor, sort of sweet peppermint, but with a spicy strong taste in it. Here. Chew the stem of this rubbery tea weeds," she explained.

Broneco held the leafless tea in his hand and then slowly chewed the long green branch. "It is good," he said.

Broneco reached for the drying wild tea plant and jerked it into the tin coffee pot. Anxiously he filled the boiler pot with pure water.

An hour later, Broneco and Annie had almost forgot the boiling of the tea on the hot stove. Broneco poured the tea into the glossy cup. He drank the tea and looked in the directions of the room next to the kitchen.

"I feel nothing, except that it has a luxurious taste. Never tasted a tea that matched that," he said.

Annie started to pour the tea when she finds out that there was no tea in the pot. "We have boiled the tea so long that it vapor raise on us," she answered, in a disappointing look. "I'll boil the same tea over."

"How clever," said Broneco.

This time Annie had all the tea she could drink, but the tea had lost all of its flavor.

"I'll go back tomorrow and get more than you brought today. I'll dry them in the sun," she said.

Broneco felt sleepy that afternoon, but he didn't sleep until nightfall. He stood by the porch, watching the stars winking in the milky way out in the space.

Grandmother then saw a falling star. Broneco watched it travel in a great force of speed south.

"Broneco, you are never to watch a falling star, for it brings sickness among our people," she said, toiling into the front door.

"Now, you tell me!" reply Broneco, entering after Grandmother into the house.

Annie and Auntie were already in bed. Broneco was the last to cover up himself before Grandmother blew out the lamp that set on the window shelf.

The next day, Broneco woke up as he always did. It was early. The crowing rooster woke him up. "That rooster! Just like being back in Ignacio," he murmured. Sitting in the bed, then he threw the pillow into the corner of the room wall covered with plaster. Then he remembered, "The dream I had last night!"

He thought, trying to remember everythings. "Oh," he said harshly. Now the dawn of early light was clearing the scene. Then Broneco heard the radio turn on in the other bedroom. It sounded sharp and clear.

Broneco listened to the morning news translated into his own native language. The announcer on the air playing records of all sorts—classical, western, popular, and rhythm and blues.

Broneco layed on the bed, silently listening, when Grandmother knocked on the door, saying, "Broneco, are you awake? It's time for breakfast."

Broneco, full of appetite, walked into the kitchen. "Annie," he said.

Annie sat at the table still blinking her eyes, barely waking up from the night of eight hour sleep. Annie used to sleep more than that, but she was up this morning with the rest of the family. She finally answered, "Yes."

"Are you wide awake? If not, snap out of it, will you?"

"I'm awake. I'm just sleepy, that's all."

"I got something to tell you this morning."

Annie yawned, arousing to know what Broneco has to say. She asked, "What is it?"

"I had a dream last night. I dreamed that I was walking in the dirt alley street when I met someone, then another one, and another. Until I met and walked with four. We walked to an old shack beyond the tall standing trees. When I looked to the south, there was a pond. Along its side, a neatly fixed fence made of wooden thin poles. In the pond, many quacking ducks swam in the glimmering water, fill in some area with cattails. The frogs making odd sound in tunes of bass. I never saw a place like that before," said Broneco.

"You know any of the boys?" asked Annie.

"Why, yes."

"Enough of that questions! Go on and finish your dreamland story," said Grandmother.

Broneco looked about in the kitchen and started off again to finish where he left off. Sipping the hot steaming black water, Broneco was more excited to complete the story.

"The boys wore black spectacles. Did I say 'spectacles'? " said Broneco.

"Yes," said Annie.

"I must prove my point, then I'll finish the story. I must go, at once, to the place where I thought I was walking and saw The Shades in person again. I must go right now," said Broneco.

Without finishing his breakfast, Broneco very excitedly picked up his dark sweater in the next room and dashed out the door.

"I don't understand Broneco," said Grandmother, holding a piece of bread in her hand.

"He said he left his soul on the hill," said Auntie.

"Half of it," answered Annie, stirring her coffee with more sugar to give a sweet taste. "He tells me that the hill seem to glow, too."

"He's so familiar about the hill," said Grandmother.

"Maybe he needs a sing in Beauty-Way chant," suggested Auntie.

"Broneco said he'll find a joyfulness up on that hill very soon. He says that's his hill," said Annie, chewing her food patiently.

"All this talk! He . . . he . . . he's only a young boy. You know how all the young boys are," said Auntie, picking her plate.

147

·XIV·

Once in a Lifetime

B RONECO crossed the canyon made by the rushing stream when
it rain in the desert area. The rolling hills leading to different
directions would be difficult for wanderers to cross, but Broneco,
he knew every inch of the unknown area.

He came to the streams of rippling water. He stood before the
rushing water. Looking at the edge of the water, Broneco could
see and smell the tracks of sheep, horses, and other domestic
animals that comes to water themselves.

Broneco crossed the cool, flowing water, then into the thickness
of the water brushes that grew tall along the river. Crossing another
swampy water, he finally reached the top of the hill. There, from
the top of the hill, lead a dirt alley street.

Broneco's dream was coming true. Passing a block of dirt road,
he met Melvin. "How are you this morning?" he said.

Broneco only smile, for he knew the boy. Walking together for
another mile, there they met another boy, this time he was driving
a car. When he saw Broneco and Melvin, he stopped and then they
went on their way. It was Ervin, a boy with laughter each time
when one says anything he thinks that's funny.

"I'm surprised when I runned into Broneco on the road. Now,
it's you," said Melvin. "Who could it be now? That object on the
road seems familiar to me."

148

Broneco glanced at the two boys and saw that they were wearing dark spectacles.

Ervin stopped the car when the person turned his head facing the pickup in shades of light brown color with white stripe. The boy also wearing dark sun glass. Young man smiling, carrying in his right hands a drum sticks.

Without saying a single word he hop into the back of the pickup.

"All we have to do is report now," said Ervin, laughing again.

Then Broneco smile also.

Riding for another couple of minutes or so, Ervin stopped the car and the mystery person in light-complexioned tone of skin jump off the back and hasten to the gate. Quickly he opened the gate. Ervin drove the car, entering the fence. There in, Broneco saw an old shack. The house made of log. On the farther side, a few steps away from the cabin, a well with a roof scattered in splints of kindling woods. Broneco strolling in the yard, examining the place. Rusty watched him from the window through the spider webs attach neatly one to another.

"Must be the tea I drank last night. The dream is true," Broneco said, kicking few rocks. To the south, the pond patched with cat-tails mixed with water lily.

Rusty stood besides Broneco and said, "Won't you come inside? Let us all discuss a few problems."

"Excuse me. I didn't mean to keep you waiting."

"That's all right."

"You haven't told me about you living here."

"This was my father's farm. Over to your right, you can see the crop," said Rusty. "We bail hay about once a month."

"It takes that long to grow?"

"Well, it depends on how fast they bloom with blue tops. That's when we cut the alfalfa."

Broneco and Rusty had the interest talking about farming, when the rest of the boys joined Rusty and Broneco out in the shady side of the tree. "Broneco, it's a coincidence that you have come," Rusty said. "I guess you know all the boys yet."

149

"Oh, yes," said Broneco.

"Broneco, first you tell us. What are you going to do after this summer? Planning to go back to Ignacio school?"

"No, why?"

"If not, then where do you plan to go to school?"

"I don't know yet, Rusty."

"I'm going to tell you something before I go into deep detail. We are going back to school to educate ourselves. You see, Melvin needs about one more year of school. And for you, you also have one more year to go to complete your twelfth year." Pausing a little, then he continue again. "Broneco, we all have an assignment to do."

"What does that mean?"

"That means, you must do your part in reforming The Shades to eminent positions."

"How do I do that?" said Broneco, looking disgusted.

Melvin smiled a little. "You must help in any way make one more step higher than we are now. Are you willing to give us a great stride?" said Melvin.

"All right, I'll take the risk," said Broneco.

"You sure now?"

"I promise."

"You must take this mission. Make it good. Study hard and make the best effort. We wanted you to study music along with lots of writing."

"But . . . but, where do I start? I mean then that means I had to be off someplace other than Ignacio school."

"How about the school you said your teacher try to convince you to enter—The Institute of American Indian Arts?"

"Hey! I never thought of that. I'll report to my agency tomorrow, for I don't have much time to lose before all the other applications are turned in or else I'm left out."

"Now, all of you remember your duties," Rusty said, "before you all and I myself leave this hot country. Remember, in two years, please we must gather again here. By this time, I'm sure that all of you will accomplish more than what we have for the last past two years of being The Shades. By then, I'm sure if not one of you fail your orders, we'll be making stages again. And my last words, try and make the best of yourself, each and every one of you. Before closing, I will say this—I will be packing my bundles of belonging, and I will heading west. Now you may all proceed. May God be with you," said Rusty as he turned and walked away.

Broneco, blinking his eyes, stood by the tree. "I will surely do my orders. You'll see," he said, walking towards the gate.

It was an hour later Broneco came home. Showing no sadness, he sit down to eat his cold breakfast that he was supposed to have eaten this morning.

"I see you are back," said Annie.

"Annie," Broneco said in wonder. "My dream came true. That tea has great power."

Annie jumped up. "Really? Did your dream really come true?"

"All of it," Broneco answered. "Even the tall water brushes and more."

"I'm going to the hill to get more of that tea," said Annie. "Willing to join me?"

"Not this time. You go and I stay."

Annie anxiously prancing out the gate went to the hill, but she found none of the tea plant, only the roots destroyed bare down to the ground at the foot of the hill. She rushed to where the tea plant was and stood before the leafless tea. Grandmother has driven her flock of sheep and goats this way when the goats eat every bite of the wild tea. Tonight, the goat will be chewing their cuds of the delicious tea weeds. Annie stared at the beaten down tea once more and walked sadly away from the hill.

In the fall of September 8, 1963, Broneco step off the sub-Agency porch in Shiprock. In his right hand, carrying newly style brief case. The flat case, full of art samples. He paused for a few seconds, fixing his loose tie. Stepping off the porch, he met one of his classmate passing by. Broneco stopped, but the boy didn't.

Broneco, neatly dressed, characterized by the lack of his emotional was unnatural of his attitude. He walked along the green lawns neatly trimmed.

Broneco, in a qualify manner, by saying, "Good morning, gentleman, miss, and etc.," each time he passes the high officials also carrying their brief cases, tipping their high rank of decent hats. Broneco's first experience was excellent.

He was now a block away from the sub-Agency. He stood on the street walk in front of another administration department. Broneco reached into his suit coat and took his dark crystal eyeglass. He picked his brief case and went on his way toward the stream of rippling water. The rushing river splashing against marble-like stones. Watching the running water for a few seconds, then he went on. He walked along the highway, the automobiles roaring by. Broneco finally reached the top of the hill.

He looked at his wrist watch. It was reading one-thirty. "I better hurry home and gather my belonging together," he thought. He started walking faster than he was. "Tomorrow I'm leaving," he kept thinking about when he didn't know he was nearly home. Since the sun was hot, Broneco eyes begin to blur. Reached into his pocket again to place the sunglass on. "This is better," he whisper.

Approaching home, Broneco was about to fall, tripping over every other prairie brush. Climbing another rolling hills made Broneco exhaust a little. In the next five minute, he was home.

"You as if just returning from swimming in the river," said Auntie.

"I did, but it's just the opposite. It was a sun bath."

"What did you do, race with your shadow?"

"No, I was trying to beat the time," said Broneco, pressing the button to the brief case when it pop open. "Is my breakfast still sitting on the table as I have left it like the day before yesterday?"

"This time, we gave it to the dogs."

"What do you say, I'm leaving tomorrow. Then I'll be heading east, if I'm correct about it."

"Better talk to your grandmother about it before you leave."

"She won't mind."

"This is your last year. To me, I think it's best that you go back to Ignacio," said Auntie, sitting before her loom, beating down her yarns of strings. "I wonder what's Annie doing in school by now."

"I suppose she's dreaming in school."

"She had better not," said Auntie.

Grandmother step inside. "Will you take my donkey to the corral and feed him some of that fresh alfalfa?"

"Grandmother, you're back an hour behind schedule," said Broneco.

"I was hunting down half of the sheep. I didn't know they were already at the watering place all fill with fresh water. Resting under the steep sand canyon."

Broneco took the donkey to the corral and did just exactly Grandmother had asked. He raced back to the house. "I have something to tell you," he said, stopping by the door.

"What is it?"

"I'm going to Santa Fe, New Mexico. My Agency head said, 'Have to leave tomorrow morning on the eight-thirty bus from Farmington.' That means I have to get ready tonight."

"Broneco, this is your last year. You should finish it in Ignacio. Besides, your friend, Johnnie, the boy you used to come home with, is also finishing his twelfth grade year."

Broneco sat besides his Grandmother and held her hands, thinking about it for a minute, then he answered. "Grandmother, I had to. Once in a lifetime, one must go someplace. I wanted to see how it is. If I do not like it, I can always come back. I will always come home, there's no other place."

Grandmother poured herself a cup of coffee. "Broneco, first you must eat and then we'll talk about it."

Broneco, blinking his eyes, understanding what his Grandmother condition and situation she's trying to point out, held a roll in his hand.

Auntie put her work off to join Broneco and his Grandmother at the table.

Then Grandmother sat quietly. "If you must go, my dear child, what you aiming for I cannot force you to do, or I cannot stop you." she said.

Broneco didn't speak for he know. His Grandmother was in her seventy now. Although she didn't look very old as she is, she looked younger than she was. Her gray hair showing a little on the side of her head neatly knotted with brown yarns. Broneco give a little smile and held his Grandmother close to him.

For Grandmother, tears fell on Broneco's arm.

It was lately, all of a suddenly, her right leg struck with a sudden pain in the knee. Broneco, during that time, did all he could to have the pain relief. Broneco has been working with the Physical Health Department when he was told that his Grandmother was very ill. So he quit his job and paid the expense for his Grandmother in Farmington Clinic for all the treatment that was given. Annie's mother had a brand new pickup truck which was used most of the time.

Auntie was getting a little worried about the knee, but then Grandmother said that she would be all right in another week. So Broneco wouldn't be so worried.

Broneco, the very next day, packed his belonging in the back of the pickup. The days were getting colder and colder. Broneco was taken to the bus depot around eight o'clock.

There, Broneco happily said his greeting, leaving for Santa Fe. "I'll see you very soon. Be looking forward for my letters, will you?" said Broneco, waving his hands, rushing down the street toward the bus depot with his luggage.

Grandmother and Ronnie waited for a while for the bus to depart. Broneco seated himself in the bus and looked back smiling.

Broneco very excited, wondering when will he reach the place where he was heading to. He's glancing here and there as the bus roar along the black pavement, moving eastward. "Will I be satisfy or will I be disliking the place?" he asked himself a question. During the traveling hours, he keep falling asleep.

Broneco was all tired out when he reached the town of Bernalillo. Waiting there for another hour, he was more tired.

Then, catching another bus, which rattle along with various

kinds of sounds jingling. Broneco in his dark glasses. Some people, mostly Spanish, making mistake by talking to Broneco in Spanish.

"I don't understand you," was the best answer.

Broneco felt strange, being with all the Spanish-speaking tribe. He fell asleep again, then the bus reached Santa Fe.

Broneco walked a little ways and looked up and down the beaten-down street made of bricks, some out of place and other neatly placed. Smelling the permeating odor of different scent made him sort of a little dizzy.

"It sure doesn't smell like Farmington. This city, I can smell everythings. I could smell the clean air in my home town, but not like this," he thought, struggling down the street and then back to the depot.

Waiting for an hour, trying to find where the school he was heading for. Then he got an idea of what he will do. "I'll phone to the school and ask them how do I get there."

Broneco smile and went up to the phone directory, but he couldn't find it. There was only one thing to do, so he asked the ticket agent.

The boy picked up the phone and dialed it. "Another gentleman's waiting here at the Greyhound depot," he said. Then, smiling, turned toward Broneco. "There'll be someone here to pick you up in a few minutes."

·XV·

So This Is the Institute of American Indian Arts!

A LL EXCITED, Broneco's knees couldn't calm down as it kept trembling vertically. Broneco strolled back to the waiting seat and rubbed his knees as though they were cold.

Across from him the dusty trash of candy and gum wrappers, tobaccos—some half chewing off and some still moistured edge— lying scattered on the floor. A lady with a brilliant eye-catching red she wore on her lip kept staring at Broneco as he got more nervous.

Then she covered her purse, hiding it underneath her heavy coat. Broneco looked down at his feet, not bothering to face her again since he can tell that she didn't like Indians as you could tell by the way she swallowed her wrinkled lumps. He can see also that she could smell Indian as they pass by her, she would again wrinkle her powdered nose, not knowing she was overdone with face makeup.

"Why does she have to hide her original white skin?" Broneco asked himself, grinning a little.

Just then, Broneco sighted a Mexican entering the bus depot. "Maybe he thinks he's great too," thought again Broneco, turning his eye from the dark, curly-haired man wearing a jet-black shaded eyeglasses. Never could tell whether he's looking at you or not.

Broneco got up from his seat, walked up to the ticket counter again to ask for information concerning the Indian School, when he notice the Mexican talking to a young man, then another one.

156

"Sorry, I made a mistake," he said, moving on, walking down the aisle of the waiting people.

Broneco turning into a pale of smile he return to his seat, when he sighted the madam staring again. He decided to return his looks when she notice herself. Instantly she turn her powdered pink face into the shades of the evening red sky. She give a gasp of a sound and looked away astonished.

Suddenly, Broneco notice a Mexican was standing before him. Feeling the nervous creeping up his spine again, Broneco looked at his feet, then up to his head.

The man in heavy black spectacle stared straight into Broneco eyes.

Broneco lost his mind, half frighten that he could just burst in between his two legs then out the back for an escape.

Then the Mexican spoke up. "Are you the new student to the school?" he asked.

"Y - yes," said Broneco, releasing his breath. Then Broneco smile as he stands up to introduce himself to this strange Mexican. "My name's Broneco," he said, reaching to shake hands with this "Mexican" he thought he was.

"Mine's Mr. Paris [Perez], the bus driver from the school," he replied, taking off his gloves so he could shake hands with this young man who just arrive from the southwestern state.

Introducing to the strange man, Broneco felt much secure and homelike again after meeting another Indian. He was very different from Broneco's relatives. Smiling, Mr. Perez picked the small luggages, while Broneco takes his pieces of stubs to the ticket agent to receive his heavy luggages.

Broneco feeling all excited again. Came around the corner of the tall building which was across the depot, then onto the intersection on the next right of way turnoff. Coming down the main street, viewing the modern Spanish style architect, with a lookout tower pointing toward the darking sky of the evening descending into the twilight.

"Like the town?" asked Mr. Perez.

"Oh, yes," replied Broneco.

157

"That's the New Mexico State Capitol there."

"I thought that was a college campus," Broneco said, adding, "How far is the school?"

"About six blocks," said Mr. Perez, searching for a cigarette in his pocket now. Finding it, he striked it with a penny match. Giving a little whirling of drifting light smoke, he exhaled. "The building here to our left is the Highway Department."

"I see," said Broneco.

Coming to a slow moving, then turning right, entering the school campus, Broneco felt the chills again. Facing the north white peaks tipped with snow, Broneco picked up his luggages.

Stepping onto the sidewalk, a boy stopped. Without a word, he picked up the suitcase. Then another stopping by also picked the heavy packed suitcase.

"My name is Ray," he said. "I am from Santa Domingo, and that kid back there is Michael."

"My name is Broneco, and the—"

"Oh, that's all right. You don't have to. We cheer those who comes in. Might be that they are feeling strange . . . well, ah . . . you know what I mean?" said Ray, interrupting what Broneco was going to say.

Entering the Dormitory hall, Broneco stopped on the patio step to give a pause. He step into the main floor, walking into the office. He put his suitcase down. Studying the man sitting back on his comfortable chair, chewing half of his cigar. Leaving the cigar to the left of his mouth, then giving a sip of puff to it, he straighten himself in his seat finally.

Leaning on his elbow now, he picked up his pencil, placing it between his heavy and rusted thumb and fingers. He pointed the pencil into the small ink container. Pressing it down into the small bottle of ink, he notice.

"Excuse me," he said, laughing now. Pulling out his desk drawer, he searched for his desk pen. Finding it beneath the papers, he insert the pen into the heavy black ink.

"Oh yes, my name is Mr. Jones. And yours?"

"Broneco."

"I betcha you don't know where I'm from," he said, teasing.

"Couldn't guess, sir, except The Four Corners Area, and that's about it."

"You're half right."

"Oh, am I?"

"You bet, son," said Mr. Jones, laughing again. Reaching below the desk drawer, he drew a slip of pink paper not bigger than his palm of his rough fist. "Sign here," said he, placing an X where Broneco could sign his name.

Feeling the headaches, Broneco blinked his eyes, then scribbled his name after X.

"Think you can find your room?"

"I think I can," replied Broneco, lifting up his luggages.

"I'll show you," Mr. Jones said, swinging his easy chair clockwise, passing through the narrow space behind the office desk, spitting the enlarged mass of wads into the empty basket. As the black form of ball hit the bottom of the shining can, the high-pitched note irritated through Broneco's ears.

Stepping onto the waxed clean floor, Broneco stopped. Mr. Jones following behind walked into Broneco which almost made Broneco tripped over the luggages.

"Excuse me, son," Mr. Jones said as the words came apologetically. Then, smiling again, patting Broneco's back.

"I think I can find the room myself, sir."

"Just go straight farther down this hall and you always find your room by looking at the numbers in front of each door."

Broneco pick up his suitcase and headed down the hall. Finding the room, he smiles to himself. He knocked on the door, but there was no answer.

Broneco entered the room. Walking about, he studied a little, standing before the large painting that hung on the wall, which was in two dimensional. Crossing the room, Broneco glanced from the bed, ceiling, windows, and closets. "My, my, this seems to be very lively and homelike. This must be the painting of my roommate," he thought, still strolling noiselessly in the room.

The painting on the wall Broneco studied a little, standing before the drawing in the colors consisting of red, yellow, orange, and clear opaque of dark and evening twilight. The picture itself showed a figure of dark masked head, it could be, a body of a dancing mountain spirit as on the chest a light gray paint showed in a form of a four-pointed star shaped, wearing a yellowish skirt with various bells and shawls on the edges.

Broneco decided to feel the texture of the rough form of the oil painting, but not exactly it was water color either.

He was reaching for the picture. A boy came in. Broneco jerked his hands away from the painting, stepping back to the middle of the floor.

The boy smiles. "You must be my new roommate, and—and nice to have you for a roommate," he said, adding, "I'm Wallace."

Broneco turned around slowly and shaked Wallace's hand.

"Please to meet you, and my name is Broneco," he said, smiling. Turning, Broneco seated himself on the chair, thinking of what to say next to have this boy bring a deep conversation. "I notice your painting," said Broneco. "I like the style of it."

The roommate now walked up to the painting, unhooked it from the wall, held it in his hand, staring. Then turning, facing Broneco now, he said, "I've done this painting last year which then it was my first year here."

"Tell me, are you an Apache?"

"Yes. How did you know?"

"I notice that you must be, half guessing according to your painting on the wall."

"You must be an artist then," Wallace said, leaning back against the soft plastic cushion on the broad back of the blue chair which set near the bed close to the window.

"Might say that, but it depends."

"Just arrive today?" he asked, grinning into a youthful smile.

Broneco almost smile, as he glance again toward the open window then back to where the boy was. Broneco also notice the boy, with his medium pitch of voice, pay attention. Giving a little sigh, Broneco replied, "I just arrive in about thirty minutes ago from this present hour."

160

"Hungry?" Wallace asked.

"A little."

"It's just about time to eat."

"At this time of the evening, supper?" asked Broneco surprisely.

"Shall I guide you to the dining room?"

Broneco, turning slightly, he stood facing the large clear mirror across the top of the drawer. Combing his misplaced hair, he now glimpse again to where the boy was, then seeing him with eye shut, resting his head against the palm of his both hands made into a pillow style.

"Oh yes, please do guide me, for I'm not acquainted with the campus yet. Show me," said Broneco, honoring his new roommate with gesture made with his hand.

The next morning, Broneco stepping out into the morning sun, looking about the campus his eyes rolled, studying, exploring, and examining. His mind also wandered away excitedly. The cool air of the morning blew steady, shaking the tall trees as the few ripen leaves whirl into circle, parachuting down onto the dark green lawn.

"So this is the Institute of American Indian Arts," said Broneco, whispering.

"You must be a new student," said a strange voice from behind.

Broneco amazed, stand facing the busy traffic street across the small grass patched against the small-rising hill which was guarded by the fence within about fifty feet away from the street. Broneco bited his lip, then turned.

There, a boy sat resting his leg above the other. Smiling brightly as the arch of the teeth neatly setted, colorful dark eyes, pale of smooth face and a lip of light rose. The hair neatly combed of woolly like in black.

Broneco grinned, said only, "Good morning . . .?"

"Ramus," the voice said, finishing what Broneco was going to say.

"And the last?"

"Suina," the boy said, laughing.

161

Broneco seated himself beside Ramus, asking a few question for a minute, when the two fell in love with a deep conversation as the sun traveled high, when the clock striked twelve.

Straightening out the wrinkle of the neatly ironed shirts, they started down the porch steps. Stepping to the bottom, the clips of Ramus kept up a good rhythm of beats, then reaching the dining room.

Broneco and Ramus stood before a highly smooth-finished dinner table with a girl standing at the other end. She kept shifting her weight, balancing her hip weights to one side which made her look more prettier than before. Especially when she giggled, bowing her shameless face.

Ramus and Broneco smiled, looking at each other. Ramus blinked his eye, then there was silence for a moment when three more boys stood before the table.

Seating before the lunch tables, Broneco glance across the table when a boy with a heavy acne and rusted-white, freckled face ignored Broneco. Then there was another who seated besides the other. Again Broneco glanced when the other boy whispered softly to his partner besides him.

"These Pueblo boys, they sure can stare sometimes like this one in front of me," he said in his own language, which the other boy thought Broneco was a Pueblo too.

"See how him and his friends are dressed?" said the other.

Broneco pretend that he didn't understand, so he went talking to Ramus about the school, when the hostess passed on the lunch evenly divided onto each plate.

Broneco, understanding his people, he knew what was the trouble with them was they like to intrude on other people's business. Complaining, they even would attempt to challenge others, beginning with a stare also. Broneco didn't bother, since he understood what the two said.

After the lunch, Ramus showed Broneco around the campus area. Coming to the round step towards the Art Gallery, Broneco sighted an unusual form of a tree. The tree remind him of girl he used to know. Reaching the steep step, Broneco paused when Ramus stopped by the weak thin tree.

"Say, you haven't tell me what your name was."

Broneco laughed. "So, you are interested in knowing my name. It's Broneco."

Ramus wanted to ask next was to know where he was from. But Broneco sensing, he interrupt again. "Please don't ask yet," he said.

Ramus laugh. Then, strolling out onto the other side of the gallery, they headed back for the dormitory.

Then, it was Monday when the school began to roll. First three days of the week, it was orientation in case some newcomer might be interested in different fields.

Broneco entering different arts departments. He first came into weaving studio, when everyone seated themselves before the weaving loom. Students, in groups of thirty, tried out their skill.

Interesting it was, but it occurred to Broneco thinking, "Must be only for the girls."

Spending half an hour, the group C (which was the identifying alphabet), move on to another studio which was Traditional Technique, just across the weaving studio.

Here, Broneco walked about the room. "Interesting, very interesting," he said, standing before a blanket dress.

Then the teacher suggested that everyone should be seated, so they could try out their skill working with the tiny beads.

Broneco played with tiny colored beads, trying to thread them onto a leather.

Then it was time to go on to the next. Crossing the dirt road to the Ceramic, Painting, Jewelry, and Sculpture. Broneco first entered Ceramic Studio. Here, he tried to make a bowl out of wet clay. Each time he finish the bowl, it would lump inward.

Just then a young girl stood besides Broneco. "Need help here?" she asked.

Broneco smiled then answered, "Yes," pointing at the dispositioned bowl.

163

She only smiled, then started the round table rolling into a spin with her right feet. The more she spin the round table, she put forth her cute little hands, pressing, raising her hands upward, the clay shaped into a form.

Broneco couldn't believe it, seeing the hollowed bowl setting before him.

"There," she said, moving on to the next to show the others.

Broneco walked on to the next room which was Jewelry. Without being told to continue on to the next class, he sneaks into the Jewelry class ahead of the others.

A blond-headed teacher greeted him and offered him a seat to try his skill on jewelry. "Would like to make yourself a ring?" he asked.

Broneco answered excitedly, "Yes." Testing his skill, he finds that he couldn't cast a metal together.

Then, entering next was the Painting Studio which lastly he give up. He tried to paint, but instead, he put the paint of sticky oil paint all over himself. Broneco being through for that day, he finds that he wasn't interest in any.

The next morning, Broneco visited another department. Again he entered the classroom with only four teachers setting at each corners of the large room. Seating before one of the teacher, Broneco was only interviewed concerning a Commercial. Explaining what it consist of and the requirements in that field. Still, Broneco didn't decided, so he move on to the next.

Broneco this time meeting a new teacher before a desk in the color of gray. "I'm Mrs. Terry Allen and I teach Creative Writing," she said.

Broneco this time shook hands this teacher and seated himself before her. "My name is Broneco. Glad to meet you, Mrs. . . . ?"

"Allen," she said, since Broneco has forgotten already.

Broneco then asked a few question which she answered in a few words. Broneco excited him deeply to his satisfaction.

"It's been a long time I have waited for this kind of work. At last, I have found the choice of my own to dream as I please,"

164

Broneco thought. To put the past history in writing so it will always be remembered someday! Yes, he will major in writing.

After three days of orientation, Thursday came when the school begins enrolling the student. Broneco sat near to the entrance of the doorway when he saw a teacher dressed in light sky color blue. A bright rosy lip, she smile as the student met her, shaking hands with them.

Broneco waited patiently. He went up to the registrar and started enrolling. Spending almost seven hours in that one room was exasperating. After Broneco all tired and wore out, he walked out into the hall, then out the academic school building. Sniffing the fresh air made a great different after his boring day enrolling.

Hearing the birds singing obvious melody in the trees, Broneco took his time shuffling along the sidewalk. Ramus caught up.

"How did you come out on your subjects?" he said.

"Fine, except I spend my day in one room, trying to get my subjects straighten out," said Broneco, blinking his eyes to clear his eye vision.

Being in another school was very exciting. Broneco was carrying more subjects than he thought he would have. In some subjects there was fun. On his leisure time, he would play piano. It was his favorite instrument.

A week has gone by tediously as the hours of the day stretched into long moments of time. The endless hours come to Friday. Broneco, in Creative Writing class, sat before the long table, facing the yonder wash packed with adobe villages. Not knowing what to write about or how to start off a story.

Since it was in the afternoon, the sun glitter its ray through the classroom window, made the students in the large square room yawning and closing their eyes fallen asleep.

All of a suddenly, a cool summer air blew gently across Broneco's face which half wake him. Mrs. Allen, the writing teacher, let out of her soft pink hands a seed pod of milkweed.

Whirling in circles above the students' head it drifted. Then landing atop the long table it skid, then walking, prancing. Broneco's eyes rolled, following the furry seed dancing before him. Though as someone ice skating in a ballet form of presentation it whirl, spinning, and then stopping.

In a sudden emotion, Broneco's pencil begin to wiggle in jerks. He begin writing his experience in writing a free verse poem.

Mrs. Allen, seated in front of the long table, smiled then took off her eye glass. She paused a minute. "That's it. You doing fine," she said, resuming her daily work, checking and marking papers which was piled high in front of her.

Broneco didn't know he has been thinking and attracted to the seed. He wrote his first poem.

The long boring hours seemed short. Broneco knew it was after school. Smiling, he handed his paper to Mrs. Allen, ready to be graded.

"Broneco, you wrote a poem," she said, adding, "This is good."

"I'm glad you liked it," replied Broneco, leaving the room.

"A poem, yes. It's a poem," thought Broneco, walking back to the dormitory. He begin to smile.

His friend, Ramus, spoke out, "Hi, Broneco. What's all the smile about?" he asked.

"Guess I was daydreaming. You know what I mean?"

"A girl, perhaps—maybe back home?"

"Might say that. Could be anything, you know," said Broneco, facing Ramus, then stopping by the entrance of the porch.

Ramus and Broneco had nothing else to talk about, so they both laugh and went on into the building.

It was Saturday. Broneco in the room was writing a letter to one of his friend when someone knocked on the door. Turning away from the desk he was working on, he slowly raise out of his seat. Then hiding the letter beneath the other papers, he answer, "Come in." It was only his friend Ramus.

"Broneco, aren't you going to the dance tonight?"

"No, Ramus, I don't know how to dance."

"You can watch."

"I still get the cramps, involuntary," said Broneco, grinning.

"Broneco, you're no good," said Ramus, coming over to where Broneco sitting beside the long standing lamp, still having his pencil in his right hand.

"Next time. Okay?" asked Broneco.

"Next time, next time! You said that four time now, four times," said Ramus, showing his fingers of four.

Broneco got out of his chair laughing at his friend. Pacing across the floor, then back again. "Patience! You have to wait till I get to know more students. Okay?"

Broneco could have gone to dance that night. Only if he had a suit coat he would have. He at last nodded. "I can't go," he said. "Maybe next time," he thought, sinking back down into his chair.

Then Monday come. Broneco very excitedly entered his favorite classroom in the afternoon. Seating himself again before the long table for writing, he waited patiently to be given an assignment.

Mrs. Allen, in the first hour in the afternoon, give her lectures in writing. Using her expression, "Hey, You, and See," trying to pound these word into the listening students' heads. If one goes to sleep, she would use her usage of the word strongly which would wake up the sleeping student.

Broneco was given an assignment to write about himself in the past tense, present, and future. Broneco didn't like to write future because he feared, if he did write about the future, he thought the day may not come, and he believed that when one plans for future, things always comes wrong.

Broneco, for the first time, was to try out his skill of writing in first person. He sat quietly listening to the voice of the wind. He begin to dream, recalling the past. Remembering, they returned to him. Choosing the best words, he start off on a story writing.

Each morning, coming out on the small patio, he notice the rippling leaves on the tall trees began to lose its attraction of green. Now it was turning its shades of color into an autumn yellow and partly orange.

The leaves drifted downward until it piled, covering the green lawn, protecting underneath the stack of corrupted, useless leaves. Sometimes Broneco thought the snow was falling, yet it was only the leaves falling from the trees.

Broneco writing his past history, he completely forgot what was going on around the campus. It was like a dream of nightmare. Understanding what his teacher, Mrs. Allen, describe concerning the sensory impression, Broneco using this description, he went on writing.

Finishing few long pages of story, Mrs. Allen returned the handwritten manuelscripts, stating she would like to know more. Broneco continued. Not knowing, his papers of written manuelscript, supposedly a short script, became a chapter of pages.

At times Broneco remembered there was snow, then there was sunshine, then the weather would turn into the blowing chills of colds.

The school work begins to tighten with homework. The more the students turns in their work, the teachers began to struggle some assignment. Then, one day in December, Broneco threw his book he is reading to the corner of his room where one of his roommate caught the book flying straight at him. He move away from the window which viewed the school building and the middle men's dorm.

Since his eyes began to ache following the tiny letters in the books he was reading, Broneco quietly lie on the bed, calming his nerves. He listened to the cold air blowing against the window. The voice of the wind began to whisper, then singing the winter songs. Afterward it was quiet again, except the dropping of the rain made it sound as of the spring. He could even hear the ripples of the drops.

Broneco, blinking his eyes, the roll of tears form on the eyelash. Letting it roll down freely, soaking into the fluffed feather cushioned pillow.

Broneco's roommate, Edd, spoke. "Broneco, who do you think you are, hitting me with that book of yours right on my chest?"

"Because the book is too interesting to stop reading."

"I agree with you B," he said.

"I didn't mean to throw it."

"But why?" shouted Edd.

"I just want you to caught, to see how alert you were. After all, it just goes to show me that you can see even though you having a red eyes," said Broneco, smiling now.

"Broneco, sometimes you remind me of my brother."

"Oh yes, I'm your blood brother, remember?"

Edd smiled and fell back on the bed and started reading the book. Then, putting the book aside, he looked at Broneco again. "Broneco, are you going home for Christmas this coming week? In fact, your Guidance Director's secretary, Mrs. Cook, mentioned that she would have to sign our leave slip in the absent of her boss."

"Oh, that nice dark-haired looking woman? The one who has a rosy red cheek? You know, when she smiles, her cute little dimples shows on each side of her heart-shaped pink lips. She's real nice to me. Of course, she always buys me sweet rolls."

"Ha! Is that all? She always buys me a cup of coffee too, along with a roll."

"Oh, she does! My teacher, Mrs. Allen, always treats with a real sweet cookie," said Broneco, standing up then making an unusual baby face which made him looked like a ten-year-old kid.

Now Edd stand up, stomping his feet, he started a little ways from Broneco.

"Oh yeah," he said, inhaling more air to pop up his chest. "I work for her too. Every after school she gives me cookies too."

"Well, ain't that something!" said Broneco, pointing at Edd, almost reaching into his eyes.

Just then a lady came in. Her hair in stripes of gray. She smile. Not very stout, but little. She had a pencil in her hand. "My goodness! What's all the noise about?" she said.

Broneco laughed, pointing at Edd. "Ask him," he said.

"We're just playing," said Edd.

"A grownup boys like you, behaving like children!"

"He started first," said Edd.

"No, he did," said Broneco.

169

Then Edd pointed at Broneco, soon the arguments became greater, pretending as though serious. Then beginning to fight when Mrs. Gala steps in between the boys.

"Listen, listen . . . children!" she said.

Broneco and Edd stopped, giving a little smirk of smile. They both looked at each other. Then, all at once, Broneco and Edd spoke. "See what she call us!"

Understanding the jokes, now they all laughed. Broneco, Edd. and Mrs. Gala all left the room and strolled together down the hall, heading for a cold drink. Edd held onto Mrs. Gala's arm while Broneco held onto the other. As though a mother taking her two young kids to a store, they all walked around the corner of the hallway.

Coming down the hall, a young boy's attendant walked into the hall, checking students. When he sighted the three coming down the hall, he laughed.

"So, you two are Mom-mom's boys," he said, teasing the two.

Then enter the small room where the coke machine stand was. Enjoying the flavor of the cold drinks, Broneco and Edd now returned their room. Broneco, relief of headaches now, returned to his desk. Now they quietly sat in the room, letting the cold winds do all the whispering against the windowpane.

The snow was now falling, drifting past Broneco's front window. He smiled. "Nice to go home again to my beloved country." He thought of home at last.

His mind seems to be calm and dreaming, facing the invasioning white snowflakes. "I'll come home and spend a great deal of time with my grandmother. I wonder how is she. What will she send me for Christmas, I wonder," thought again Broneco.

He waited a few days before he made his destination for Christmas. With all the wonderful and joyful moments, he departed.

·XVI·

Tears Raining in My Heart

Soon it was Christmas. Broneco more excited and full of joyful feeling. Anxiously Broneco came back to the dormitory from school, carrying loads of books in his left hand. He looked at the calendar on the wall and notice it was Friday.

"I'll make arrangement tonight for I'll go home tomorrow and see my family. Then I'll come back to continue with my school work again like I have been before," he thought.

The next morning he checked himself out on leave. Again it was like going to school on the bus, but this time the bus was heading northwest.

Exactly seven hours later, Broneco was back in his home town. Shopping a little in town made a great difference of his feeling.

Broneco couldn't walk for twenty-five miles to his Grandmother's winter camp, so the best thing to do was stay with his mother, Emma, for a few days. So, he stayed for a few day and then asked his uncle to take him back to Grandmother's place, but he refused him.

Broneco made up his mind that he would walk in the deep icy snow, if he has to walk that far, when finally his uncle took him.

It was only a few days left to return to school. Broneco wanted to spend a few days with Grandmother and Auntie, but he couldn't.

He stood before the old house which was there for eighteen

years. Just then Grandmother approached the corral, riding her beloved donkey.

Broneco walked a little ways and stood there waiting as the wind kept blowing against his long jacket.

Proudly and thrill, full of cheerfulness, Grandmother rode forth and lean down to where Broneco was and kissed him on the cheek.

"It's nice to see you come back like you said that you will always come back to the old place," she said.

"Grandmother, are you all right? I mean is your knee all right?"

"Don't worry about it. It's perfectly fine, my child," she reply, holding Broneco's hand. "Are you going to stay for a while? We needed some firewood. Perhaps you would help Annie and Auntie get some wood today."

"I would like it, but, Grandmother, I have very little time. I had to return back to school tomorrow. I could stay, but . . . but my uncle said he's going in the next five minutes. I would get wood if . . . if he did wait that long. Grandmother, you got to understand, he refused to bring me here, but I said I was going to walk, when he decided to bring me here and then go back with him right away."

Grandmother blinked her eyes and thought about it for a minute. "We could take you back today after tomorrow on your Auntie's pickup," she said. "We could today, but the water in the engine is deeply froze."

"But - but I can't," said Broneco, staring up at his Grandmother. He wanted to stay and help, but there was some other things to think about.

Broneco was forbidden to return to his Grandmother in certain conditions which he didn't understand, but for himself he knew what his stepfather told him were mysterious.

Broneco didn't feel right about it, so he thought about it for a long time. "Grandmother, I couldn't."

"Must you go so early? It's too soon," she answered.

Then Broneco's uncle called, "Broneco, it's time to go."

Broneco held his Grandmother's hand and asked her to wait for a minute. He rushed to the car, feeling temper of angry.

"Can't you wait for another minute?" said Broneco in a madly tone voice.

"Your aunt is angry, very angry. Must go right away," his uncle said.

"Just one minute."

Broneco runned back to where his Grandmother was. She was waiting for an answer. He held his Grandmother's hand tight.

"You have to understand. My uncle says we must go right away, saying my aunt is mad."

"All right, but before you go may I ask when will you be back?"

"I'll be back again in April. This time, I promise you that I will spend a week here with you, my aunt, and myself. And I'll have me a present with me, just for you," said Broneco.

"What day of the week will it be?"

"I'll be on Easter," said Broneco.

"Oh, I wanted to ask you a question before you go," she said. "Broneco, I had a present for Johnnie. I thought you might be coming home with him, but you didn't. What happen?"

"Nothing, Grandmother."

"I think he was a very nice boy. I miss him. Come home with him again sometimes, will you?"

Broneco looked down at the ground, bowing his head, blinking his eyes. "I will, Grandmother. I promise I will. Will you be waiting here for me? Just wait for me until I return. This is my last year to complete my twelve years of schooling. You'll come to my graduations, won't you?"

"I sure will. I planned that for several months. I'll be waiting here for you. Once you were so small, herding my flocks of sheep for me. Now you are grown up. I hope someday you'll take care of me like I did before. Sometimes an old person get so discourage, but one thing you must not forget. Don't forget this beautiful countryland here where you were born," she said, reaching into her bags hanging besides her. "I've got a present for you on this Christmas."

Broneco picked the package and gently held it in his hand, pressing it against his chest.

173

"Thank you," he said and kissed his Grandmother cheek. "I'll be back very soon. It's not that I don't want to stay, but, as you know, what one plans it doesn't come out right sometimes. I'll send you some money just as soon as I get back to Santa Fe, enough to paid for you expense throughout the year until I return. Wait for me and I won't forget my promise. I'll be here with Johnnie. Now, I must say good-bye," said Broneco, still holding his Grandmother's hand, pressing it nervously.

"Good-bye," she said, wiping her tears a little.

Broneco walked few yard away and stood there and waved his hands. The cold winds blowing against her clothing as they flatten. Sitting on her donkey steadily.

Broneco ask his uncle if he could just another minute. He slam the car door. They were off on the road again. Broneco only looked back when he saw the object outside the home, it was Grandmother still sitting on her donkey, waiting.

Broneco didn't like the idea, but he was going back tomorrow. He had made the arrangement only for a week and didn't have enough time.

Broneco went back to school, feeling unhappy about the home situation. He was about to rush home. One evening, he looked out the window, watching the moon. As it glitter high in the space, he sense something was deeply wrong back home, but he couldn't seem to figure it out. What could that be, he asked and he kept asking himself, but still the answer wasn't clear. The next day he went to school with the sense of a troubled feeling.

"I'll make my arrangement to leave tomorrow night," he thought about it.

It was Friday. Broneco kept thinking about it. He sat by the window again, when he heard a phone ringing in the office. He could hear sharp and clear.

"That's for me," he whisper and rushed out the door. He came around the corner and glance down the hall and raced down the main hall into the office. There was no one in the office.

Broneco slowly picked up the phone. "Hello," he answered. Then there was a little clicking sound.

174

"Long distance calling Broneco," said the operator girl.

"Speaking," said Broneco.

"Broneco?" she asked.

"Yes, indeed."

"Hold on a minute," she said. "Deposit one-sixty, please."

Broneco held the phone in his hand, rolling his eyes up and down the side of the wall, blinking and rubbing his eyes.

"On the line, yes," the operator whisper.

Then came the jingling, tingling, and crashing sound. Broneco waited to have the extensions connected, shaking a little from the nervousment, stir of chills running up his spine. Finally the line was clear.

"This Broneco speaking?" said a voice with the sound of mysterious.

"Yes, it's him, and who's this speaking?"

"Ronnie speaking. Please just calm yourself and don't get too excited for I have somethings very important to tell you," he said.

"Go right ahead. I'm listening."

"Your aunt and mother wants you to come home immediately."

"Why?"

"Please don't ask question, just come right on home, will you?"

"Why?"

"Your aunt states that it's very urgent!"

"O.K., I will on Tuesday, if they would let me."

"Not Tuesday, but come home tomorrow, immediately, and be quick about it."

Broneco wondered what it was all about, holding the phone in his hand. Then he added, "All right, I'll be home. Tomorrow."

"Good-bye. May you be on your way tomorrow. Good luck," Ronnie said and hung up.

Broneco held the phone, patiently placed the black bar back in it's position carefully. "I'll be there tomorrow, exactly twelve," he whisper.

Broneco waited in the office until the matron returns. Mrs. Gala came in and smile as she always does.

"Good evening, my sweet child, you looked worried," she said.

175

"I had an emergency call. If possible, may I be released from the school and dormitory right away for the morning four-twenty bus?"

"I'll call the main office first. Just wait here," she said.

For half an hour Broneco waited, walking back and fore with a stroll down the hall.

Then she answered, "You sign this slip of paper and you'll leave tomorrow at four-twenty as you requested. Remember, you are to be back Sunday."

"I understand, thank you," he said, rushing back to the room.

Broneco's traveling expense wasn't enough. The bank was close and the money couldn't be check out. Broneco sat in the room, trying to figure out another way. He had one friend he always trusted. He was Broneco's only hope that he would give a loan until he gets back.

Broneco rushed down the hall to the other end. Stopping before Room 225, he knocked on the door.

"Come in," answered someone in the room.

Broneco rushed the door open. "Keith, I needed a help from you. There's no one that I can ask," he said.

Keith only sat back in the chair and smile. In his right hand holding a pencil, chewing a little on the eraser. "A help from me? From a poor guy like me?" he said. "Well, what can I do for you? I'll do all I can, if I have what you wanted."

"You're my only hope."

"No, no, there you go again. My friend, don't go through all of that talk. Just ask for what you want."

"I just wanted to borrow some money from you for a couple of days and paid you back a week from now."

"How much?"

"I'm short of eight dollars," said Broneco.

"Here's ten, and have a nice trip," he said.

"How did you know really that was the amount I needed?" ask Broneco.

"Intelligent." He smile.

Broneco was on his way down the hall again to the opposite of the north side. He had enough to paid his expense on a round trip ticket. He didn't sleep that night, wondering about why he has to come home immediately.

It was three-thirty in the morning. Broneco started to pack a few things to take with him when he picked his Grandmother's picture. When he held it up, the complexion of the skin, he notice has somehow changed into more darker. He knew then.

It's my Grandmother," he thought.

Broneco dropped the picture and went before the window. Staring into the distance of darkness, still it didn't help. He picked up the picture and placed it between his packed clothing.

He rushed out the door again and headed down the hall. Into the main office and the night attendant took him to the bus depot.

Broneco was shock of what he knew. It was unbelievable, but Broneco was taught of all these tricks by his Grandfather long ago. He knew very little and yet it worked.

Around eleven-thirty in the morning, Broneco was back in Farmington town. He walked down the street and met one of his friend, Ernest.

"We were expecting you. Luckily we met. I'm here to take you home right away," Ernest said.

"Well, please hurry."

"O.K., right away."

Broneco and Ernest walked across the street. Then stopped by a parked sky blue car and left the black lines of tar on the pavement down the main street.

Broneco didn't talk much all the way to Shiprock.

Ernest asked, "To the hospital or straight home?"

"Home, please."

"If you want me to take you to the hospital and then home, I'll be glad to do so."

"I better get home first. I'll make it there later."

Ernest drove away and Broneco stood in front of the door. The house was lock and no one home. The wind blew strongly and whirling into dust storm. Broneco ran to his next door neighbor. He knocked on the door.

177

A lady, very casual, opened the door and then she said, "Come in."

Broneco slowly, unwillingly entered the house.

"Your mother and aunt are at the hospital right now. They told me in case you should come home, we are suppose to take you there," she said.

"There's no need to. I can make it," Broneco replied.

The lady wanted to help, but the car wasn't there. Broneco only said a few more words and shutted the door behind him and left.

He walked down the road and soon he started to run. He rushed to his uncle's wife's place and asked her if she could take him to the hospital immediately.

She took her time. Finally, she came out of the house.

Shortly after, Broneco rushed into the hospital and few relatives were waiting there. One said, "That must be the boy whom my sister once spoke of. I see he has come home."

Broneco disobeyed the rules of visiting hour. He passed by many room and walked into the right room as if he was told which room his Grandmother was in.

He stopped by the room and opened the door. His eyes narrowed, walked in silently. Emma sat by the window.

Broneco walked and stood before his Grandmother and held her hands, but she didn't look nor felt his hands. He held on tight to his Grandmother's hand. He glance to the right of him and saw his mother's tears rolling down her cheeks.

Grandmother was not dead, but she was completely unconscious. Broneco forgotten about everythings, when someone took his hand off Grandmother's hand.

"Broneco, let's go home now," said a young woman whom Broneco knew since he was young. He came home not quite remembering anything.

The next morning, Broneco and Ronnie went back to the hospital. But Auntie came out and took Broneco by the arms and lead him away from the entrance, back to the car.

"Broneco, don't go in there. We'll come back later. We must make our fast trip and pick up your sister, Annie, today," she said.

Broneco didn't say much. Ronnie drove all the way to Colorado and picked up his sister.

During the afternoon, the sun was high and the wind didn't blow anymore all of a sudden. When Ronnie was motioned to the side of the road by his stepfather. Ronnie walked to the other car, when Broneco rushed to the side of the car and heard, "They want all of us back at the hospital right away."

Broneco walked away from the car feeling numb.

Back at the hospital, Broneco held onto the door handle while Annie and her mother headed for the hospital entrance. Auntie went in first, then Annie. Broneco waited by the car until everyone was in. He slowly walked into the hospital last. "Now I must go into the hospital," he said.

Inside, Broneco's tears rushed, deep in the heart. Now the loneliness was within Broneco.

He stroll across the floor into the emergency waiting room. There, he put his arms around his mother and aunt's neck.

He said, "One must go—mother, aunt, and relatives. We are given life and is taken back as it has been request. Now she is out of misery. Without a single pain, she left us. They say somewhere in the universe, one's father is there where love is love."

Then Broneco walked away. It was on Washington's birthday. Then followed by his aunt, mother, and other relations.

That very day, Broneco and his family went back to the winter camp and stood by the long pole. Broneco's tears bursted into rippling tears rolling down his face. He could hear her last spoken words, as he looked to where he stood before his Grandmother during the short moment of visiting, promising that he would come home with Johnnie.

Across the small rolling hill towards the north, there her sheep still grazing in the prairie land. Broneco held onto the small pole.

Just then, Broneco's cat, Moon, approach him. Moon always loved by Grandmother. She always worried about Moon to starve or being hungry.

Broneco fell against the wall of the house and cry. "Oh, why does it have to happen? Why?"

179

Seeing Broneco wept, Moon jumped into Broneco's arms and licked his cheek. Broneco took Moon in his arm and walked back to the car.

"I'm taking him back with me and I'll bring him back next week," he said.

Broneco and his family were off on the road again. Auntie and Emma came back to the old place to pick up Broneco's Grandmother few belonging of jewelry.

Tuesday came. Broneco attended the funeral.

Sitting in the car, Broneco's big sister mention that Grandmother has said once, saying, "Grandmother once said to me— she was very proud, holding me in her arms—she has made a plan, states she was going to Broneco's graduation this coming May," as her tears dripping down her cheek.

Broneco stood before the grave as the dirt fell into the dug out area. He stood, tears raining in his heart, the wind started to blow with cold air. Broneco didn't show his tears anymore; only the unshown tears tremble in him.

There was about forty people in all as the relations gather.

Broneco walked a little ways and looked back. "Good-bye. As for me, I'm going back home and take care of the sheep for the rest of my life. Things shall remain the same. Someday people shall remember and read about you as I'm your author as well as my own."

Only the dust blew across the grave where Broneco's unforgotten Grandmother laid. Broneco strolled away.

·XVII·

Graduation

THE NIGHT before graduation, Broneco sat by the window watching the stars twinkle. Hearing the cool mountain air blowing, making billows of disturbed sea waves into frightening force. He sat by the window, thinking about the past. Blinking his eyes, he listened to nature's sounds of variations. It sounded like back home, standing on the hill.

Out in the open, in the yards of the adobe buildings, built in heavy structure, fitted its name Santa Fe. The tall standing trees barely fluttering their leafs each time the wind blows toward the east. Once in a while the curtain in the room kept drifting, twisting itself over Broneco's head. Resting his chin into comfortable relaxation, he kept recalling the dreaming nightmare.

Sitting on the soft bed, he felt the bed cover. Feeling the texture made him think of the day when he kissed his pet lamb. The soft furry cheek stiffed with cockleburs. Broneco was lucky that none of the thorny seed case didn't injure his lip. Many years it was— the day Broneco discovered what English meant to him. He could visualize the image of his family gathered around the morning glittering fire.

Still sitting by the window, the cool spring air blew the light drapery curling unevenly, strike Broneco across the face. His mind cleared itself to present. The cars were roaring in the street across. The street only a block away. The lights of speeding cars passing as if he's seeing a falling star. Cruising police car racing after another speed breaking rulers down the main highway, soaring pitched into high impressions.

Winking his eyes, he stood up by the window, glancing through the darkness of the night with few lights shown in the porch of every houses. Just then, he heard a sound of footstep in the main hall. It became louder and louder. It sounded like the day he was in the room alone when Johnnie entered the room during his seventh grade year. Broneco picked up Johnnie's picture.

"It can't be Edd. He walks with different rhythms of step. It can't be Johnnie," he thought as his eyes stared at the door with fear. "What will I say? If you're come, Johnnie, I'll die of shock. I'll die of your approach," he whisper, sweating.

The footstep kept stumping nearer and nearer. The step of the unquestionable stranger kept beating through Broneco's head.

When the door opened with a quick force, Broneco rushed to the window, in ready position to swing out the unscreen window. He was froze.

"Broneco, what are you looking at?" said Edd.

Broneco dropped Johnnie's picture on the floor.

Edd, unbuttoning his shirt, made a glance to where Broneco was standing. "What's the matter?" he asked.

"Oh, it's you! I was just thinking."

"Why?" said Edd, teasing like he always does.

Broneco moved away from the window. "I thought . . . thought somebody else other than you was heading this way," said Broneco, picking up the photo on the floor.

"Just think! You and I are graduating tomorrow night at this time. Aren't you happy?"

"Not exactly," Broneco answered.

"Why?"

"My teacher, Mr. Simpson, said I was failing my grades. I asked him still if I'm passing at least, and you know what he told me?"

"What did he say?"

" 'Why worry about it? I'm not the one whose graduating.' "

Edd laugh and took off his shoes. "Your folks coming tomorrow?" he asked.

Broneco sat on the bed, folding and packing his clothes. "I don't know, Edd. Maybe so, yes."

"I don't know about mine either."

"Coming back next year?" Broneco asked.

"Oh shucks, I'm tired of this place. I better go someplace else."

"Maybe I am, but really I don't know yet," said Broneco, holding another shirt half folded. He looked at Edd and watched him for a second. He then knew that Edd's footstep didn't sound like his because he tripped. "How did you fall?" he asked.

"How did you know, or were you looking out the window when I fell on the slippery ice out there?"

"No, brain work does it."

"What do you mean?"

"I mean that by the way you walk down the hall I can tell by the step you make. This time, you made your stepping rhythms different."

"I don't get you."

Broneco was now through packing. Suitcases from big to small neatly rowed by the doorway. As usual, he picked up a book and placed his head curl on the feather cushion pillow. He was tired so he turned off the light to fall asleep.

Edd roll over with blanket paralleling with his head facing the wall. He was in his deep sleep now, snoring as though a ravenous lion in the jungle, roaring and looking for food of his appetite.

The next day, Broneco went to school as usual. Around the Institute campus, student oncoming and passing, all thrill of excitement, since it the last day of school.

The day was sunny, except clouds stretching high above the mountain in the north. Broneco, stepping off the academic building, on a stroll. He begin to smell the first cut of alfalfa. He sniffed air. "It's going to rain, I see," he thought. He almost forget that he was suppose to report to the commencement exercise during the seventh period.

He went back into the academic building. Down the hall, he met Edd. "We are suppose to have our caps and gown," he said.

"You have yours?"

"No, are you?"

"No," Broneco answered. During the whole two hours, the commencement exercise was practice.

The senior sponsor announced that every seniors were to be in the dressing room by seven-thirty that evening.

Broneco and Edd went back to the building.

Then, after supper, Broneco sat by the window, wondering again. The sun begin to sink behind the west Santa Fe mountain. In the evening sky, the colors of autumn yellow, orange, and red showed its delirious attraction.

Broneco looked down at his shoes, remembering that he only had a school shoes which was in the color of buckskin tan.

"I can't graduate in this shoes," he thought. Disgusted, he reach for his suit coat which lay on the bed neatly spread. His cousin, Gladys, gifted him his first suit coat for his graduation, yet he didn't have a new shoe to match it.

Trying on the new suit coat, Broneco then looked at himself in the mirror hanging over the bureau. Pausing a little when he remembered something that he never thought of for a long time. He pull the drawer out and unpack his sweaters from the drawer.

Broneco held a package in his hand wrapped in a red Christmas wrapping, neatly tie with a blue ribbon. "Why did I waited so long?" he thought.

Holding it for a long time, Broneco started unwrapping the package which he received from his grandmother during his short visit with her.

"I should have stayed longer, just a little longer," said Broneco, opening his present late after Christmas. "What could it be?" he asked himself.

He brought his present back from home during his Christmas vacation. Evidently he was too excited during the New Year's night and forgot all about it, placing the package in the drawer underneath the pullover sweaters. Following the New Year's, many activity took place around the campus area. Since then, Broneco completely forgot about the package in gift wrapped, hidden in the drawer.

"What could it be?" he asked himself again.

Shaking the package didn't answer Broneco's question. A little excitement quivering his nerve, he pull the blue ribbon. Again, Broneco thought of the day, how he receive the package from his grandmother, picturing her image sitting on her gray donkey in the heavy cold wind, blowing her coat, fluttering of quick ripple. Broneco's eyes filled with tears. He held a brand new shoes in his lap.

Placing the shoes besides the bed, he whispered, "Thank you. I'll wear the shoes tonight for my graduation."

Looking at the shoes again, he spotted something else in the shoe. Curiously, he reached for the small rectangular shaped piece of paper. Patiently, he unfolded the note and read, "Present for Broneco on Christmas, love, Grandmother."

Broneco wipe his tears, then placed the note in a small envelope and sealed it.

"It's a miracle," he said, putting on his suit tie. He heard a footstep in the hallway. Then, there was a knock on the door.

"Come in," said Broneco, slightly turning sideways.

"Hey, you look just great, since I never saw you wearing a whole outfit," said a voice.

Broneco, in his new shoes, swing to see who the visitor was. Smiling then, he wink his eyes. "Sit down and have a seat. Glad to have you visit," said Broneco.

"Graduating tonight?"

"Oh-oh, yes . . . yes!"

"Congratulations."

"Thank you, my friend Ramus. Aren't you going to sing a dedication song for me tonight before I leave?"

"Which one?" ask Ramus excitedly.

"Raining in my heart," said Broneco, laughing.

Just when Broneco and Ramus are ready to play their musical tune in the boys' lounge, someone knocked on the door.

185

"Come in," said Broneco.

A young boy came in, Broneco's classmate, Michael. "Someone wants to see you down the hall in the waiting section," he said.

"I guess that means we have to wait," said Broneco, departing his friend, Ramus.

Broneco, coming around the corner, there he saw his sister [cousin], Gladys, sitting with his mother, Emma.

"I thought you did never come," said Broneco, seating himself.

"We weren't sure either," said Broneco's sister.

"Come, I'll show you around the campus and then take you to the academic building," said Broneco. Strolling with his mother and sister down the concrete walk was wonderful. It was exciting. "How's everythings back home?" he asked.

"Your Auntie is taking care of the sheep until I get back," said Emma.

Just then Broneco's favorite teacher, Mrs. T. D. Allen, came in sight with her husband, Mr. Allen.

"Wait, I want you to met my teacher," he said, stopping along the walk.

Mrs. Allen gave a smile.

"Mrs. Allen," said Broneco, all excited.

"Oh, are these your folks?" she asked, interrupting.

Broneco smirk in a soft grin. "Yes, this my mother and this is my sister," he said. "She's a Navaho—has five fingers, too," said Broneco, whispering to his mother.

Mrs. Allen blinked her eyes as it sparkle with twinkle.

Broneco talking with Mr. Allen for a moment when they all depart and headed down the sidewalk into the academic building.

"There should be two seats available for you," said Broneco, heading back to the boys' dormitory. The time was going by fast.

Broneco made his fast trip back and dressed himself into cap and gown shortly after. Then the music was on. Some students started on with their rhythms of stepping down the aisle marching.

Broneco stood behind his friend. He looked to where his seat was. "At last, I am approaching, getting ready to receive my diploma," he kept thinking, walking off on his left feet.

186

Then he was in the chair. Taking a deep breath, he seated himself. The others followed behind. When the time came, Broneco was called upon the stage to receive his diploma, he couldn't believe his eyes. The folded black book covered with leather! He held it in his left hand and walked off the stage.

After graduation, Broneco and his mother and sister went back to where they were going to stay overnight in the hotel. Broneco feeling happy stayed with them for a while before he went back to the school campus.

The next day, Broneco on his way home, looked at his diploma many times. Coming home was exciting but, there again, was something to think about. Approaching home, he looked at the hill and smile.

"I have come back. I been waiting to come back," he thought.

Since he was young, he has been familiar with the hill. What could it be, no one knows. Many times Broneco's aunt would asked, but she still doesn't understand as Broneco explains each time, "Not now, until you make my dreams come true," he'd say.

Stopping the car before the house, Broneco slowly step out. Looking everywhere—to the corral, the sheep corral, and last to the house again—Broneco said to himself, "It's no use thinking about it." He looked toward the house where Grandmother used to sit. The words, "Wait for me," kept recalling again. With a little fainting feeling, entered his room.

·XVIII·

After Graduation

B ACK ON the reservation, staying with Auntie for a couple of days Broneco was happy. Then Annie returned from school. Broneco started packing his clothes again to return to Santa Fe to work for the summer.

"I'll have to return, Auntie, back to Santa Fe, but I'll come soon when I make enough money to last us for the summer not running short on food expense," said Broneco, kissing his aunt on the forehead. In his right arm, holding his suitcase and a sweater.

Auntie took Broneco back to Farmington to catch his bus from there. "We'll take good care of the sheep until you return and then you can help us out," she said, leaving Broneco on the sidewalk.

Broneco stood in the street, holding his suitcase, waving his hand. Then he went into the depot. For half an hour he waited, finally the bus arrive. Seven hours after, he walked across the street to the Institute campus.

"Nice to be back. This is my home," he thought, entering the campus ground.

Anxiously Broneco strolled along the sidewalk. Then he entered the building. Stopping in the office, there sat Mr. Jones, chewing his tobacco leafs as if it was sweet. Giving askance of glance, he stop chewing, exhaling the carbon smelling fog of smoke straight into Broneco's face.

188

"I'm a new student here," said Broneco, teasing.

"Well, hello, —"

"Broneco," answered Broneco.

"I'm Mr. Jones," he said, giving another puff of smokes. "Let me see where we'll put you." Taking his time, looking a long list of names when he came to the last name. "No vacancy," he said, crossing his arms above the other.

"But - but—"

"Well, I'm sorry," said Mr. Jones, leaning back in the lazy-man's chair.

"Surely there must be a room," said Broneco.

"You can sleep in the living room," said Mr. Jones, sitting, inscrutable. Then he smile. "Did I get you worried?"

"I knew you got something on your mind," said Broneco, picking up his suitcase.

"Room 227," Mr. Jones said, speaking stentorially.

"See you later."

Broneco headed down the main floor and went into the living room. He seated himself before the piano setting by the window. Gently touched the keys, pressing one key at a time. He shutted his eyes and fingered various keys. Then he chorded with three whole step of notes. He opened his eyes again and, this time, slowly beating on the chords, started an introduction.

It was getting dark now. Where Broneco was sitting there was little light, since the lamp was on. He started his vocal very lively.

"After graduation," he began to sing.

In another room, Broneco's friend, Keith, recognized the tune Broneco was playing. "That must be Broneco," he thought, heading for the living room. He entered the room and watched for a minute. "Excellent," he said, clapping his hands.

Broneco sensed that someone was in the lounge, glanced to the side of the door and saw Keith. "I was just trying to play a tune."

"Sounds wonderful."

"I didn't know. Thank you sir-e-e," said Broneco, smiling.

Keith seated himself on the couch, waiting for Broneco to finish

189

his music in chords. "Go right ahead and finish what you were playing." Keith sitting, crossing his legs above the other.

Broneco unwillingly started again. "After graduation," he said again like he mentioned before. Then he stopped.

"I never heard that song before," said Keith.

Broneco looked at Keith and answered, "That's my after graduation song."

"You mean you just made it up?"

"Oh yes, I sure did."

"I can't believe it," said Keith.

The song Broneco wrote was something great to Keith. For Broneco, it was just another piece of paper with a scribble of writing. He held the paper in his hand and placed it on the holder. "Join me?" he asked Keith.

"Me-e-e? Oh, I can't sing." He laughed.

"Just join me."

Keith stood up and went to where Broneco was. Broneco started his chords again. Keith and Broneco looked at each other and both stopped laughing and said, "After graduation." They both laughed.

"It's after graduation, and it is," said Broneco.

"Let's try again," said Keith.

Broneco rolled up his sleeves and walked right up to the eighty-eight piano keys. "Here we go again," he said, smiling.

"It was after graduation," said Broneco, as Keith started humming the sound deeply. Broneco blinked his eyes and said, "After graduation."

"What happen after graduation?" asked Keith, still singing.

"She held me tighter," said Broneco.

"Is that all?"

"And her tears drop onto my arms," said Broneco, still singing. "After graduation it was," Broneco smiled again and ended the music.

"Shall we go and rest up for tomorrow's days work?"

"You needed very badly," said Keith.

Broneco was excited to go to work in the morning. He wondered about his work he was doing in school. I'll finish it this time, he kept thinking. Half smiling, he went to sleep in the room he was assigned to.

The next morning, Broneco reported to his teacher, Mrs. Allen. Mrs. Allen Broneco's favorite teacher of the year. It happen to be Broneco's trusted teacher. Mrs. Allen understanding this light-brown, complexed student. She taught this young, intelligent Indian boy with the best effort that she can give. By the end of the year, Mrs. Allen much surprise how much she has gotten into Broneco's unread mind.

Mrs. Allen sat in her studio, as usual sitting before desk.

Broneco entered the room. "I'm ready to go to work again. I hope I'll do much this morning," said Broneco.

"You'd better," she said.

Broneco smiled and sat the table with pencil in his right hand. Scribbling and erasing, he started on his manuelscript which he has been working on for the whole year now. He worked hard every day and still there were only a few pile of papers stack up in numbers from one to fifteen clipped together.

During the afternoon, Broneco goes to work in publication under Mrs. Allen. He sometimes feel so disgusted. Mrs. Allen would come around in the Publication Department and talk with Broneco, teasing, making jokes, making him forget about smelling all the glues that he work with. The strong permeating smell of the cement glue would make Broneco dizzy. Sometimes objects in the room looks blurry, even makes him walk like a drinking man, walking up the back alley of the street.

Broneco would sit out in the sun during the weekends, watching the birds singing their best musical tunes in the trees. Many times listening to the birds, Broneco would write out songs in lyric style of writing. The different tones of music he hears gives him more and more quality of music. Music was his leisuretime hobby. When he has the time, for his convenience he would sit at the piano for hours.

Other times, Broneco has time to think about other things. He would sit at his desk writing for many hours and falls asleep, sitting before his desk still fingering the keys of his typewriter. Many times, night watcher would spot a light in the window while guarding the campus. When it's time to report to work, many times Mrs. Allen would ask, "Broneco, didn't you have enough sleep last night?" That's when she sees Broneco making involuntary reaction from the three hours of sleep.

"I sleep only for a few hours," said Broneco one day.

"Why?" Mrs. Allen asked.

"I was working on my script of writing."

"Why so late?"

"Well, let's say during the night when everything is still and quiet, Broneco's mind is at ease and full of imaginations."

Mrs. Allen laugh. "I stay up late too," she said, pouring herself a cup of coffee. "Want to taste my Navaho coffee this morning? Might help you wake up."

"Better be careful of the way you use that word," said Broneco, giving a sleepy smile.

He walked up to where the coffee was boiling with a little whistle of tooting sound. He lift the large coffee pot off the gas burner. With a sizzling sound, he poured the dark rippling coffee into a gleaming paper cup. Broneco stood by the desk and said, "I wonder . . . Why not boil the bean instead of draining the grinded black beans?"

"I suppose to give more flavor," Mrs. Allen said.

"Why didn't Hasteen Yazzie grind the black beans instead of trying to boil the tropical shrub for days and nights? Thinking it's going to soften as the Mexican beans would!"

Mrs. Allen giggle, laughing. "That's because he didn't know much about the use of the beans," she said, taking her eye glass off. "Now, where did you get that idea?"

Broneco, sipping another of the hot coffee, standed before the long table. Then he turned around and faced Mrs. Allen. "I just happen to read NAVAHO HAS FIVE FINGERS," replied Broneco, blinking his eyes a little. "The - the book was wonderful! I wish I could write a book like that."

Mrs. Allen grin and picked up her eye glass again and placed

192

her spectacle halfway down. Then looked straight at Broneco in stare. "Thank you. You will, only if you try," she said.

Broneco smiled again, seated himself before the long table covered with scattered piles of hand-written scribble of writing. Chewing his pencil eraser, glancing through the writing he had done, smiling to himself, making correction of his errors.

Mrs. Allen sitting at her typewriter with a speed of popping sound as if someone in the kitchen is making a popcorn.

Now the coffee has coolen down, Broneco took another swallow. "Oh, this is Friday, isn't it?" he asked, scratching his head.

"Yes, this is Friday," she answered.

"I think I'll head west today."

"How are you going?"

"That old hound dog," said Broneco, gathering up his written script of writing.

Mrs. Allen again with her glass placed halfway down her smooth nose, she look up. Then she stop typing. "You don't mean right now, are you?"

"Yes, right now I'm going to lunch. It's five till twelve," said Broneco, smiling again.

He gently closed the door behind him. The sun was bright. As for the tall standing trees, waving their heavy leaves, Broneco stroll down the shady side of the walk. Out on the lawn, water sprinkle turning their cycle from east to west directions.

Broneco's friend, Keith, met him on the walk. "I feel like taking a ride for the first time," he said.

"I feel the same."

"Where were you this morning? I went into Publication Department but I didn't see you there."

"I was in the written arts building, working on my script—the one I was talking about," said Broneco, stopping by the small patio of the boys' dormitory. He sat on the adobe wall of the patio.

Keith seated himself on the wooden bench. "Still got five minutes yet," he said.

"I thought it was time for lunch."

193

"What are you two waiting for? It's time to eat," said Alfred, tucking in his shirt, walking out of the building. He was tying his belt, then combing his dark hair shining with oil.

Broneco frown a little and jumped off the patio wall. "I'll put my folders away," he said.

"Hurry! We'll be walking very slowly down the sidewalk," said Keith. Alfred laughed as he always did.

Broneco rushed back to the room. In the room, he almost trip over a long cord hitch onto the hi fi radio. "Excuse me," he said, speaking to himself. He quickly changed his shirt and ran down the hall. Then he saw Mr. Jones walking up the step to the office. Broneco stopped running and came around the corner of the hall as if he didn't run down the shiny floor.

After lunch, Broneco and Keith went to the living room. Broneco stood by the doorway. Then he said, "I'm leaving today."

"Why?" asked Keith.

"Oh, just for the weekend. Be back Sunday afternoon."

"I guess I'll go to the movie tonight," said Keith, lying on the couch, kicking his shoes off.

Broneco went to where the piano set by the window. He seated himself and touched certain keys, pressing one or three out of eighty-eight. Then he started playing few chords.

"You still know how to play 'Rhythm of the Falling Rain'?" asked Keith.

"I suppose I do. Why?"

"It reminds of the girl I used to go around with for a while until she left. Why? She didn't say. Maybe she didn't like the school."

"How was she?" Broneco asked another question, still playing chords, touching here and there.

"She had a blond hair, sort of red-headed," said Keith, and continue talking.

Broneco went on playing various tones of music, keeping up with the rhythms of what Keith was saying. Then Keith finished.

"I used to love a girl and now she's gone with the wind," said Broneco. Suddenly he touched the keys with a roaring sound of attention, then with a rolling sound. He blinked his eyes and started

194

singing. The music echo in the atmosphere of the room. Broneco stared out the window, pressing another rolling sound into a tingling rhythms of raining pattern of vibrations.

Watching the birds singing up in the trees, singing their best melody of their creative scale of music, Broneco played an introduction to "After Graduation." Broneco raised his voice a little with sound of the piano. Once again he reminded himself of the day he used to listened to Johnnie play his special music, also sitting by the window.

Broneco reached into his shirt pocket and took a paper neatly folded out on the piano book holder. Keith sat up and joined Broneco at the piano.

It was after graduation all the odd things were happening to Broneco. Ending his song, "After Graduation" he kept repeating it as it decrease slowly. Then he stop. He blinked his eyes again as he always did.

"Well, I guess I better be on my way heading west to return again to the land of my ancestors," he said, standing up. Then he smile. "Good-bye, I'll see you Sunday."

Shortly after, Broneco, wearing his dark spectacle, walked out of the dormitory. "Here I go, returning from my mission of one and half years of doing my duty," he said. Carrying in his right hand a small briefcase, and in the other hand, traveling suitcase. Broneco was going home for a few days. The birds flew about him. He walked down the sidewalk.

·XIX·

Stranger on the Hill

EARLY in the morning, three weeks after Broneco has gone back to Santa Fe to work there for the four more weeks, Annie was in the kitchen back home. With a pencil in her hand, she skim through the numbers on the calendar months.

"Only a few more days and my brother Broneco is going to be back for the summer vacation," she said, speaking to herself.

When it was only a week away for Broneco to return, Annie went about her cooking, looking through recipe. She added a little bite of ginger to her ingredients, making a pumpkin pie. In her left hand, she held a cookbook. When she looked at the clock that hung on the wall, "Not time for lunch yet," she thought.

Annie finished her pie. Carefully she slid it into the hot oven. She decided that she would stroll outside in the flower bed. Sniffing and wrinkling her nose, she went outdoor. Walking in the yard, she was kicking loose sand off the side of the mud bricks which was built for holding the ponds of water after a heavy rainfall once in awhile. Sometimes, when it get so hot in the summer, it would rain. The water would run in the small handmade canal into the pond.

The sun was getting hot in the morning. Annie started watering the small plant. On the side of the house, on the north side, there were group of morning glory climbing higher and higher up the wall. Annie usually water the glory every morning. About a few yards away from the main entrance to the kitchen, there a yucca plant, sending up the long stem up so high. The fresh fruit hanging like a banana was riping early in the month of June.

Annie went to the pointing yucca plant and took one fruit off of it. Biting the piece of it, the taste of it's in comparison in sweetness to a golden banana. Her saliva in tingling taste flew [flowed] beneath her tongue to flavor. Then Annie, rounding the corner of the house, she glance toward the hill and spotted an object, but she didn't care [think] much about it. She went on sprinkling water on every other plant. Then she thought about it for another minute. She decided to look. Skeptically, she faced the hill and saw someone on the hill.

Throwing small rocks, aiming it down the hill. The stranger walked around, picking up rocks. Annie was awe-struck, seeing someone on the hill. Since it was distance away, she couldn't tell who it could be.

"I'll get my mother's binocular and see who it is," she thought. Annie was now getting clever.

She haste into the bedroom and took the binocular off the book shelf. Anxiously wanting to know who it was, Annie looked at the hill and saw no one on the hill.

"It can't be. It can't be," she said to herself.

Decided to go up the hill, but she wasn't too sure whether it's some friendly stranger upon the hill. Annie made up her mind several times to go up the hill, but she refused. She forgot all about the pumpkin pie in the oven, when she scented the smell of the burning pie. She rushed into the kitchen.

Nervously she grabbed the pot holder and took the pie out of the oven. The pie was baked right. She kept glancing out the window. Now she was curious about the stranger on the hill. When there was a knock at the door, Annie dropped the knife to the floor. Sweating a little, thinking about the stranger on the hill, she said, "Come in, whoever you are."

The door opened. Slowly it swinging open wide.

Annie was about to faint when her mother came in. "Oh my, I smell something very delicious from the kitchen. Or is it something else that I smell?" she said, carrying her bundle of wool ready to be spinned into strings of yarns.

Annie picked up the knife from off the floor and placed it back on the table. She cut the pie with her hands shaking.

Auntie saw that Annie was very nervous. She asked another question. "Annie, is there anything wrong?"

"No, mother. I was just thinking."

"Thinking about what?"

"Mother, I saw a stranger on the hill today. Did you see it, by any chance?"

Auntie layed her bundle of wool on the side of the table and took her scarf off. "No, my child, not at all."

"Well! I just saw someone on the hill. I was going to see who it was, came into the bedroom and picked up the two-eye-pieced binocular. And when I rushed out the door and looked again, I saw that no one there. I only saw the usual everyday crows, flying around up in the air," said Annie, telling her story of what she had seen.

"Maybe it was the crows you saw and thought that they were boys," Auntie said, laughing, nibbling on her piece of pumpkin.

"No, mother, really I saw someone."

"Are you sure?"

"Yes."

"Maybe it was one of your boy friend that you went to dance with last night."

"No, it can't be Parrie."

"How do you know?"

" 'Cause he told me that he won't be seeing me until my brother, Broneco, comes home a week from now."

"Let's eat now and not talk anymore about this foolishness," said Annie's mother.

Annie smile and served her mother a roast leg of a mutton. With a brown gravy, mashed potato, and for the vegetable, she served her golden corn. Annie then seated herself to eat with her mother.

"When did you say Broneco was coming home?" asked Auntie.

"Next week."

"That means we have to wait for him in Farmington to pick him up. I suppose he has a lot of luggages to haul as he always does."

Annie chewing a piece of cut-off square mutton, she said, "I don't think Broneco needs us this time."

"Why?"

"He wrote me a letter the day before and told me about it," said Annie.

"You never told me about it."

"I just forgot to tell you."

"Pass me another piece of that pie," Auntie said.

Annie, simpering, beginning to smile, passed the pumpkin pie. The pie was baked neatly brown with bites of brown sugar on it. Most of the time this school vacation Annie would do the cooking at home while her mother looks after the sheep. Either she would go shopping in town for that day, still Annie would stay home and tend to chores of looking after the sheep and housework.

Another week passed, Annie sat outside the house and decided to glance at the hill when she saw someone on the hill as of the last time. She stared and wondered. "Could it be that someone I know, or is someone roaming the hills for a walk?" she asked herself these question in her mind.

Patiently Annie waited for the stranger to walk off the hill. Again throwing small rock down the hill in every directions. "I can't believe it," she whisper. She slowly walked into the house and pick up her mother's binocular, just as she had done before.

When Annie stood outside, she saw no one on the hill. She decided to go up the hill, yet somehow she refuse again. "Who could it be?" she asked herself. "Parrie? No, it can't be."

Annie strolled through her flower bed, carrying the binocular in her hands, swinging it by the long leather strap. "Broneco is coming home tomorrow, if I'm correct about it. When he comes home, I'll tell him what I saw on the hill. I'll tell him all about it, and he would believe me. My mother doesn't believe me, and if Broneco doesn't believe me, this time I'll go up the hill and speak to the person or whatever he is," she thought, feeling discourage, thinking about the stranger on the hill.

Annie went back into the house and setted the table, placing a plate of fried chicken which she just kill this morning. Expecting her mother any matter of minutes now, she seated herself at the table, when there was a knock at the door.

Doubtedly, Annie said, "Come in."

The door swinged open. The bundle of wool tumbled into the bedroom. Annie got out of her chair and walked to the doorway and saw her mother, sitting under the tree.

"What's the matter, Mom?"

Nothing much, my child. It's that I have walked in the hot sun."

"What about the hot sun?"

"Give me cold glass of water and then we'll talk about it," she said.

Annie walked back into the kitchen and dipped a cold water out of the water cooler. She walked back into the bedroom and then outside. She gave the dipper full of cold water to her mother and seated herself on the small bench.

Annie's mother drinked the cold water. "I been stuck in the mud, trying to pull one of the lamb out of the mud today. I guess I was too heavy. I kept sunking lower and lower until I grabbed ahold of my own dog, Blacky, and pulled me out. I don't know what I could have done without Blacky," she said, smiling.

"You shouldn't go after the sheep alone. From now on, I'll go with you after the sheep. Until Broneco comes home, he'll help us then."

"How many more days is he coming home?"

"It'll be tomorrow," said Annie, counting her fingers.

Sitting under the tree, it was cooler than inside the house. Annie went back into the kitchen and brought the serving plate and other necessary dishes outside and set a small coffee table under the tree. Annie and her mother ate their lunch under the tree.

Annie told her mother about the stranger on the hill again. This time, she didn't make any objections. She asked Annie if someone she knew could come and wait on the hill, but Annie's answer was, "No."

The next day, Annie and her mother went herding sheep five miles away from home. The grass was glimmering. The sheep scattered far apart from distance. Annie's mother sat there underneath a small greasewood brush, growing its richful green ripples of leaves. Resting, she spinning her yarns of wool strings.

Farther up, canals made from the rushing streams after a heavy rainfall. Annie played, jumping across the deep, narrow canal.

Soon it was time to gather and round up the sheep. Annie and Mother headed back for home. When it gets so hot, the sheep would head for the corral also.

Annie and her mother were approaching home, the dust of cloud showed in the air from behind the hill. It was from direction where they were coming from.

"Must be the sheep heading this way, too," said her mother.

Just then, Annie heard a sound from the wash. "There must be a car coming across the wash to our way," said Annie excitedly.

"Must be some visitors."

"Not while wearing our dirty clothes like this!" said Annie, standing there behind her mother.

"Let's race for the house before the car comes across the wash," suggested her mother.

"Well, come on," said Annie, grabbing her mother by the arm.

Annie and her mother raced for the house. Before they reached the corral, the automobile appear in the open. Annie was so excited that they ran into each other, entering the fence.

"Oh, my blouse is torn on the side," cried Annie.

"I'm stuck to this fence. I need your help," said Annie's mother, trying to loose herself.

The car was now approaching. With a tearing sound, they kept pulling on her dress. Annie, too, getting her shoe loose.

"How in the world did my feet ever get stuck into this fence?"

"Because you runned into it, trying to get ahead of me, when your feet got caught in between those two woods," said her mother, pulling her dress away from the fence to loosen it up.

The car stopped right by them.

"Help!" said Annie, remembering that her blouse was torn on the side.

"What are you two up to now?" said unidentified voice.

"It's all our fault," said Auntie, whispering.

Annie glance to where the car was parked and saw Broneco laughing.

"Broneco! Come and help us get ourselves off this fence," said Annie, giggling.

"What's all this about, Annie?"

"It's Broneco. He's coming to get us loose," said Annie, speaking to her mother.

Now, they were loose from the fence. Annie picked up her shoe.

"Tell me, what were you two trying to prove, or is it some kind of a game you two playing?" asked Broneco, still laughing, then adding, "That's what you two get, trying to hid from me before I get home."

"That wasn't our plan at all," said Annie.

"Yes sir, not at all," said Auntie, laughing now.

"We were just trying to get back into the house before you got here. We thought you were some visitors coming to see us. So we raced for the house and we automatically got stuck here to this fence," said Annie.

"Well, I'm a visitor, ain't I?"

"Yes, and we are glad that you aren't a white visitor."

"Shall we go inside the house and talk about it?" said Broneco, now smiling.

Broneco and Annie followed Auntie into the house. Inside the house, Annie washed her face and set a big mixing bowl on the table.

"I had made my promises to make a pie today, and it is suppose to be special for today," she said.

Auntie put the coffee pot on the stove to heat up the cold coffee.

Broneco helped around with the dishes. It was nice to be home again. Broneco was happy and so was Auntie and Annie.

"Where's Moon?" asked Broneco, glancing out the window.

"He's probably sleeping in the tree, as usual," replied Annie.

"Does he still eat in the baby chair?"

"Once in awhile he does, yes," answered Auntie, making a flour into a roll of rubbery dough.

Annie was through mixing her ingredients into the bowl. Then into the oven she layed a two plate of pies. Annie's specialty was pumpkin pie.

An hour later, Broneco was hungry. The baking was done. Annie started setting her table with various size of plates, forks, spoon, and knives. They were ready to eat, when Annie mentioned the stranger she seen on the hill twice now.

While they eat, she told Broneco all that's happen since four weeks when she was baking that pumpkin pie and sees someone on the hill.

"When do you think you'll see the stranger on the hill again? If you see him again, I'll surely take him off my hill," said Broneco.

"That suits me fine," replied Annie, stirring her cup of instant grape drink. "But who do you think it is?"

"I really can't say."

Broneco kept thinking about the hill for the rest of the day. In the evening, Broneco and Annie sat by the doorway under the porch. Auntie joined Broneco, talking about the amazing hill.

Broneco, this time, try his best to explain something about the hill that his aunt didn't understand. "I know it's been a long time. This hill, it's mine and belongs to no one but me. At one time, I remember when I was only a small child we used to lived in a tent here. I didn't know what a water tower was until my grandfather told a little about it. Before that time, once my grandmother said the word "six." I didn't know what she was talking about until she counted her finger from one to six.

"The life was hard since I remembered. A girl I used to know that lived a mile away from our house, she never wore a slick, tight

203

slack. Until one day I saw her wearing a men's levi's pant. It was the first time I seen a girl or a woman wearing a men's clothing. As you can see now days, every girl, woman you see—they would be wearing pants of some sort, either tight or overdone with fats," said Broneco, explaining what he knew till this present day.

"Until I went up that hill, I saw the view of Shiprock. How glorifying it look to me! Beyond, river flowing with games of fishes. I went back to the tent and asked question about it. Sitting with my grandfather on the hill for whole hours, I saw you arriving on that black horse you used to own. I knew it was you because of the way you used to ride horses.

"Those days were wonderful and, for once again, I hope it will be wonderful like the old days, but this time it'll be the modern way. It'll shall be soon. Now I know what my grandfather meant when he said, 'Someday, my child, you'll come back here to the very place and find cheerfulness.' This was what he said to me and together we stroll off the hill," said Broneco, looking toward the hill.

Broneco entered his room, thinking about the hill. Still thinking about the hill, he put his head against the soft pink pillow. Covering himself with a light blanket for a comfortable sleep, Broneco fell asleep. While in the other bedroom, Annie and Auntie were snoring in their deep sleep.

The rooster crow in the morning, fluttering his wing, flew up on the tall corral post. Broneco opened his eyes and thought of the hill first thing in the morning. He jumped out of bed and went into the other bedroom and out the door. Rushed to the corral and stood there, looking at the hill in a distance, hearing the wind blowing upon the hill. He seen nothing on the hill. It seemed to glow a little, but not too bright.

Broneco walked around side the sheep corral. Looked once more toward the hill and said, "I'm not coming. It's too soon."

Broneco knew there is something about the hill, but he doesn't know what it was. He knew that he will find a cheerfulness there, but still didn't know what kind of happiness. It was hard to answer that question or to solve that problems. Reaching the gate to the corral, he smile and opened the gate and let the flock of sheep out for grazing.

Broneco ran back to the house, feeling excited about something. He entered his room and went back to sleep, covering himself again.

By now, Annie and her mother wake up and turned on the radio for the morning program. Listening to the radio every morning, usually they listen for the news. The speaker in the morning program was Mr. and Mrs. Blue Eyes, announcing in his tribal language, so that every Navaho in the surrounding area would listen. Since some of them didn't not speak English, they would rather listen to their accustom native language—listening to announcements, news, appetizing, and other commercials.

Annie and her mother in the kitchen started preparing breakfast. Annie's mother decided that she would go out and get pail of water for the used of hot water. Annie making a scramble eggs on the hot grill, Aunties came rushing in.

"The sheep, they are gone!" she shouted.

"They are gone?" said Annie, leaving the scramble eggs on the hot grill.

"No, wake up Broneco."

"Broneco, Broneco, Broneco!" said Annie, tripping over her own shoes in the bedroom. Walking on her knees, she reached the door handle and knocked on the door calling Broneco.

Broneco almost had the nightmare. "What, what?" said Broneco, jumping out of the bed as he just did an hour ago. "May I help you?" he said, opening the door patiently. Remembering, then he frown with his left eye barely opening from sleepiness.

"Broneco! The sheep are gone," said Annie, shouting harshly and worried.

"Gone? I see," said Broneco, scratching his head, yawning. "Gone," he said then, repeating the word, "Gone," walking into the kitchen.

In the kitchen, Auntie burned the eggs and put the cold water on the stove. "The sheep," she said, pacing back and forth, looks for her scarf.

"Excuse me a minute, and let me wash my face. Then I'll tell you all about the sheep," said Broneco, pouring a cold water into the washpan.

"Tell us about the sheep? What do you know about the sheep?" said Auntie, scrapping about the sheep.

"Just like my deceased grandmother! When are you two going to learn?" said Broneco, placing a towel around his neck.

"Broneco, better hurry."

"Be patient, will you?"

"I understand," said Annie. "Broneco let the sheep out early this morning."

"I guess I'm getting old," said Annie's mother, beginning to laugh.

Broneco was now through washing. Smiling, he put the towel up on the rack.

"Broneco, will you see about the sheep today?"

"Oh sure, I'll take my car out there and drive along the old road," said Broneco, speaking to his aunt.

Annie started serving Broneco.

"I have to go to the store and buy some more groceries today," said Auntie, chewing a hot biscuit in the morning.

"I'm staying home and rest for today," said Annie.

"You ought to go for a ride with your mother," said Broneco.

"No thanks, I'll stay. I needed rest."

"I guess I'll leave the car here. I'm not that lazy. I walk," said Broneco. "I need exercise in the open country instead of walking on the hard concrete walk all this time, wearing heels out."

"How does it feel to be in a big city?" asked Auntie.

"Just like being in Farmington, but you have to kept your eyes on the walk."

"Why?"

" 'Cause if you don't, you'll walk into somebody else that's oncoming down the street. The building are high, about sixteen times as this house we're sitting in. The towns are crowded with many nationality of peoples."

206

"I probably get lost. Even now, I'm about to walk right straight into the wall," she said.

Broneco only laughed and wiped his lip with a napkin. Auntie was through eating, while Annie taking her time fixing her breakfast very special.

Broneco went back into the room, changing his clean clothes into work clothes. He then took the rifle off the shelf and loaded it with shells.

Annie's mother was driving her pickup out of the fence when Broneco stepped outside and breathed the cool air. Broneco looked at the hill and saw the crows flying over the hill, fluttering their wings. "Are those the stranger on the hill?" thought Broneco smiling. Walked a little way and, picking up a small rock, then aiming at the post. He missed.

Walking on foot was wonderful. Broneco looking far into the distance land, seeing all kind of objects. Hills, plateau, and standing rocks. He came to the second long stretching, rolling hill and saw the sheep grazing. There the grass was plenty high and green, which makes the lambs fat. Broneco decided to rest here upon the hill and watch the sheep.

Annie, back home, decided to wash her clothes. She went out to get more water when she saw someone on the hill again. She stood there watching. This time, Annie wasn't afraid.

"I'll come and help you find what you looking for, stranger on the hill," said Annie, speaking to herself.

The stranger on the hill tossed a small rock down the hill in the direction of Annie.

"You just wait," said Annie. She looked, facing the hill. "This time you'll not escape my eye vision," she said, when her dress was caught by the wire. Annie was jerked back. She looked to see what caught her dress. The stranger walked off the hill in that matter of seconds. Annie released her dress and glance again when she saw nothing on the hill.

"I'll still come up the hill and see where you head to, even look for your tracks," said Annie when she remembered that the rolls

207

were in the oven. She went back into the kitchen to see if the rolls were done. She has forgotten all about going to the hill. This was her third time seeing the stranger on the hill.

The stranger was still unknown. Broneco couldn't guess who it could be either. Now, even Annie's mother was wondering about the hill. It aroused Broneco, Annie, and her mother. During the evening, they would talk about the hill, but still there was no answer. Even the dogs would bark, looking towards the hill during that evening.

Annie and her mother sat on the rocking chair, rocking themselves. Annie said, "What will it be on my fourth time, seeing the stranger on the hill?"

According to the custom, usually something would be expected on the fourth day. Things would happen four times, or when one sees a cotton-tail fox, no one is to wait even a day to hold a healing ceremony. Now, the talk was about the hill. Annie's mother talking about calling on a medicine man. To Broneco, it was unnecessary so he told his aunt to wait until two days later.

The moon rosed high now. Everythings was silent. Broneco waited out on the porch, watching the hill. The hill showing its brilliant shade of opaque outline in the fading twilight. Broneco kept thinking about the stranger.

"Who could it be?" he kept on asking himself. Still, the answer was mysterious. Half an hour later, Broneco stood by the door, taking his last glance at the hill before he went to bed. Then he entered the front bedroom and then into his own apartment. Squeezing his hands together, he layed in bed, looking up at the ceiling. The small wax candle glowing dimmer and dimmer every minute.

He covered himself with a light blanket. His eyes was getting narrow, then a little snores. Broneco went to sleep. The candle was still burning, as the wax ran down its side into the candle holder. The open window above Broneco's head, the air kept blowing through the screen, singing durations of ancient songs of the old ones. Suddenly the wind blew strongly, making the curtain ripple and flutter with an increasing sound. Broneco was deeply asleep, dreaming.

The candlelight went out as if someone has blown out the candle. The pile of papers on the dresser top scattered about in the room, made all kinds of furious imaginary nightmares. Then the lightning strike far in the north, roaring as if a ravenous beast loose out of its cage, dying away shortly, now it was calm. The reflection in the mirror flash upon Broneco's face. He now only part asleep that he notice all what was happening throughout the night.

It was early in the morning the gentle rain started falling. The cool air blew few drops of rain into the open window once in awhile. The cold drops of rain, dropping on Broneco's smiling face, made his cheek winked. The thunders roared in the misty white woolly clouds above. The grass in the prairie land, soaked heavy from the rainfall, begin to change their color. Since Broneco left to work in the month of June, there wasn't a single drop of rain. Yet, why on the day after Broneco return? It was obvious, though, that it was a miracle thing to happen unexpectedly.

On the top of the roof, the water started running into streams of rushing water. On the side of the house, the water started dripping into the rhythm of every second as though the clock in the kitchen is ticking. In the dug-out canal, out in the yard, water started rushing into the form of spiral glimmering streams. From the east, south, west, and the north, the rain water flowing down the open wide wash, carrying corrupted pieces of stick, tumbleweed, juniper from the far mountain. Making the roaring sounds of destructions, the muddy water ripple from every directions.

Now the rain was steady. Could even smell the freshness of the cool breezes of air in the early morning. The atmosphere in Broneco's room was damp. The pictures that hung on the wall started to wrinkle in curls. Then Broneco's cat, sitting before the door, knocking with his paw and calling, "Ann-e-e-o." But Annie sleeping comfortably nothing could interrupt her deep doze, and so was Auntie.

The cat, Moon, sat on the small porch, couldn't bear to sitting under this leaking roof, kept yawning and shivering from this cold drop of rain. Shaking himself every other minute, shaked the wet rain off himself didn't help. He was getting wetter and wetter. He licked his paw and jumped across the deep skimming puddles to find shelter where he can keep himself out of rain, since Broneco hasn't answer the door for the last thirty minutes.

Broneco was now in his light sleep, ready to wake up. The rooster didn't cock this morning. In spite of damp moisture, his wing was all wet even though he tried to flutter his wing with smooth waterproof feathers. But it still didn't kept the wet rain off. For the past few hours, since four o'clock, cocking rooster was in the heavy downfall of rain, he got a sore throat. He tried to cock, but the sound down in his throat cocked as if a speaker in the radio was torn in half.

The water dripping from the roof formed in between the window screens. It had stopped raining now. The wind started blowing again. Each time the wind blew against the window, the water that formed between the screen dropped heavily on Broneco's face. He was about to wake up now. It could be in any minute.

The hill was soaked with moisture from the rain. The hill began to change its gray side into a brilliant, verdant greenish. The grass has turned its color into a glorifying sight.

Broneco still in a gentle, rambling snores. The wind blew against the window in tremendous force. It made the cold dripping water splashed on Broneco's face.

Broneco wake up.

·XX·

Miracle Hill

B RONECO, still lying in bed early in the morning, begin to smile. Then he sat up in bed. Feeling weightless, he felt his chest, astonished, sensing that something has happen during the night. He looked at himself in the mirror and saw that his hair was more darker than he thought he had seemed the day before.

"I can't believe it. I just can't believe it," he thought, feeling his hair. Ghastly the room looked.

Looking out the window made a lot of difference. Broneco's eyes twinkled, blinking his eyes to clear the blurs, he listen to all kinds of sounds out there beyond the many rolling hills. The air smelled in the odor of freshness and of the cold rain that night. Hearing the ripples of the dripping rain water falling every seconds, dripping down from the roof. Broneco's mind was clear. He felt his head. It was cold.

The wind was blowing softly and gentle. The water forming between the window screen stopped. Broneco listened to the tiny drops of rain water falling outside. It made an unusual musical sound. Could hear the rooster flapping its wing, hens pecking insects, and pulling worms out of the moist area in the yard. Broneco looked at the dresser top and saw the papers scattered about in the room. The picture of Grandmother on the dresser look as though she was going to smile.

Broneco, still blinking his eyes, wondered about his Grand-

211

mother. All the things she used to talk about once—a better improvements on the old house, a separate rooms for each, and a new dining room with a large living room window.

These things ringed through Broneco's ears. Secondly, remembering Grandmother used to ride her gray donkey. The days were wonderful then. Those days were long in past for Broneco, herding sheep for a whole day, having all kinds of joyful games. He recalled his forgotten history of the past.

He looked out the window, staring far in the great distance. The mountains were hidden underneath the misty fogs. The sounding of the thunder. The flashing of the lightning, striking about the mountains. It looked as if somewhere in a swampy country. The fog covered the mountain tops.

Feeling much secure of rest, Broneco got out of bed and stretch his arms high into the empty atmosphere of the room, almost touching the ceiling above him. Then decided to pick up the scattered materials of papers which were all blown on the floor. He walked around in the room. After finishing and replacing items neatly back in its order properly, Broneco pick the picture off the dresser and held it close to his chest.

The cool blowing air made the curtains twisting and drifting gently. The sun was now peering over the East Mesa. Broneco placed the picture back upon the dresser and opened the door.

Without making any sort of a sound, he creep out. Standing out in the front of the main kitchen door, Broneco faced east. Walking farther away from the house he stood there. Reaching into his pocket he drew out a small bag. Untying it, he held it steady in his hand.

Waiting in that tedious hour for the wind to calm and stillness, he drew his small finger into the bag. There, a grains of yellowish, golden corn pollen he held to the East. Broneco stood facing the bright rays of the morning sun, sensed that the air was still now.

Looking among the heavy thick clouds gradually opening into the blue heaven of the universe, Bronceo stared at the opening of the dark clouds as though expecting an object to appear before him

212

in the opening. His eyes begin to glow in chills of tears. Broneco choked in whispers of speech:

Wondering of the yonder distance,
Thinking, When will I reach there?

The wind whispers in my ear,
I hear the songs of old ones.

My loneliness I wrap around me,
It is my striped blanket.

Sending out touching wishes,
To the world beyond hands' reach.

The bluebird that flies above,
Leads me to my friend, the white man.

At last, I know the all of me—
Out there, beyond, and here upon my hill.

"I'll come again, Miracle Hill," said Broneco as the pollen at the tip of his small finger descends.

Broneco turned clock-wisely, walked back to the entrance, then into the kitchen, passing on to the bedroom of his own.

Annie and Auntie were still giving off their soft buzzing snores.

Broneco opened the door to the south. Standing under the porch, he faced the hill in fear and expecting a miracle.

The glorifying hill was now covered with green grass. The gray-sided hill no longer showed. Broneco, winking his eyes, stared at the hill. He couldn't believe it. Looking toward the corral now, he could hear the different bells jingling and tinkling on the neck of the sheep.

Shaking themselves, the sprinkle of rain water dropped. The dogs sat before the gateway to the corral as though they were smiling.

Broneco walked through the puddles of water, then right on, passing the water. The permeating fruit odor on the yucca plant where were now ripen, as Broneco can see since they were falling off and the smell of it. Walking through the small garden bed, the

213

morning glory on the side of the wall. They also, were showing their respective colors of variations in blue, pink, and white.

Broneco could smell the sweetness of the circulating odor in the air. The wild flowers Annie used to water were blooming at last. Glancing here and there, it was amazing. Broneco, strolling about the house, kept seeing different things.

The sagebrush, neatly trimmed, has overgrown again, but this time it was showing its frisky seed pods in rough formation in groups. Interesting it looked as Broneco walked through the growing flowers and others blooming in decorative shades.

The sun was now high in the sky. Broneco looked to the south again. "I'll never forget my first white friend," he thought. "If Dale was still here in this community, I would shake his hands and thank him for what he once tried to teach me, sitting under the tree with him. But, those days are over. Now I must use white man's method to explore their dignity."

Just then, Broneco saw his cat, Moon, upon the heated side of the roof, all curl up. Moon was wet, as Broneco can see, since his soft furs was still shining in the sunlight, bristling.

"Moon, will you come down? Who do you think you are, sitting upon the roof?"

"A cat on the hot tin roof," said Annie, teasing her brother from the kitchen window as she was lighting up the stove.

Broneco furiously turned his head toward the roof, facing Moon who was now licking his paw, pointing south toward the hill. Broneco, for a moment, thought Moon was speaking.

"What did you say?" asked Broneco in fear.

"No, it was me, Broneco," said Annie from the kitchen window.

Broneco didn't smile, instead ignore Annie. Now she was fixing herself a breakfast, including Broneco's and her mother. The near tree in heavy coated leaves kept waving. Resting under the shade of the tree, Broneco stared at the hill.

The voice of the wind upon the hill seems to whisper. "Come, Little One, for you may find your happiness here upon me, the miracle hill. For I am the mother earth who rules nature. Come."

Then Broneco remembered, "I must tell my Aunt and Annie

about the dream I had last night before I forget." He went rushing into the kitchen.

Annie's mother was pouring herself a cup of fresh coffee. Broneco seated himself besides his aunt. Annie placed the prepared breakfast on the table and also seated herself besides Broneco.

Broneco pulled the shades aside and, glancing out, kept looking at the hill.

"I see the hill is covered with verdant green," Annie's mother said. "Water still rushing in the rivulet stream down the hill, yet they are slowing their speed. Out there beyond, I also see the land with fertile soil," she said. Then, turning around again, poured another cup of coffee.

"I got something to tell you this morning," said Broneco.

"What is it?" asked Auntie, anxiously to know.

"It's about the dream I had last night."

"What about the dream—bad, good, or bad?"

"It was a good dream."

"Then tell us about your wonderful dream," she said.

"I dreamed that I was walking toward the hill. Then I was upon the hill. I met a stranger. Facing away from me, he stood."

"Said anything at all?" Auntie asked.

"He didn't say anything. Just when he was turning around to face me, the dropping of the rain water from the window splashed on my face and wake me up. I didn't see who, or what he looked like," said Broneco, finishing his dream story.

Annie didn't say anything about the hill. She only went on eating her morning breakfast.

"Yes, it's a miracle, since everythings this morning seems to be different," said Auntie.

"You ought to look around out in the yard this morning. It look just beautiful and every flower that Annie watered for the last six week in this drying desert country are sprouting and blooming. Especially the morning glory on the side of the house," said Broneco.

Attached to their deep conversation, Broneco didn't know it

was getting late for the sheep to graze out in the open country as usual. When he remembered, he went out to the corral and opened the gate.

Walking through the corral, the sheep moved out into the open freedom. They scattered on the side of the sandy hills. As hungry as they are, they eat to their mouthful of greens to satisfy their appetite. They nibbled on the small gray greasewoods.

Broneco walked back to the house. Entering the gate, he looked at the hill again.

While out in the yard, Annie and her mother were picking off the fruit from the yucca plant. Carefully they picked the fruit off, making sure that the pointed needle will not puncture their hands.

Broneco crossed the small wooden bridge. The clear water in the dammed area glimmered during each blow of the air. The tree kept waving its heavy leafs. Moon was now climbing up the tree, using his sharp claws.

Broneco went back into the house. Entering his room, he picked up his summer shoes and a white shirt together with dark-colored slack. He changed his clothes in the room and combed his hair neatly.

"I'm going to the hill and sniff the great-spirit air," he thought. Taking up more of his time, he fixed his dark blue tie and walked into the bedroom. Glancing on the chest drawer, he decided to close the drawer. He saw his grandfather's picture in the unfolded photo album. Broneco held it in his hand and smiled.

"I'm going to the hill where once you told me that I will find cheerfulness there on the hill. I remember the cheerfulness you talked of. I remember," he said, placing the picture back in the chest drawer, then closing it afterward.

Standing under the porch, giving a little stretch and a deep breath of fresh air, he walked across the small wooden bridge. Reaching the post, Broneco lean on it.

Standing there, Broneco begin to think of his youthful days again. The land was wide then, now the days for Broneco were short. For many ways, Broneco wanted to spend his time at home with his family. Now, was it the time to stay with the family?

216

Thinking back in the month of December, during the winter of nineteen hundred and sixty-three, Broneco recalled the day he stood before his grandmother, for the last time, speaking to her. It brought deep sorrows which formed tears in Broneco's eyes. Blinking his eyes, the drop of tears dried within his eyes.

Watching the corral over the south side of the hill, Broneco could smell the drying scent of odor in the corral and its surrounding. Sniffing and wrinkling his nose, he glance about the area, searching with his eyes.

Broneco kept recalling the past and its history. "The world out there and beyond the hands' reach . . . " Broneco thought about it again.

These objects in the distance used to make Broneco wondered. The yonder hill made Broneco think more and more about the civilization where there was cheerfulness, where there was lot of interesting things—the city, the school, the piano, the writing on his manuelscripts. Broneco held onto the post quietly.

The post was cold from the night's rain. Still covered with twinkling bubbles of water. Feeling the post, Broneco could feel the texture of morning dews. Along the side of the twenty-gallon barrel, there were moss of green color, the water dripping down into the pan below. Then Broneco look over to the horse corral where Grandmother's donkey used to scratch himself against the rusty post.

Broneco could still picture the sacrificed gray donkey during the death of his Grandmother. The stable still full of dry hay made Broneco lonely.

Ever since the gate was close, only the big glossy dark blue rooster flies upon the gate when the light begin to show. There he would flutter his wing and cock early in the morning, but this morning he didn't cock because of the heavy rain that night.

Broneco smiled a little when he saw the rooster walking across the open area in the yard. He looked weary, stretching his wing high, trying to flutter the dews of his wet wing.

The bells on the few sheep kept jingling within the gray grease-

217

woods. The dogs wrestling among the moisted sandy hill, crawling and barking. Broneco glanced back to the hill.

The wind was quiet, except once in awhile, the cool blowing air blew wildly. The sun was now high up in the blue heaven. Far to the west, the clouds started moving toward the north. They looked as though a giant sheep grazing in the meadow, nibbling on prairie grass, moving slowly to another grazing country. Broneco's eyes dimmed, looking about.

Along the side of the fence, the tumbleweeds stack—the most enemy of many human beings who lives on the prairie—pointing their needles outward, turning their gray long-stretching arms into the greenish shades. Then, hearing the birds tweeting in the trees, seems to brighten up the day. Broneco grinned and faced the trees, wondering what kind of birds were up in the tree, singing their harmonized music that he never heard before. He like the sound of the birds singing in the treetops.

Just then, Annie and Auntie came around the corner of the house on the east side. In their hands, carrying shovel. Digging fresh dirt onto a new position to hold the rain water for a longer lasting to keep the trees soaked with plenty of water for at least a few more days. Making a new dam, they worked together.

Broneco still holding the cold post, feeling the texture of the post again, gently rubbing it with his fingers. His cat, Moon, came across the wooden bridge, welcoming him. Rolling himself at the edge of Broneco's feet, he played.

"Go play with Annie, Moon," said Broneco, speaking to his cat.

But Moon didn't listen to Broneco. He went rolling himself, scratching Broneco's feet.

Broneco looked to where once the family sat together, eating early in the morning, talking together. What he sees there is only the wash away fireplace. Farther he looked into the distance. He saw the two rolling hills, and the wide wash area. Now he remembered once racing along the side of that particular wash. Riding his horse, Pinto, which he owned once. Broneco picture himself receiving the necklace on his Grandmother's birthday.

Then, recalling the day he first killed a gray fox, when he used to carry his bow which he no longer carry in the year of nineteen hundred and sixty-four. He rested his head against the post. Thinking of the past wasn't a happy feeling. Those days were wonderful, but those days happened in the past. The time was now nine-thirty. The sun was high off from the East Mesa.

Broneco shutted his eyes, listen to the sounds around the house. The sounds became present from the past, but it made no difference. It was present. Barking of the dogs far over the hills kept reminding him of the day he was getting ready to go to school. He had almost forgotten his mother, Emma, since he never seen her for a long time now. He kept thinking about all the things that happened in the past. He felt tears and sorrow inside his heart.

But then he thought, "Why should I think of the past which exist no more?" He straighten up. "This should be the day I feel stronger and happy about all the things that had renewed by the heavy rain last night. I should be happy and thankful for the rain. It brought the nature's cheerfulness to all the plain that was starving from the hunger for thirst. Even the surrounding things are cheering up, full of pride. Then, why shouldn't I be happy?"

Broneco lifted his head and looked toward the hill—the hill in the distance as if someone was going to appear at the top. He stared away from the hill, still holding onto the cold post. He whispered, "It's been a long time since I've seen Johnnie. I wish I could see him again, just to greet him with the word of welcome. I wondered whereabouts is he."

Broneco squeeze his hands together against the roughness of the post. Now his mind seems to clear.

"The dream last night. I wonder if it's true?" he asked himself several times. "I wonder if it is someone living or is he just another dream spirit," thought again Broneco, standing straight and looking at the hill.

Annie and Auntie were now worried about Broneco been standing out there for the whole hour. Annie and Auntie went back inside the house and sat by the window, waiting for Broneco to come inside the house.

Auntie decided to go outside to see if anything was wrong with

Broneco, so she did. "Come, my child, come inside the house and have a cup of coffee. Might feel better then," she said.

Broneco reached for his aunt's hand and said, "One minute."

"Is there something wrong?" she asked curiously.

"No, Auntie, I was just thinking."

"Thinking?"

"Yes," said Broneco.

Then she smiles and crossed the small wooden bridge. Quietly close the door behind her and entered the kitchen.

Broneco waited. Sometimes he had a strange attitude and difficult to understand. Again, he was strange, but he seems to smile. He would never show a single otherwise.

Waiting another few minutes, Broneco wondered why he was known as a "mystery boy," and the other, "the unknown boy," then there was another one by the name of "Little One."

Recalling his given name from distance relatives, Broneco almost giggled. Even in the heart of civilize American people, he played joke with other people. He did play his part of being a mystery boy to his people, yet his white friend were too smart to play with.

He started to walk, passing the garden, leaving his tracks in the moist wet earth. Walking a little ways, he stopped and reached down to the ground and dipped the fertile soil into the palm of his hand. Cupping a handful of soil, he kept rubbing it together, feeling the moisture of the dirt.

He looked toward the hill and walked on in a shuffle, shifting the dirt in his hand. Engaged to the hill, his memories kept recollecting in dreams of flowing fog mist. Picturing the forgotten history, again the distance remind him of the day he sat with his grandfather, many years ago. When Broneco was five, he used to think that the world was small. He remembered since he was four.

Slowly he walked, approaching the first rising hill. He stopped to caught his breath. Stepping on, he stroll, crossing the second low flat stretching hill, he begin to fear and, startled, glancing at the hill.

Come to the third rolling hill. Broneco's frightening fear deformed in his nerve. Although the chills of fever left his body, he kept refusing to reach his fourth hill. Squeezing the displaced tangled fingers against the other, his nerves were now alert and aware. Forgetting about the existing world and the gifts it contained, Broneco was now whispering the word, "Miracle Hill."

He stood at the foot of the high slanting hill. The fear was now gone. Again, the wind began to whisper through the stunted and rusty arid brush. Whishing of the cool summer air blew upon Broneco, waked him out of his numbness into a pleasant alertness. He glanced beyond.

There, the stranger stood, faced away from Broneco!

Broneco, thinking it must be the blurrness, doubted the object. He rubbed, blinked, and winked his eyes. The object was still there.

Broneco, curiously, glanced to the left of him, remembering the magic tea growing there once. It was an unbelievable sight, the tea was there. Showing its glorifying tiny yellow berries in the form of bells, struck immediate attention in Broneco's eyes on the side of the hill. Waving in the stiff formation, it vibrated in silent still.

Broneco tried to speak, but the word couldn't come out. The stranger seems to smile as Broneco bowed his head down, looking at his feet, thinking, "What in the world is happening to me? Am I fainting to die?" He whisper the words clearly, at last.

"No, brother, it's me," he heard.

"For heaven sake! God of All Mighty, help me," said Broneco, thinking he was dying as the earth bounds to whirl in a spin. He thought this was the end of his life.

He glanced toward the house and saw that, in the north, the clouds of fog like cotton still remain. The rainbow showing its four different colors in red, blue, yellow, and dark purple. Though it was far in the great distance, the rainbow seems to be nearer. Then sees the sheep, grazing along the sandy hill, nibbling on the green prairie grass. The grass waving and glimmering, as Broneco never before has seen the old place looked so in tiding of green.

221

Broneco bited his lip and faced the stranger again. He looked straight at the stranger's face and spoke. "Is this the end of my days?"

The stranger only smiled as of before, and then answered, "No. it is only the beginning."

And then the stranger was the great rock, standing in the far distance among the dark southwestern mountain about fourteen miles away. Showing its terrifying sight, it stood high and great. Although it stood far away in the great distance, it looked as though it was nearby, just behind the horizontal hill. In the foggy white mist, it showed its unforgettable memories, since Broneco's time of birth. It looked like a ship caught in a waving sea of rolling tide, during a heavy hurricane storm for an endless hours.

Broneco, blinking his eyes, watched the great standing rock, remembering again of his youthful days. "I used to think of that distance standing rock when I was young and away from the civilization. I guess I was still untame, living among the nature's gift and half wild yet."

When he was five and a months old, he used to think and wonder of the far standing rock in the shade of heavy ash color, intercepting the clear horizontal prairie. Isolated and alone it stood, yet known to all its surrounding. "Yes, I was young then," he thought.

He transposed his eye vision into a distance where he couldn't see no farther. Going beyond this point, Broneco, curious of his yonder mountain, then thought, "If I ever reach that far mountain, there will be another mountain."

Now, on this hill, Broneco knew that he must be going on to explored something more valuable than the first. Coming to the top of this small ordinary gray and sun-baking arid desert hill of his traditional life, Broneco was now amazed. It was there— another mountain.

"At last, I know a little, I have accomplished, and achieve the knowledge and wisdom of my distance friends. Ever I shall use their tongue to understand and to communicate, exchange gifts. for their tongue is the barrier of destruction to my people. Now,

I have learn their signs and ways of living, I can see another mountain."

Now, Broneco turned, leaving his footprints on the Miracle Hill. The wind blew for once again, blowing, singing the ancient songs.

The birds in the near treetop of the yard sang their best melody of music. Broneco left the hill thinking, "It's been a lonely years. Miracle Hill, in the glory of hope, I thank thee. I will always return and share the nature's airy freedom upon you."

Leaving the hill behind in a far distance, showing its merry sight. No longer after, Broneco ever would be lonely. Till this present day, the wind still whispers, singing the songs of the old ones. This is the Miracle Hill, and Broneco walks on, learning about the world beyond hands' reach.

Index

Academic building: 165, 183–84, 186
Adobe: 165, 193
Agency: 150, 153
Alfalfa: 149, 153
Alfred (Broneco's schoolmate): 194
Allen, Don B.: 186
Allen, Terry D.: 164 ff., 186, 191
American Indian: *viii*
American people: 220
Amy: 11 ff.
Amy's father (Broneco's grandfather): 10
Amy's husband (brother of Broneco's father): 10
Ancestors: 26, 195
Annie: 10 ff.
Apache Indian: 160
Applications: 150
Arizona, state of: 3
Arrow: 33; *see also* bow and arrow
Arrow, evil (taboo): 29
Art: 128, 151
Arts department (Institute of American Indian Arts): 163
Aspirin: 99
Ass: 33
Assignment: *ix*, 150, 167–68
Atlantic Ocean: *x*
Attendant (dormitory): 140, 177
Aunt Amy (Broneco's mother's sister, also wife of his father's brother): 10 ff.
Aunt (Aunt Amy): 9 ff.
Auntie (Aunt Amy): 44 ff.
Aunt Nonebah (hypothetical): *xv*
Autobiography: *ix*
Avery Hotel: 118
AWOL: 88

Ballet: 166

Band: 103 ff., 121–22
Bar lounge: 92
Barney (nickname, Emerson Blackhorse Mitchell): *vii* ff.
Basketball: 37
Battery radio: 119
Broneco: 11 ff.
Beads: 163
Beans (Mexican): 192
Bear Dance (Ute): 59 ff.
Bears (Three Little): 58–59
Beauty-Way chant: 147
Beginners' class: 54
Beginning: 222
Benally, Johnnie: 54, 85 ff.
Bernalillo, New Mexico: 154
Bernie (Broneco's girl friend): 103 ff., 113 ff., 124; *see also* shared love
Bernita (Broneco's girl friend): 122 ff.
Berry pudding: 30
Binocular: 197 ff.
Birthday: 3–4, 31, 66, 68, 72, 82, 84, 87, 106, 218; *see also* March 3, 1945; necklace
Black beans: 192
Black stallion: 24
Blacky: Amy's horse's name, 30; dog's name, 68, 200
Bleeding: 19
Blessing: 44
Bluebird: 213
Blue Eyes, Mr. and Mrs.: 205
Boss: 169
Bottle: 92
Bow: 219
Bow and arrow: 4, 7, 12 ff., 21, 27; Annie taught to shoot, 28 ff.
Boy friend: 198

225

Bread: 8, 30, 40, 46, 60, 96, 128, 141
Bread (nickname for Annie): 141
Bridge (at Gallup, New Mexico): 128
Brief case: 151–52, 195
Broneco (narrator of story): ix ff.
Bronka (Grandfather's mare, mother of Pinto): 26ff.
Brother, blood: 169; see also Ronnie
Brown, Mrs. (dormitory clothing room attendant): 99
Brush made of grass weed: 22
Bucket: 6–7, 39, 88
Bus: 78, 113ff., 153ff., 171, 177, 188
Business college: 114
Butane: 109–10, 119, 125

Cafe: 90, 105
California, state of: 114
Cameras: 48
Campus: 158, 161–62, 168, 183, 185–86, 192
Cap and gown: 184, 186
Cat (Broneco's): 14, 34–35, 209, 214; see also Moon
Catholic Center: 95
Cavalcade: 69
Cedar trees: 26ff.
Ceramic: 163
Ceremonial dance: 15
Ceremony: 208
Chair: 141, 189
Chapter House (Chinle, Arizona): 131 ff.
"Chili crackers": 128
Chinle, Arizona: 124, 127ff., 132
Christmas: 199ff., 124–25, 169ff., 184–85
Christmas tree: 113, 116, 119
Church: 90
Clock: 85, 102, 109, 119, 162, 209
Clockwise: 17, 50, 84, 112, 159, 213; see also Navaho Indians, customs
Clothes: 7, 16, 38ff., 44, 46, 49, 56, 72, 79, 84, 87, 97, 112, 131, 140, 183, 188, 201, 207
Cockleburs: 181
Coffee: 8, 27, 34ff., 45–46, 95–96, 110, 112, 143–44, 147, 153, 169, 202, 215, 220
Colorado, state of: x, 3, 48, 94, 179
Colt: 11, 23ff.
College: 114, 158
Commencement exercise: 183–84
Cook, Mrs. Carmen: 169
Corn pollen: 44, 212
Corral: 3, 14, 18, 21–22, 30ff., 45, 66, 68, 79, 96, 143, 153, 172, 187, 201ff., 213ff.
Cousin: 10, 13, 19, 28, 30, 128, 186
Creative writing: viii–ix, 164–65
Cricket-nose (He-who-has-the): 56

Crows: 7, 29, 198, 207
Cup, grandfather's white: 110–11, 144–45
Cupie Dollie: 142
Curley, Dale: 17ff., 37; see Dale (Curley)

Dale (Curley): 17ff., 37, 47, 214
Dance: 60–61, 92, 95, 101ff., 120ff., 166ff., 198
Danny (Broneco's schoolmate): 92–93
Daughter: 10, 41–42
Daydreaming: 98, 166
Delores, Colorado: 98
Death: grandfather's, 77; grandmother's, 178–79
Delores (friend of Ronnie): 122–23, 129ff.
Depot: 113, 155, 157, 188
Desert: 148, 215
Dining room: 51, 57–58, 83, 139, 161, 212
Diploma: 91, 186–87
Distance: 3ff., 29, 45, 68–69, 96, 143, 177, 197, 207, 213, 218, 221ff.
Diurnal: xiii, 41
Dogs: 4, 8–9, 19, 30, 41, 66, 68, 76, 96, 117, 138, 152, 200, 208, 218–19
Donkey: 26, 56, 143, 153, 172, 174, 185, 212, 217; see also Tellie
Dormitory: 49, 52, 55, 62, 73, 78, 88, 90, 93, 98, 138ff., 158, 163, 166, 171, 186, 193, 195
Dough: 6, 41, 75–76, 203
Dream: 60, 97, 137, 142, 145ff., 164, 167, 187, 215, 219
Dreaming: 110, 170, 181, 209
Dream spirit: 219
Drink: 130
Drinking: 136, 191
Drunk: 93, 130
Durango, Colorado: 110, 113, 116

Easter: 173
East Mesa: 212, 219
Edd (Broneco's roommate): 168ff., 182–83
Emergency: 176
Emma (Broneco's mother): 9, 41–42, 171, 178ff., 186, 219
Enchanters, the: 129
English: viii–ix, xii, xv–xvi, 5, 7, 18, 46–47, 49, 55, 61–62, 74–75, 101, 181, 205
Ernest: (Broneco's friend) 177; (Delores' brother) 124
Ervin (friend of Ronnie's): 123, 148ff.
Eve (Annie's friend): 139
Eye glass: 152, 156, 166, 192

Fairchild Company (Shiprock, New Mexico): 143

Family: 42, 45, 146, 171, 179, 181, 216, 218
Farmington, New Mexico: 47, 109, 112, 116ff., 153, 155, 177, 199, 206
Farmington Clinic: 154
Farmington High: 115
Father: 9ff., 41, 149
Father of light (the sun): 44
Feather: 6, 61, 210
Flocks of sheep: 24; *see also* sheep herding
Footprints: 223
Ford: 127; *see also* "Night Train"
Fork: 58
Four: 3, 167, 221; *see also* Navaho Indians, beliefs
Fox: 13ff., 208, 218
Four Corners Area (where four states meet): *x*, 3, 159
Fourth: 208, 221; *see also* Navaho Indians, beliefs, customs
Frankie (Rusty's girl): 122, 131–32
Friend: 55, 62, 75, 82, 90–91, 94, 98, 166, 176, 186, 189, 196, 213–14, 220
Friendship: 83, 92
Freedom: *xv*, 223
Future: 76, 91, 167

Gala, Mrs. (dormitory supervisor): 170, 175
Gallup, New Mexico: 113, 127–28
Gift: 69, 82, 111, 113, 115, 119, 221–22
Girl friend: 77, 139
Gladys (Broneco's cousin): 184, 186
Glasses, dark: 155; *see also* eye glass, spectacles
Goat: *xi*, 3, 21, 46
Goatskin: 5, 31
God: 151, 221
Gooney bird: 39
Graduation: 91, 173, 180ff., 184–85, 187, 189–90, 195ff.
Grammar: *vii*, *xi*
Granddaughter: 42
Grandfather: 3ff., 26–27, 29–30, 34, 36, 38ff., 48, 57, 74, 77–78, 110, 177, 203, 204, 216, 220
Grandmother: *xii–xiii*, 3, 5–6, 8–9, 11, 19, 21–22, 25–26, 28, 30, 33ff., 39, 42–43, 45ff., 53, 56–57, 66, 68, 70, 74ff., 95, 97, 109ff., 118, 125, 135–36, 143, 145–46, 152ff., 170–71, 177, 178ff., 184–85, 187, 203, 206, 211–12, 216–17, 218
"Gray dog": 110
Grave: 180
Greasewood: 216–17
Great-spirit air: 216
Great standing rock: 222

Green light: 115, 117
Greyhound: 155
Guidance Director's secretary: 169
Guitar: 123, 127, 129, 140

Haircut: 18, 27, 37–38
Hand's reach (the world beyond): 213, 223
Headband: 6, 27, 69
Highway Department (Santa Fe, New Mexico): 158
Hill (The): 9–10, 44, 72, 78, 142ff., 147–48, 151ff., 181, 187, 197ff., 204, 212, 213, 220–21
Hogan: 3, 6, 27, 30–31
Home: 13ff.
Horse: 5ff.
Horseback: 9, 24, 69
Horseman: 12–13
Horse race: 75
Hospital: 177ff.
Hotel: 187
Hound dog: 193
Husband: 49, 56

Ice cream (Navaho corn): 30, 120
Ignacio, Colorado: *xii*, 97, 145, 150, 153
Indian: *xii–xiii*, 14, 27, 76, 100, 128, 156–57; *see also* American Indian; Apache Indian
Indian Community Center (Gallup): 128
Indian school (Institute of American Indian Arts): 139
Inscrutable: *xiii*, 41, 189
Institute of American Indian Arts: 150, 156, 161, 183
Intermountain Indian School (Brigham City, Utah): 86

Jazz: 92
Jewelry: 138, 163–64
Joe (Virgel's brother): 56
John (Broneco's uncle): 38–39, 41ff., 49, 74; *see also* Uncle John
Johnnie (Broneco's schoolmate): 28, 97ff., 113, 118, 137–38, 153, 173–74, 179, 182, 195, 219
Joker (Annie's nickname for Mr. Veldez): 141
Jones, Mr. (dormitory supervisor): 158–59, 194
Junior High gym (Chinle, Arizona): 129
Junior High School (Ignacio, Colorado): 101, 141

Karl's Shoe Store: 118
Keith (Broneco's schoolmate): 176, 189, 193–94

227

Kin terms (in Navaho culture): *xvii*
Kissing: (Bernie) 107; (aunt) 188

Lamb: 3, 7, 14, 21, 45, 66, 200, 207; pet, 4, 44–45, 181
Land of Enchantment: 3
LaPlata Mountain in Colorado: 125, 142
Lazy-man's chair: 141, 189
Leather: 12, 187, 199
Legends: 76
Letter: 77–78, 154, 166
Little One: 4ff., 9–10, 16, 46, 214, 220
Little White Horse: 15
Loneliness: 51, 78, 179, 213
Lonely: 51, 92, 141, 223
Loom: 3, 10, 37, 163
Lost: 44, 51
Luggage or luggages: 49–50, 140, 154, 157ff., 199

Makeup: 115, 139, 156
Manuel script (for manuscript): *xi*, 168, 191, 217
Mare: 23, 33ff.
Martin, Mrs. (dormitory supervisor): 49–50
Masked head: 160
"Matilda" (song title): 106
Matron: 139
Medicine man: 208
Melvin (friend of Ronnie's): 123, 148ff.
Merriam, Miss (Broneco's first grade teacher): 54–55, 58
Mesa: 4, 7, 24, 35, 45, 67, 125, 212, 219
Mesa Verde: 14
Mexican: 79, 156–57
Michael (Broneco's schoolmate): 158, 186
Mike (Rod's friend): 82
Milkweed: 165
Mission: 150, 195
Moccasins: 11, 69
Mom: 200
"Mom-mom's boys": 170
Money: 174, 176, 188
Moon (Broneco's cat): 179–80, 203, 209, 214, 216, 218
Mormon tea: 125; *see also* tea
Mosquitoes: 12
Miracle: 185, 213, 215; thing, 62, 209; way, 87; Hill, 105, 211, 213–14, 221, 223
Morning glory: 196, 214–15
Mother: 9, 19, 21, 24, 30–31, 37–38, 41ff., 56, 65, 119, 171, 175, 178, 186–87, 197, 201, 206, 219; Pinto's, 31; earth, 44, 214; Annie's, 143, 154
Mountain (another, yonder, far): 222–23

Mountain spirit (Apache): 160
Movement (Navaho concept): *viii*
Movie: 90, 194
Music: 93, 102, 106, 112, 116, 122, 124, 128, 130, 133, 135, 150, 186, 190–91, 194–95, 218, 223
Musical: 136, 185, 191, 211
Mutton: 6, 8, 25, 198–99
Mysterious: 44, 143, 172, 208
Mystery boy: 220

Name: 11, 26, 72, 118
Nataani Nez: 110
Native language: 205
Navaho Indians: *viii*, *xi–xii*, *xv–xvi*, 51, 128, 186, 205; world view, *viii*; family and social life, *xvii*, 119, 126, 201; taboos, 29, 130, 140, 143, 145; protection of name, 54; customs, 59, 111, 113–14, 121, 128, 130, 140, 156ff., 163, 167, 193, 216–17; war with Utes, 87; beliefs, 143, 151, 177, 208, 212, 219, 221; *see also* school, sheep herding, hogan, summer camp, winter camp, tent
Navahos Have Five Fingers: 192
Necklace: 63, 66, 70, 218
New Mexico, state of: *x*, 3, 48, 136: capitol, 158
New Year: 121, 125ff., 134, 184
Nightmare: 60, 168, 181, 205, 209
"Night Train": 128, 131–32; *see also* Ford

"Once in a lifetime": 148, 153
Orientation: *xiv*, 163, 165
Oven: 25, 30, 75, 96, 196–97, 208
Owl: 8, 40

Painting: 159–60, 163–64
Pale-face: 37
Pants: 6, 16, 46, 204
Parrie (Broneco's cousin): 95–96, 198–99
Past: *xv*, 165, 167, 181, 212, 217, 219
Perez, Mr. (Paris): 157ff.
Phone: 155, 174–75
Photo album: 216
Physical Health Department: 154
Piano: 99, 106, 165, 190–91, 194–95, 217
Pickup: 7, 38, 41, 46–47, 98, 141, 149, 154, 172, 207
Pie: 202; *see also* pumpkin pie
Pig-pen: 139
Pine River Boys (a band): 103
Pinky (dog's name): 30, 34, 68
Pinto (pony's name): 31ff., 66ff., 76, 218
Plateau: 207
Poem (Broneco's first): 166
Pollen: 44, 213
P-jay: 90

Police: 130
Potato pull (a game): 57
Potato sack: 56
Prairie: 218
Prairie dog: 7, 13, 57
Prayers: 44
Present (gift): 112–13, 115–16, 119, 167, 173, 181, 184
Present (now): 219, 223
Prize: 63, 72
Publication: 191, 193
Pueblo boys: 162
Pumpkin pie: 196ff., 203
Punch: 92–93, 104

Quarter horse: 13

Rabbit: 4 ff., 12, 27–28, 65, 118
Race: 5, 9, 63ff., 75, 201
Radio: 119, 145, 194, 205, 210
Rainbow: 221
"Raining in my heart": 171, 185
Ram: 68
Ramus (Broneco's schoolmate): 161 ff., 185–86
Rasping stick: 61
Ray (Broneco's schoolmate): 158
Ray, Mr. (dormitory attendant): 87–88
Registrar: 165
Relatives: 74, 178, 180, 220
Reservation: vii, 3, 47, 59, 76, 188
Rhythm: 37, 133, 162, 183, 186, 194–95, 209
Ricky (Broneco's schoolmate): 100–101, 138
Rifle: 207
Ring: 15–16, 61, 134, 164
Roadrunner: 13, 22
Rod (Broneco's schoolmate): 80 ff., 84, 89
Rodeo ground: 66
Ronnie (Broneco's brother): 41–42, 122, 127ff., 131–32, 140, 175, 179ff.
Roommate: 85–86, 160–61, 168
Rooster: 27, 137, 145, 204, 211, 217
Rope: 23, 25, 33, 39, 67
Round Rock, Arizona: 56
Rusty (Broneco's uncle's young boy): 122–23, 127ff., 131–32, 149ff.

Sagebrush: 23, 214
Salt Creek Wash: 66, 75, 127
Salt trees: 12, 25–26, 36, 75–76
Salt Water Canyon: 19, 25, 45, 66
San Juan River: 40, 64
Santa Domingo, New Mexico: 158
Santa Fe, New Mexico: 153ff., 174, 181, 188, 196

School: argument about, 38ff.; first grade, 53ff.; second grade, 73; third grade, 74, 77; fourth grade, 77; seventh grade, 79, 91, 182; tenth, 95; eleventh, 137; twelfth, 150, 153, 184
Script of writing: 192–93
Sculpture: 163
Seagram 7th: 123, 130
Secret: 83
Seed: xiv, 165–66, 214
Shade house: 10, 16ff., 38, 44, 46, 74
Shades, The (a band): 122, 129, 131 ff., 147, 151 ff.
Shared love: 95, 98, 107, 114
Sheep: 4, 7–8, 14, 16, 19–20, 27, 33 ff., 56, 64–65, 69, 74–75, 142, 151, 153, 173, 186, 199, 200–201, 205, 212
Sheepskin: 19, 27, 45, 51
Shepherd: 70, 96
Shiprock, New Mexico: x, 8, 110, 116, 135, 143, 151, 177, 204
Shoes: 87, 92, 99, 102, 136, 183; Grandmother's present, 185; Annie's caught, 201
Short cut: 5, 22, 67
Sign: 61, 223
Silver squash blossom: 72
Simpson, Mr. (teacher): 182
Sis: 69
Sister: 19, 24, 42, 118, 178ff., 186–87
Sister-in-law: 44
Sister's son: 74
Six: 5ff., 63, 68, 203
Slack: 204
Smile: 91, 98
Smith, Mr. (dormitory attendant): 73–74
Snapping fingers: 69, 81, 90, 128
Snow: 3, 31, 124ff., 132, 142, 168, 170 ff.
Son: 41
Songs: 5, 208, 213, 223
Spanish: 155, 157
Spanish Trail Fiesta: 110
Spectacles: 48, 131, 146, 149, 157, 193, 195
Spirit, dancing mountains: 160
"Split the scene": 123
Spotted Heart (a story title): 87
Spring (water): 5, 8, 22, 24–25, 34
Squash blossom necklace: 70
Stallion: 25, 31, 72
Standing rocks: 207
Stepfather: 172, 179
Steve (Broneco's schoolmate): 79
Story writing: 167
Star, falling: 182
Stranger: 15, 81, 87, 98, 182, 197ff., 121–22
Strawberry patches: 99

229

Stud: 23
Studio: 191
Sub-agency: 151–52
Suina, Ramus: 161 ff., 185–86
Suitcase: 7, 38, 46, 49, 50, 73, 79, 84, 86, 90, 96ff., 140, 158–59, 183, 188–89, 195
Suit coat: 167, 184
Summer camp: 35, 37, 117
Summer home: 7, 74
Sun (father of light): 44
Sun glasses: 130–31; *see also* spectacles
Surprise: 4, 31, 37, 74–75, 106
Sweet rolls: 169

Taboo: *ix; see also* Navaho Indians
Tales: 76
Tall standing rock: 125
"Tank" for tent: *xi*
Tea: 40, 56, 126, 137, 143ff., 149, 151, 221
Teacher: *ix, xi, xv,* 17, 53ff., 73, 81, 163ff., 182, 186, 191
"Tears raining": 171, 180
Teddy bear: 109
Television: 86–87
Tellie (grandmother's donkey): 33–34, 36, 68; *see also* donkey
Tent: 3, 8ff., 13, 18ff., 36ff., 42, 44ff., 74, 204
Tenth grade: 95
Tepee: 60
Ticket agent: 155, 157
Tom (Rod's friend): 82
Tomi (girl Broneco met at dance): 133–34
Tool (white man's): 58
Tracks: 207
Trading post: 17, 47, 64, 66
Traditional techniques: 163
Trailway (bus): 114
Train: 128
Treadmill: *xi*
Tree-shade house: 3
Tribal language: 205
Tribe: 63
Tumbleweeds: 139, 209, 218
Turquoise: 15–16, 61, 63, 70, 72
Twist: 123, 131
Typewriter: 191, 193

Uncle: 7, 48, 74–75, 121, 171

Uncle John: 37, 47–48, 178
Uncle's wife: 178
United States: *ix*
Utah, state of: *x,* 3
Ute Indians: 60–61, 87

Veldez, Mr. (dormitory attendant): 140
Vera (Uncle John's wife): 37, 41, 44, 47, 49
Virgel (Broneco's schoolmate): 51, 55ff., 73, 82, 86
Visitor: 13, 120, 201–202
Vocabulary: *viii*

Wallace (Broneco's roommate): 160–61
Water sprinkle: 17, 50, 193
Water tower: 8, 203
Watson, Mrs. (teacher): 73
Weaving: 10–11, 36–37, 163
Whirlwind: 14
Whisky: 100, 123, 130
White Man's civilization: *xii–xiii,* 4, 16–17, 37, 45–48, 58, 63, 76; white tongue, 5–6; white friend, 19, 213, 220; white skin, 156
White mare: 23, 32, 34
Wife: 37–38, 42, 48
Wild flowers: 214
Williams, Mr. (dormitory attendant): 88–89, 98
Window Rock, Arizona: 114
Wine: 12, 92
Winter camp: 125, 171, 179
Wolf: 57
Wool: 198, 200–201
World: 12, 221; view, *viii;* beyond hand's reach, 213, 217, 223; small, 220
World War II: 9
Worship: 44
Wrist watch: 152
Writing: 150, 165, 167–68, 193; writing studio, *xiv*
Written arts building: 193

Yazzie, Hosteen: 192
Yellow (dog's name): 30, 34
Youthful days: 222
Yucca: 197, 213, 216

Zero class: 53